# TAMING AGGRESSION

## YOUR CHILD

# TAMING AGGRESSION IN YOUR CHILD

## How to Avoid Raising Bullies, Delinquents, or Trouble-Makers

### Henri Parens, MD

JASON ARONSON

Lanham • Boulder • New York • Toronto • Plymouth, UK

Published by Jason Aronson
A wholly owned subsidary of The Rowman & Littlefield Publishing Group, Inc.
4501 Forbes Boulevard, Suite 200, Lanham, Maryland 20706
http://www.rowmanlittlefield.com

Estover Road, Plymouth PL6 7PY, United Kingdom

British Library Cataloguing in Publication Information Available

**Library of Congress Cataloging-in-Publication Data**

Parens, Henri, 1928-
   Taming aggression in your child : how to avoid raising bullies, delinquents, or
trouble-makers / Henri Parens.
      p. cm.
   Includes index.
   ISBN 978-0-7657-0896-0 (cloth : alk. paper)—ISBN 978-0-7657-0897-7 (pbk. : alk.
paper)—ISBN 978-0-7657-0898-4 (electronic)
   1. Aggressiveness in children. 2. Aggressiveness in children—Prevention. 3. Bullying
—Prevention. 4. Child rearing. 5. Parent and child. I. Title.
   BF723.A35P376 2011
   649'.64—dc23

                                                            2011042011

For all the children and parents who
have taught me what I have learned about
how to make the lives of children and their parents
"easier"* and more rewarding—and our world safer.

*A mother in the project group I describe in chapter 1 said to me smiling, "Dr. Parens, you haven't made my taking care of my children easy, but you have made it easier."

# CONTENTS

Preface                                                                          xi

Introduction                                                                      I

**I    Can We Tame Human Destructiveness?**                                        **5**
My Research Project on the Development of Aggression                               6
Effects of *Parenting for Emotional Growth* on the Aggression
Profile of the Children                                                           7
The Significance of the Individual's Aggression Profile                           8
The Critical Interaction between the Child's Relationships
and His or Her Aggression Profile                                                 8
Some Effects on the Child of His/Her Internally Accumulating
High Levels of Hostile Destructiveness                                           12
Rebellion against Family and Authority Figures                                   13
Bullying                                                                         14
Delinquency and Crime                                                            15
The Tendency toward Malignant Prejudice and its Social Enactments   15

**2   What Is Aggression?**                                                        **27**
Why We Need to Know what Aggression Really Is                                     27
When Should Parents Start to Deal with their Children's
Aggressive Behaviors?                                                            28
Understanding Our Children's Aggressive Behavior Helps Us                         30

How a Child's Aggression Can Create Problems for
Himself and His Parents                                               30
So, What Is Aggression?                                               31
A Working Model for Understanding Aggression                          31
Categories of Aggressive Behaviors                                    32
There Are Three Trends of Aggression                                  35
What Is *Nondestructive Aggression?*                                  40
What Are *Hostile Aggression* and *Hostile Destructiveness?*          40
Implications for Parenting                                            41

**3   On Compliance                                                   45**
Compliance versus Obedience                                           46
What Kind of Children Do We Want?                                     47
What Makes Achieving Compliance in our Children So Large
A Challenge?                                                          47
Compliance                                                            49
The Problem with *Obedience* (or *Excessive Compliance*)             52
From Excessive Compliance (Passive Obedience) to
Insufficient Compliance                                               54
The Problem of Insufficient Compliance                                55
What Are Reasonable and Growth-Promoting Expectations?                62
Categories of Expectations with Degrees of Obligation                 63
The Development of the Ability to Comply                               65
A Timetable for the Ability to Comply                                 68

**4   Achieving Compliance through Discipline,
Limit Setting, and Punishment                                        75**
Generally, Accepting Parental Authority is in the Child's Best Interest   76
Rationale                                                             77
Setting Limits Constructively                                         79
When to Set Limits                                                    80
Principles of Limit-Setting                                           82
The Basic Limit Setting Model                                         83
A Critical Point in Setting Limits                                    85
Principles of Punishment                                              87
Limit-Setting and Punishment over the Years                           89

**5   Helping Children Learn to Express Hostility in Acceptable
Ways—and Reduce Teasing, Taunting, and Bullying                     113**
A Critical Distinction between "Being angry" and "Being mean"        115
Rationale                                                            119

Interventional Steps                                                    123
Why Reduce our Children's Need to Erect Defense
Mechanisms to Cope with their Feelings of Hostility?                     131
Teasing and Taunting, the Building Blocks for Bullying                   137
The Child or Adolescent Who Gets Teased, Taunted,
or Bullied Needs Help Too                                                148

6  **How to Handle Temper Tantrums and Rage Reactions
   in Growth-Promoting Ways**                                           **161**
   Differentiating between Temper Tantrums and Rage Reactions            162
   Rationale                                                             170
   Intervening with Temper Tantrums                                      173
   Intervening with Rage Reactions                                       179

7  **Optimizing the Parent-Child Relationship**                         **189**
   What I Know about Human Attachment                                    190
   Separation-Individuation: Becoming a Self Related to Others           194
   The Emergence of Infantile Sexuality and Its Impact
   on Child-Parent Relatedness                                          197
   Later Trends in the Evolving of Relationships in Childhood            201
   Further Thoughts on Optimizing the Parent-Child Relationship          202
   The Quality of Parent-Child Relatedness Largely Determines
   the Quality of the Child's Aggression Profile                         211

Index                                                                    215

About the Author                                                         227

# PREFACE

Our experience working with parents and children has convinced us that handling children's aggression is one of the most difficult challenges for parents. In turn, children often encounter significant problems in dealing with their own aggression, and as adults many will continue to have difficulty. The constructive management of aggression greatly contributes to both the proper future emotional development of the child and the comfort of the parents.

In this book I talk to parents, teachers, day-care workers, and other child caregivers. In the course of our research on aggression in young children, we found a number of parent-child interactions in which aggression is especially activated. In these, aggression is generated or mobilized especially in the form of anger, hostility, hate, and rage—what I speak of as *hostile aggression.* My research and clinical work has convinced me that parental input and handling significantly influence the development of aggression, in both its nondestructive form—best represented by assertiveness—and in its hostile aggressive form—best represented by hostility. The challenge for the parent is to promote what is constructive in aggression, that which is needed for adaptation, and to lessen as best as can what is hostile, that which can undermine children's well-being, their relationships, and their life at home and in our society. I am convinced that informing parents about inherent features and dynamics of aggression, and proposing to them strategies for their parenting interventions, can help them in this enormous challenge.

# INTRODUCTION

## HOW CAN WE AVOID RAISING BULLIES, DELINQUENTS, AND OTHER SORTS OF TROUBLE-MAKERS?

**B**y trouble-makers I mean individuals, children and adults, who disrupt other people's efforts to live as well as they can, to develop into people who are able to work, to love, and to play. Given that families raise individual children, here we will consider only the individual trouble-maker. By trouble-maker I here mean a bully, delinquent, or criminal. While for many reasons such as individual and societal harm, and psychological and monetary costs, delinquency and criminality have long preoccupied society, it is only recently that the potential effects of bullying have come to the attention of society. Before the Internet, bullying tended to remain localized to individuals and small clusters of kids; its painful consequences for individuals tended to remain localized in school and the neighborhood, and in many cases might not even reach a bullied child's home. But with the advent of the incredible speed with which thousands of iPhone users can access text messaging and email and webcams can spread information—often distorted and malignant—targeting a given adolescent can be widespread in moments, causing the bullied kid devastating surges of rage—often quiet—and peaks of humiliation. Some sudden explosive deadly reactions by the bullied—as in Columbine High School—as well as suicides among them have gotten widespread news coverage. These effects of modern-day bullying have fortunately led to the development of efforts at recognizing and reducing bullying and the ravages it can cause.

Bullies, delinquents, and criminals, generally, are born like you and me, that is, with healthy enough brain functions and bodily systems. But most commonly, these individuals are and have been subjected to experiences from early on in life, foremost within their own homes, that have and continue to cause them much emotional pain, be it by too frequent and intense emotional and/or physical abuse or by neglect of basic emotional needs. In all cases, excessive loads of accumulated hostile destructiveness, generated in them by such early life abuses and/or neglect, become in turn the generator of their destructive acts against others—and themselves. I will try to explain how this comes about.

This book is a more reader-friendly version of my recently published, *Handling Children's Aggression Constructively: Toward Taming Human Destructiveness*. This latter book turned out to be more complex than I had initially planned; it became more heavily documented with past research that supports what I propose, and as it evolved became more appropriate for students and readers in professional fields of mental and public health and in the humanities—including those in education, psychology, sociology, anthropology. This current book, *Taming Aggression in Your Child: How to Avoid Raising Bullies, Delinquents, and Trouble-Makers,* is intended for parents, for child caregivers, day-care workers, time-constrained school teachers, and the everyday interested reader who might trust the credibility of a mental health professional with 40 years of research and clinical experience in his field of study, without requiring that he prove then and there every thought he proposes.

I will first assert that we can do more than we think about taming human destructiveness, especially so by preventing its accumulation in kids, the next generation of adults. I have learned over the years that the adage "an ounce of prevention is worth a pound of cure" is only partly true; it's worth a lot more! I will then present the reader with my model of aggression (chapter 2), a model developed out of my research and clinical work, which taught me to understand what aggression is and what causes it. This model provides us with the means for understanding our children's aggression, what's good and what's bad about it, and it guides us to develop strategies to deal constructively with a cluster of frequently occurring parent-child interactions in which what's good and what's bad about aggression can be lessened or can be intensified. I have seen that this can help parents attain a clearer understanding of typical aggression-generating interactions between them and their children, and I have then seen parents able to apply this basic interactional knowledge not only to dealing with their children's aggressive behaviors but also to the entire challenging enterprise of their child-rearing.

The issues I address are complex, and some may not be easily assimilated at first reading. There are, however, no unexpected rocks, whirlpools, or dragons. My aim is to help parents seize the rich opportunities inherent in these challenging interactions with their children.

This is *not* a book about how to handle children who suffer from significant aggressive behavior disorders, such as teenagers who already are delinquent or engage in criminal behaviors. Books have been written to help parents and others deal as constructively as they can with such very challenging youth. This is a book about how to prevent the development in kids of disturbed aggressive behaviors. It can be very useful for the handling of problems in the making, so as to not further their becoming difficult problems to deal with.

Equally critical to its primary aim of optimizing children's aggression profiles, this book is about how to prevent the development of problems that are secondary to the development of aggression-based behavior problems. Many people are not aware of the fact that problems with aggression can lead to difficulty in learning in school, difficulty in forming good relationships at home, in school, and in the neighborhood. Ultimately, these problems can turn out to be of greater consequence than the aggressive behavior problems themselves.

# 1

# CAN WE TAME HUMAN DESTRUCTIVENESS?

I dare raise this question because we have learned that even while we are limited in our ability to tame human destructiveness, we can do much that may prevent its generation and accumulation in children (and adults), and its eventual unleashing. We have found strong evidence that humans are not born bursting to be destructive, driven by an instinct to destroy as was once held. Rather, I have found fact that human destructiveness is generated by human experience. This leads me to hold that there are ways whereby human destructiveness can be lessened. One preeminent way is to prevent the generation and the accumulation of what I have called *hostile destructiveness*. That's what this book is about.

Here I'll lay out some of the cornerstones for my reasoning that we can do more than is generally assumed toward taming human destructiveness:

- Our Research Project on the Development of Aggression
- Effects of Parenting for Emotional Growth on Aggression Profiles of Children
- The Significance of the Individual's Aggression Profile
- The Critical Interaction between Human Attachment and Aggression
- Effects on Children of Accumulating High Levels of Hostile Destructiveness
- Rebellion against Family and Authority Figures
- Bullying

- Delinquency and Crime
- The Tendency toward Malignant Prejudice and its Enactments

## MY RESEARCH PROJECT ON THE DEVELOPMENT OF AGGRESSION

In September 1970, my Medical College of Pennsylvania research team developed a project with 10 volunteered neighborhood mothers with their then newborns; it actively lasted for 7 years, and was followed at 19, 32, and 37 years from the start of the project. The mothers were told that I was teaching child development to child mental health students and that they would be helping us and the students learn about normal kids. They were also told that we would undertake non-medical and non-manipulating research based only on observation of them with their children. They had no idea what our research questions were. In fact, our research questions changed early in the course of the study, driven by behaviors we saw which we had not predicted.

The mothers and their infants, as well as their children who were not yet in school, started to meet as a group twice a week for two-hour sessions. The research team began sessions as naturalistic as possible while making observational studies of them. Mothers and children were free to act as they wished; no assignments were made; no pressures were exerted on them; no tests were given; no formal challenges were presented. The mothers talked among themselves while they tended to their infants and other children. Surprisingly, soon the mothers became interested in the comments I occasionally made to the observing professional trainees. Following several requests by the mothers that I tell them too what I was telling the child psychiatry students, I began to jointly address the students and the mothers regarding the meaning of the children's behaviors, the developmental forces that elicited them, etc. The mothers soon started to ask questions of their own about their children's behaviors and wondered progressively about why their child was doing this or that, and how to best handle some of their behaviors.

These mothers and their children who were not in school attended the group over a 7-year period. Of course, the children of age went to school; some of the mothers had 2, one had 3 children while in the project. The attitude and feeling in the group, the mothers, the children, and the research staff became increasingly friendly, mutually respecting, and fun.

Our aim soon shifted to helping the parents understand what seemed to drive their children's behaviors and to talk about options for handling these toward optimizing their child's development. Within months the mothers' behaviors toward their children seemed to be positively influenced by our explanations and discussions. The mothers' questions seemed more and more open; they showed genuine interest in and gave the impression that they appreciated our discussions. We came to realize that we were doing some unanticipated productive "parenting education."

This was often affirmed by the mothers as time passed. Expressions like "I wish I had known this before I had my children" led us to develop formal materials for "Parenting Education" focused on the emotional development of children. Driven by what we saw, in time, we developed three sets of materials:[1]

1. Parenting for Emotional Growth: A Textbook;
2. Parenting for Emotional Growth: A Curriculum for Students in Grades K thru 12; And some time later, we added
3. Parenting for Emotional Growth: A Series of Workshops for Child Caregivers, Parents, Child Care Workers, Educators.

Over time the benefits to the mothers and their children were documented.[2]

I want to emphasize that the parenting education[3] to which I am referring is not driven by racial, religious, or ethnic beliefs. I like to say that the parent and child in question in Parenting for Emotional Growth is that of Homo sapiens (the human parent and child). This is because all children, whatever the race, religion, ethnicity, or nationality, have the same basic developmental and emotional needs and the same basic development-optimizing strategies can be used without influencing positively or negatively the child's race, religion, ethnicity, or nationality.

## EFFECTS OF PARENTING FOR EMOTIONAL GROWTH ON THE AGGRESSION PROFILE OF THE CHILDREN

Aggressive behaviors are an unavoidable part of normal childhood development; they are part and parcel of the child's orientation to the world around him/her and his/her efforts to cope with it, and with himself in it. Children are not born with a ready-made program for how to deal with their aggression in socially acceptable ways. How to handle children's various aggressive behaviors and help them cope with them constructively is a most common concern for parents. Aggression develops. But how? From what? To what? I'll detail this in chapter 2.

The changes in the mothers' handling of their children's aggressive behaviors began to be evident by 18 months into the project. Their handling
of their children's aggression was distinctly growth-promoting. And we saw
evidence for the durability of the mothers' handling of their children's aggressive behaviors in our 19-year follow-up study. In this first follow-up
study, the project children's "characteristic angry and hostile behaviors" and
their "potential for violent behavior" were significantly lower than these are
in kids who come from their community.[4]

While the number of kids in our project was small (16) the tendency
demonstrated at our 19-year follow-up study is noteworthy. Equally noteworthy is the fact that at 32-year and 37-year follow-ups, these aggression
profile parameters as documented in these now adults' (the grown children's) histories and current state proved to have held up over the years.
None got in trouble with the law, all graduated from high school and most
went to college, most had jobs and families.

## THE SIGNIFICANCE OF THE INDIVIDUAL'S AGGRESSION PROFILE

It is well established in mental health that the child's aggression profile has
large potentially lifelong implications for his/her behavior, his/her adaptation and development (including education and work performance), for
his/her relationships and interactions with others, and for her/his role in
society. Many researchers have found that high accumulations of what I
call *hostile destructiveness*[5]—which is the form of aggression that includes
hostility, hate and rage—tend to lead to

1. Rebellion against family and authority figures such as teachers;
2. Bullying of others, peers and even teachers!
3. Delinquency and crime; and
4. A greater intolerance of others often leading to malignant prejudice
   and its social enactments.

## THE CRITICAL INTERACTION BETWEEN THE CHILD'S RELATIONSHIPS AND HIS OR HER AGGRESSION PROFILE

For nearly a century many mental health professionals have held that
infants come into the world with an inborn aggressive drive that compels

in them a tendency, even a need, to destroy. Aggression-research theorists of varying disciplines including psychoanalysis have not accepted this assumption.[6] My own research has led me to assert that this assumption cannot be supported by observable or inferable evidence from healthy-enough normal infants and children and that rather than an inborn destructive tendency being the formative factor in a child's aggression profile, it is the child's experiences that over time are the largest factor that shapes each child's aggression profile (see note 5). More detail on this in chapter 2.

There is much agreement among neuroscientist and mental health researchers as well as clinicians that given the endowment with which the infant is born, the development of the central nervous system of the child (the brain and its bodily extensions) and the child's personality formation are most shaped by adapting to the world into which the infant is born.[7] Once born, the child's largest development in brain functions occurs in her/his first 6 to 8 years of life. This applies as well to the child's mental health and personality formation. The more positive the emotional and physical beginnings during these earliest years, the healthier will be the child's mental health and his/her personality formation.

While a large numbers of studies have documented that the earliest years of life are the most formative of the child's mental health and personality, this however, does not diminish the fact that enormous developments in personality, in adaptive capability, in intelligence and learning (education), and more, are still in front of the child as she/he develops into adulthood. The time and the opportunities for development in humans are awesome and never-ending. Even in the late years of life, creative individuals continue to grow. But parents must know that just because much development continues after 6 years of age—many more easily recognize development beyond year 6—these earliest 6 years, by establishing baseline bodily reactive systems including brain patterning and neural networks that shape the child's personality, are of critical importance. And this is so for the child's aggression profile and its effects on personality.

Considering the basic factors that form the child's aggression profile, namely the child's inborn givens (including his or her genetic make-up) and early life experiences, and that the foundation of the child's personality gets formed during the first 6 years, home is where the child's aggression profile first gets formed. And, the largest determining factor of every "home" is the quality of the relationships between the child and his nuclear family. This applies equally to very early life adoptive parents. Long-term substitute caregivers who emotionally value the child also play a part, a greater or lesser part in the young child's home-world-based aggression profile development. This can include long-term, favorable foster care.

The emotional investment the parents make in the child, with few exceptions, is most determining of the character of the child's developing an attachment to them. Many studies[8] have documented the critical role of the quality of the child's attachment to his/her primary caregivers in the child's emotional life and personality formation. The child's development is significantly determined positively by the degree to which the attachment is affectionate, respecting, secure, and predictable; and it will be negatively determined by the degree to which the attachment is laden with stress, hostility and hate, and unpredictability.

While this next thought may stir some controversy, I have found from clinical work that the quality of the attachment to the mother (biologic or adoptive) is of "utmost importance," commonly, having a greater influence on the child's well-being than that of other family members, including the father.[9] This may change because in the past couple of decades more and more fathers have gotten involved in the direct care of their infants and young children in which case the attachment of the young to their father may well achieve equivalent emotional importance as to the mother. The trend of fathers' direct-care-involvement has, I believe to the benefit of all, come so far as to include that fact that more and more, some fathers elect to be the stay-at-home parent, and care for the child from infancy on. While studies are limited to date, findings that have been reported[10] are quite positive and tell us that these children are equally well developed psychologically (and physically) as primarily-mother-reared kids.

As I found in my research on aggression, there is "a stable positive correlation between the quality of the child's attachment to his/her mother and the child's aggression profile."[11] In this, I found that the degree to which one is hurt by one's own parents has a direct bearing on how hostile an individual child, adolescent, and adult one becomes. I have even taken the position that when children are traumatized by their own parents, they suffer more and therefore become more hostile than when they are traumatized by any other individual or groups. And, as a Holocaust survivor, to the surprise of many, I have asserted that being traumatized by one's own mother or father is worse than being subjected even to genocidal abuses. Of course, degree of traumatization plays its part. Nonetheless, to be traumatized by one's enemy is expectable; even kids know that. But to be traumatized by those who are supposed to love you, nourish you, and do the best they can to protect you against hunger, cold, and evil, that is the worst. Who then can you turn to? Kids know that too. I know some readers will be skeptical of what I am saying here. But I am not the only Holocaust survivor child who is a child and adult psychiatrist who holds this view.

Pertinent to this, in their study of child survivors of the Holocaust, Judy Kestenberg and Ira Brenner[12] found that children who prior to the Holocaust had had good family relationships, endured the genocidal abuses of the Holocaust better than those whose relationships prior to the advent of the Holocaust had been troubled, laden with neglect and maltreatment. Furthermore, they found that those who had formed good (secure) attachments before the Holocaust were able to form good attachments after, recreate families and achieve good lives. Those who had troubled attachments before the Holocaust were generally less able and even unable to rebuild their life and family after.

Another related remarkable finding has also been reported in a number of studies of resilience.[13] Those who had come from troubled families but who had learned to, and could optimize their relationships with others outside of their families, were highly advantaged in surviving well-enough. This came from the many human beings who despite a troubled childhood and even adolescence have been able to draw on their internal resource and, forming gratifying enough attachments outside of their families were able to make their life rewarding-enough. In these cases, good later attachments helped them tame the hostility and hate that had been generated in them by hurtful childhood family relationships. Thus resilience studies, yet from another vantage point, point to the positive link between the quality of attachment—even if to persons other than their own parents—and the quality of the child/adolescent/adult's aggression profile. This positive correlation has also been found again and again in many studies spanning the last century on the relation between insecure and troubled early life attachment and delinquency and criminality.[14]

Specifically addressing the intimate link between the quality of the child's attachment and that of his/her aggression profile, in one of his studies (Egeland et al. 2001), Byron Egeland remarked that "A very large number of studies have found an association between parental neglect or harsh treatment and later conduct problems, as have we" (in Sroufe[15] et al. 2005, p 256). And in that same volume, the lead author, Alan Sroufe, writes that "aggressiveness is highly predictable from early in life, but from patterns of organization in the infant-caregiver system, not from . . . behaviors [inherent in] infants" (p 26). This fact is clearly visible in the work of researchers as Brazelton[16] (1981) and Beebe[17] (2005) for instance who have recorded infants' reactions of irritability, distress, turning away from the mother during adverse interactions. These emotionally painful experiences over time organize, within the child, in angry or other negative reactions toward the primary caregiver.

Put simply, there is consensus among researchers in sociology, psychology, psychiatry, psychoanalysis, and attachment theory that the quality of the child's relationships with his/her primary caregivers correlates strongly with the quality of the child's aggression profile—*from constructive to hostile destructive.*

## SOME EFFECTS ON THE CHILD OF HIS/HER INTERNALLY ACCUMULATING HIGH LEVELS OF HOSTILE DESTRUCTIVENESS

I said earlier that when the child accumulates high levels of hostile destructiveness within his/her psyche it tends to lead to (1) rebellion against family and authority figures; (2) bullying others; (3) delinquency and crime; and (4) a greater intolerance of others that often leads to malignant prejudice and its social enactments. Let me briefly explain. Because I have not defined the concept of hostile destructiveness in this chapter (I do in chapter 2) and I am using it here, a word is needed to understand its role in the assertions I just made.

In chapter 2, I propose that there are 3 major trends in aggression: *nondestructive aggression, nonaffective destructiveness,* and *hostile aggression.* I have decided to settle for a further clarification: I now want to specify[18] that the trend hostile aggression contains the subtrend hostile destructiveness, so labeled because not all hostile aggression is both hostile and destructive.

Let me illustrate these trends:

1. When a child pushes aside or climbs over an obstacle to his goal, or when he asserts himself in a disagreement with a peer and stands his ground, he is protecting his right to strive for his goals and what he thinks is right; he is being neither hostile nor destructive; this behavior is fueled by *nondestructive aggression.* Such aggression is most evident in properly played sports. In a quieter way it is also what drives kids (and adults) to achieve in school, in their studies and work.

2. When a lion chases a gazelle, catches it and destroys it, the lion is not being hostile; it is hungry and has to have food in order to survive. The lion is being destructive but not hostile; that is *nonaffective destructiveness,* which means it is aggression that is not driven by negative emotional feelings but, in this case, by physical need, by hunger.

3. *Hostile aggression* is that familiar range of aggressive feelings that increases in intensity from annoyance, irritability, and anger, to hostility, rage, and hate. These feelings all have a negative quality; they feel unpleasant, make us look and, too often, act unpleasant. But not all these various levels of hostile feelings lead to the wish to harm or destroy. I hold that only those feelings that pertain to hostile destructiveness, that is, hostility, hate, and rage lead to the wish to harm and destroy. These are the feelings that lead to bullying, delinquency, criminality, and malignant prejudice.

What our research has taught me is that the most critical factor that generates hostile aggression in humans is the experience of psychic (emotional) pain; and when that emotional pain is intense, it crosses a subjective line of experiencing that pushes into wanting to cause harm and destroy; it becomes hostile destructiveness. In the course of growing up, children experience much emotional pain. It's part of life. It is important to note that while physical pain, even intense physical pain may make us angry, it is especially intense emotional pain that makes us feel hostile and destructive. Here is how this has a bearing on rebellion, bullying, delinquency, crime, and malignant prejudice.

## REBELLION AGAINST FAMILY AND AUTHORITY FIGURES

As I said, much research and clinical work documents that the foremost accumulation of large loads of hostility and hate tends to be generated at home, most commonly by children's being *emotionally* and/or *physically* abused by their own parents during their growing years.

*Physical abuse* is easily identified—although it will not be acknowledged by the parent who rationalizes, makes excuses for his or her loss of reasonable control, and believes "I'm just doing this for your own good." It should also be borne in mind that intentionally causing one's child physical pain is also experienced, perhaps even more so, as emotional pain.

Even more problematic is *emotional abuse*, which is often carried out without inflicting physical pain. Because no physical pain is inflicted, many a parent fails to recognize how injurious emotional abuse is. For instance: "Why don't you ever do anything right!" Or, "You'll never amount to anything!" Or, "Do you know how much I bled giving birth to you!" Remarks as these, expressed in moments of exasperation, injure the child's or teenager's sense of self, his/her "healthy narcissism" (see chapter 3), which wound especially deeply when said by one's mother or father. Being insulted and humiliated causes acute emotional pain—"narcissistic injury" we say—and sharply generates hostile destructiveness in the child or teenager.

Parental abuses often lead kids, especially teenagers, to reject even well-meaning authority figures as teachers who they unavoidably perceive as being "just like Mom/Dad." To kids, all grownups are automatically perceived to be "like my Mom/Dad." And the resemblance does not need to be large. It then has become the child's common experience that "grown-ups maltreat and hurt kids" and/or that "adults hate teenagers!" Who wants to listen to them!

## BULLYING

What makes a kid bully another? Because hostile/hate feelings are painful to harbor—just as the body finds physical pain unpleasant to bear—it is difficult to cope with accumulating hostile destructiveness within oneself. I discuss in chapter 2 that hostile feelings are biologically generated, self-protectively, to rid oneself of the noxious agent that is causing the (psychic) pain one experiences. Given the intolerance we generally feel for internally accumulating hostile destructiveness, these press from within us to be discharged. As a result, a child or adolescent who is unable to modulate (psychologically resolve or just sufficiently tone down) or govern his own accumulating hostile feelings will feel pressured and seek ways, consciously and unconsciously, to discharge them. There is always the risk that one's own hostile feelings may be discharged inwardly (turned against oneself); or that they will be discharged outwardly (turned against someone else). Since the child cannot afford to injure or estrange a parent—which the child needs for survival—or a person in authority or bigger than him/herself— who can inflict punishment—the child/adolescent seeks to discharge that hostility toward someone (or something) who (that) is weaker than the self and/or is least likely to retaliate. *Bullying*, while socially highly undesirable, is one of the ways to safely-enough discharge hostility outwardly. When done individually, the bully invariably picks a "safe target," someone weaker than him/herself. When the bullying is done by a group, while different discharge methods are used, these nonetheless are fueled by the collective accumulated hostility of the group.

Of course many life experiences bring with them high levels of emotional (psychic) pain which in turn generate hostility in us (see chapter 2). Being hurt by others is not the only way we are made to experience psychic pain.

Another major source comes from the child himself/herself: poor school performance, excessive frustration with himself when the young child attempts to do something and fails, envy of others who seem to do with ease what the child can't do, envy of what another one has which one can't have, poor self-image, be it due to weight or some bodily defect, etc. All these negatives can make a child or adolescent bully another who is viewed as having those good things.

## DELINQUENCY AND CRIME

Well-established and reputed studies I noted before have found strong correlations that document the finding that, in the histories of delinquents and criminals one discovers that, at home, growing up, they were neglected, physically and emotionally abused, and suffered no end of insults and humiliations. There is significant consensus among professionals in pertinent fields of study who hold that the hostile destructiveness that gets generated[19] by these maltreatments is a large motivating factor in individuals who turn to antisocial and criminal behaviors.

## THE TENDENCY TOWARD MALIGNANT PREJUDICE AND ITS SOCIAL ENACTMENTS

My studies on prejudice[20] have led me to propose that we all have prejudices. Prejudice, defined as a pre-conceived negative[21] judgment about others, is experienced by all of us. Having become who we are, we tend to feel less at ease with people we perceive to be "different than we are"; we prefer to be with people like ourselves. Why does being with people "different than we" tend to cause us some discomfort, even anxiety? And how do we come to prefer to be "with our own"?

Two normal psychological developmental factors cause this. One is *stranger anxiety* and the other is *identification* (to be like someone we value). Let me explain.

### Stranger Anxiety

A normal baby comes into the world equipped with instincts to attach to her/his caregivers. We can assume that this is fostered by Mother Nature's biological mandate that "you must preserve the species." It's simple; if we don't reproduce, our species, Homo sapiens, will die out. Equipped to attach, the human infant must attach to humans in order to eventually reproduce. But then more demands are made on the infant.

Given that humans, like many other mammals, are "pack-animals," they must attach to their own pack. Without this, stable packs—families and communities—would not form. How much this became inherited over time, we can't answer. The fact remains that it is advantageous to society formation that stable families be formed. There are other types of packs than families, such as peer groups, or even communities organized around principles like Communism or National Socialism that attempt to minimize the role of the family; but it is questionable whether these are as stable as communities that are formed by clusters of families. Now, in order to form families, infants' attachments have to be specific; the infant will have to attach to members of his particular family. So, the infant is prescribed, probably genetically, to attach to those caregivers that most care for the infant. The mother seems to universally be the chosen candidate for this role. Pretty good thinking too, because overwhelmingly, no one is likely to be as eager and devoted in fostering the baby's attaching to her/him than the baby's own mother/father.

So, the baby's brain is pre-wired to push the baby to attach to his/her primary caregiver(s). But there's this other nice lady next door who smiles at him nicely and the baby smiles back at her. In fact, as Rene Spitz found,[22] at the very beginning, at about 5 or 6 weeks of age, the baby will smile at any face, even at a drawing of a face. That won't do! If the baby is to become a member of his family, the baby can't just go on smiling at any face. It's got to be a family face. And lo and behold, as the weeks pass, the baby begins to sort out which faces are—and all that comes with these faces—part of the family and which is not. And by 5 or so months, the baby knows: this is the one who cares for me most and seems to want most to have me around: she's my mother! And then, there's that one with the loud voice who always seems to want to play; well, that's my Dad. And that smaller big person, who seems to sometimes be nice to me and at other times not, that's my brother or my sister. Of course babies don't have these thoughts but they seem to act as if they do.

The next thing that happens is that the 5-month-old begins to rely on her/his mother. Oh, she just disappeared! Actually she just went into the kitchen but the baby can't see her from where he is, so he believes she has disappeared. He/she believes Mom has "disappeared," because as Jean Piaget taught us,[23] the 6-month-old baby's memory development is such that she/he can't yet remember the image of her/his mother when she is not in the baby's field of vision, but can recognize her when the baby sees her, when she "reappears." Now that she just "disappeared," the 6-month-old feels abandoned, outright scared, and feels separation anxiety!

Side by side with this development and the emergence of *separation anxiety*, whereas the 6-weeks-old baby used to just smile at almost everybody who looked at him/her, now the baby seems to get frightened when someone the baby doesn't know smiles at him/her. This person may well be the child's grandfather whom the baby has not seen for 3 months. And much to mother's shock the baby starts to cry when Grandpa tries to pick her/him up! Now along with *separation anxiety*, the baby also experiences *stranger anxiety*. Why?

I propose[24] that *stranger anxiety* is in the service of channeling the pre-wired infant's attachment behavior toward a small number of people that are consistently in the infant's immediate world, his family world. If Grandpa was a frequent visitor during these months, the baby would not have experienced stranger anxiety; he might not have been as warmly responsive as to Dad or one of the siblings, but it would not have triggered the "I don't want to be with you" reaction. So, while stranger anxiety secures the infant's becoming a member of his specific family, it has potential negative implications for the infant's future reactions to "others." In other words, while stranger anxiety protects the infant's attachment to persons who constitute his immediate family, it also generates the reaction "I don't want to be with you!" to those who are not commonly seen family. This is a key factor then in the child's fear of strangers; and this fear of strangers, while decreasing over time, continues throughout life, especially when the child's environment maligns strangers—as too often happens in militant religious, nationalistic, and ethnic education of children.[25]

## Identification

Infants come into the world equipped with a pool of genes half of which come from their mother and the other half from their father. We expect from this that the child will have features like one parent or the other or both. A parent with red hair is likely to have a child with red hair. Such features, both physical and behavioral, will make it easy to assume that this baby is probably this mom's/dad's child. This is the genetic contribution to the child's being like his/her parents.

Identification, being like, not just looking like, goes well beyond that. Infants imitate their caregivers. Even in infancy, when mother holds the baby and looks at it, opens her mouth, if she waits patiently enough the weeks-old baby will open his/her mouth. It's not fair to try this with a smile, because a smile will yield a smiling reaction; that's not imitation; that's reacting to Mom's smile. In our documentary DVD,[26] I show a movie clip of a mother sitting on a couch holding her baby on her shoulder in order to burp her; standing next to her a less than two-year-old girl is leaning against the couch's back rest, turned toward the baby, smiling at the baby softly. As the comforting mother is gently patting the baby on the back, the little girl too, begins to pat the baby on the back, much like the baby's mother is doing. You might say she is imitating the mother.

Yes, but she is doing more than imitating. She is grasping a complex scene: a mother comforting her baby. She wants to do it too. She is not just imitating, she is taking in the function of doing this; she is identifying with the comforting mother. Some day she will be a comforting mother. Step by step, taking in parents' reactions, ways of doing things, views on all sorts of matters, doing what her/his mother does, what father does, the child becomes like her/his parents. And the child will note over time that some other parents do not do what his/her mother and/or father does. The child will progressively find that many other people do things differently. Some of these ways of doing things the child will find congenial; some the child will not.

Thus, *stranger anxiety* and *identification* combine to make the child a member of his/her specific family. It will produce a child who, as I have said (borrowing on what Freud said), will bear the stamp "Made in the H Family," where H = His/Her family. And with that comes "the distinction between my family and that of others'." And similarities between the child's family and other families will bring a feeling of connection with these families. By contrast families that are seen by the child as different from his/hers along a variety of features will bring with it a feeling of difference between "them and us."

Given these developments, it is unavoidable that we all have preferences, that is, prejudices. But these are not prejudices that of themselves bring the feeling that "others" are not as good as we are. They are different and I feel more at home with my own; but, I wish them no harm. This is why I have called these prejudices, *benign prejudice*.[27] Given that family formation is central to community formation and that as pack animals this serves us well, it would not be desirable to try to eliminate the form of prejudice I speak of as benign prejudice.

But how do we get from benign prejudice to that other type of prejudice, the type where one person or group wants to cause harm or even destroy another person or group, because they are Blacks, or Armenians, or Jews, or Tutsis, or Muslims, or . . . ?

This is one of the key concerns of this book, of our children's aggression profiles. Study of prejudice has led me to propose that two factors lead to the conversion of *benign prejudice* into *malignant prejudice*. These two factors are (1) the displacement and projection of a person's own accumulated hostility and hate onto innocent others, and (2) militant education.

## The Displacement and Projection of One's Own Hostility and Hate onto Innocent Others

Hating those we love creates difficulty for all of us.[28] Even being very angry with someone we love causes us distress and anxiety. Unfortunately, it is impossible to rear kids well without causing them some distress and therewith they experience anger toward us. Having to leave a young child to go to work, setting limits (see chapter 4), demanding that the child eat, or go to bed, or do his/her homework, etc. all tend to make children angry with their parents.

Consider then how difficult it is for the young child whose ability to control his own very angry feelings is only beginning to develop. In both research and clinical work I have often seen how *the child's experiencing hostile feelings toward those he loves creates in the child a large dilemma.* After all, if a child is angry with his mother, the child will be very worried about the reaction he might get if he were let loose on Mom. It's also worrisome when the child's angry with Dad. So the child will swallow his anger and it will accumulate inside his psyche. But what often happens as well is that the child will find ways to get rid of the accumulating hostility and hate by using some strategies we call "defense mechanisms."

In our observational research, we saw a striking cluster of defenses young children erect when very angry with their mother. For instance, already by 12 months of age we had seen much evidence of *displacement* (when angry with mother, Jane picked up a block and threw it, not at her mother but at the woman sitting next to her mother!) By 18 months of age we saw clear evidence of *projection* (a strategy where the child projects her own hostility onto someone else: "I'm not angry at her, she's angry with me"), *rationalization* ("I'm angry with her because she was mean when she told me to brush my teeth"), and *denial* ("I didn't do that; it was an accident"). Then, especially organizing of prejudice, starting from 5 to 6 years on, we saw behaviors from which we could infer *"reality-distorting defenses,"* including *reductionism* ("All Blacks end up in jail!"), *caricaturing* ("All Jews are greedy!"), *depreciation* ("All Spics are lazy and don't deserve to be paid like us."), and *vilification* ("All Muslims are terrorists!"), defenses that play a key role in the organization of what I call *"malignant prejudice."*

## The Role of Trauma in the Predisposition to Malignant Prejudice

Given that even in normal-average homes rearing children leads to their getting angry with their parents, consider the amount of hostility and hate children accumulate when they are neglected or abused at home, be it physically or emotionally.[29] We'll talk more about this in the course of the chapters. For now, I want to say that

> *Being traumatized by one's own parents is a major contributor to the generation of hostility and hate in humans.*

Of course, much hurtfulness happens to people; but most people are vigorous so that not all intense pain is traumatizing. It is when one feels overwhelmed by a highly painful event of shocking meaning to the self that we experience it as traumatizing. Various factors determine the degree of psychic pain we experience: (1) the *nature* of the traumatic event, (2) the *age* and *state of self* at the time of occurrence, (3) who is the perpetrator, (4) whether it is episodic or chronic, (5) what meaning we give to the event, and, highly critical, (6) *whether the event is perceived as intentional or accidental.* All these combine to determine the degree to which we are traumatized. For example, abuse at the hands of one's own mother or father causes much more psychic pain than when the abuse is caused us by a stranger or an "enemy." Neglect or abuse by those we count on for love and protection multiplies the degree of psychic pain experienced and as I said before, drives many an individual to bullying, delinquent, and criminal behaviors.

I don't want to oversimplify how traumatized humans may behave. As has been amply documented, many cope with severe trauma with remarkable resilience which brings out in them noteworthy creativity and productivity. Nor do most who are traumatized become delinquents and criminals; many become depressed and self-punishing, and some become emotionally very disturbed. In addition, although many will erect the cluster of defenses I have noted, these defenses may not result in their developing malignant prejudice. These individuals may not target a given group of "others" toward whom their hate is discharged; in fact, they may not share their outrage with others; they act alone, sometimes with particular, sometimes with any random target victims. Regrettably, many who are heavily traumatized develop a pressing need to discharge their hate in the form of "revenge,"[30] which creates in them *the need to have enemies.*[31]

In sum then, the more children are traumatized, the greater the load of accumulating hostility, the more the defenses set up to cope with heightened levels of hate and rage persist, the more they become patterned. For the past two decades, neurobiological findings have taught us that patterns of reactivity and behavior become structured in brain neural pathways[32] early in life and thus become part of personality formation. But in addition then, there is the role education plays in our developing the tendency to feel *malignant prejudice* toward others.

### The Role of Education in Our Developing Malignant Prejudice

Yes, high loads of accumulated hostile destructiveness may transform our benign prejudice into malignant prejudice. But malignant prejudice can be greatly facilitated, even in individuals whose accumulating hostile destructiveness is moderate and is not sufficient to of itself lead to the formation of malignant prejudice. I have said[33] that education is programmed to socialize the child, tending to mandate that he/she be like the other members of their community. This can be a major contributor to transforming benign prejudice into malignant prejudice. A German friend, painfully distressed while and after reading my Holocaust memoirs[34] wrote to me that, when he was young, even thought he did not even know one Jew, he had learned to hate Jews because he was taught that "the Jews had killed Christ."

This teaching, to hate someone we are made to believe is our enemy, is driven in large part by the demand that the child identify with his/her parents and the society the parents represent. This teaching of dogma often carries with it "malignant distortions" of the "enemy" brought about by "reality distorting defenses" that justify malignant prejudice toward them. Here education is put into service to compel malignant prejudice. *This form of teaching dishonors education!*

Let's get to the central issue of this book. What is aggression? And, how can parents and other child caregivers and educators optimize children's healthy aggression profiles and, especially, how can we prevent their becoming trouble-makers?

## NOTES

1. Parens, H., Scattergood, E., Duff, A., & Singletary, W. (1997). *Parenting for Emotional Growth (PEG): The Textbook©.* and *PEG: A Curriculum for Students in Grades K Thru 12©.* As well as Parens, H. & Rose-Itkoff, C. (1997). *PEG: The Workshops Series©.* All these *Parenting for Emotional Growth (PEG)* materials are available on one CD entitled, *Parenting for Emotional Growth©,* which can

be obtained on Amazon.com and at the Thomas Jefferson University Book Store in Philadelphia.

2. Parens, H. (1993). Toward preventing experience-derived emotional disorders: Education for Parenting. In: *Prevention in Mental Health*, H. Parens & S. Kramer, eds., pp. 121–48. Northvale, NJ: Jason Aronson, Inc.

3. Since 1970, our work with parents and their young children has formally turned to education for parenting. We have developed two methods for this work. First, we use a group method for teaching parenting to people who are already parents (Parens, H., Pollock, L., & Prall, R.C. [1974]. Film #3: *Prevention/Early Intervention Mother-Infant Groups*. Audio-Visual Media Section, Eastern Pennsylvania Psychiatric Institute, Philadelphia, PA). A group consists of seven to ten mothers (and fathers, where feasible) with all their very young children, who meet for a one-and-a-half-hour weekly session with two mental health professionals knowledgeable in child development. In our group, members continued in the group, which was open-ended, from infancy until their children were 5. In a natural setting, we talked about the behaviors occurring in the children that were puzzling or troublesome to the parents. We also discussed any questions the parents had about their children or their parenting. Some groups of this kind have met for several years, others are of limited duration, in the course of which we have seen mothers of all educational levels acquire much understanding of their children's emotional experiencing and the psychodynamics of their behaviors, and from that develop a good basis for growth-promoting child rearing (See 37 years' follow-up remarks by mothers and their grown children of our original group in *The Urgent Need for Universal Parenting Education: A Documentary*, produced by H. Parens & P. Gilligan. Thomas Jefferson University, Media Division, Philadelphia, PA, 2008). Such parenting education groups have been carried out for years by a cluster of mental health professionals associated with the Psychoanalytic Center of Philadelphia in the Philadelphia area.

The second method is to teach parenting to students—parents-to-be—from kindergarten through grade 12. We have developed a curriculum encompassing the emotional sector of parenting (Parens, H., Scattergood, E., Duff, A., & Singletary, W. [1997]. *Parenting for Emotional Growth: A Curriculum for Students in Grades K Thru 12*. © TXu 680–613). Preliminary field applications of this method by us and ongoing applications of such derivative educational materials developed and used by Educating Children for Parenting® have been very well received by students and have shown gratifying results.

4. See H. Parens (2010). *Handling Children's Aggression Constructively*. Lanham, MD: Jason Aronson/Rowman & Littlefield Publishers, Inc. See chapter 1 for details.

5. In developing my model of aggression, I have made efforts to be as clear as I have found to be useful. In this, I distinguish between trends in aggression that are critically different and have distinguishable functions in human (and other animal) adaptation. I discuss the model of aggression in detail in chapter 2. For now, I will

say that there is a trend I label "hostile aggression" which for reasons I explain in chapter 2 also includes the sub-trend "hostile destructiveness," the specific form of hostile aggression which includes hostility, hate, and rage.

6. For an extensive documentation and discussion of this decades-long debate, see chapters 2 and 3 of H. Parens (1979 [2008]), *The Development of Aggression in Early Childhood.* Lanham, MD: Jason Aronson/Rowman & Littlefield Publishers, Inc.

7. Of course, the greatest degree and rate of development occurs before the infant is born. Imagine the miraculous degree and rate of development from the fertilized egg to the 9-month-old fetus! This is why, given that the fetus' health and development is *totally* dependent on the environment the mother provides her fetus, her self-care is so vitally important.

8. Referenced in *Handling Children's Aggression Constructively*, chapter 2.

9. Referring especially to the work of D. P. Farrington from Cambridge, England and his colleagues, Emmy Werner (Werner & Smith 1992) notes that "The more successful men were likely to have [had] mothers [who] had high opinions of their sons" (p. 9). I have heard from Holocaust survivors, as from Henry Krystal, Anna Ornstein, and know from my own Holocaust experiences, that we ascribed our sense of self-value in the face of the humiliations and abuses to which we were subjected: "I knew that my mother loved me." Sigmund Freud is known to have said as much. I have also found the converse which is that, even in the face of being loved and thought-of well by one's father, the pain of not having felt well-enough loved by one's mother may have lifelong painful reverberations.

10. Pruett, K. D. (1987). *The Nurturing Father*, Warner Books. Pruett also made this point in a lecture he delivered in Philadelphia on May 4, 2002 entitled, "Fathers and young children: Longitudinal lessons in autonomy, gatekeeping, overnights, etc." at the Annual Margaret S. Mahler Symposium.

11. In a lecture I gave in Munich, Germany, at an international conference held in November 2008, I spoke to this point. The lecture, entitled "Attachment, aggression, and the prevention of malignant prejudice" appears in German in *Bindung, Angst und Aggression* (2010) KH Brisch & T Hellbruegge, Hrsg. Stuttgart, Germany, pp. 12–46. It will appear in English in *The Psychoanalytic Inquiry* (in press).

12. Kestenberg, J., and Brenner, I. (1996). *The Last Witness: The Child Survivor of the Holocaust.* New York: American Psychiatric Press.

13. Authors of such studies include among others, Norman Garmezy, E. James Anthony, Emmy Werner, Boris Cyrulnik, and Stuart Hauser.

14. Aichhorn, A. (1944). *Wayward Youth*. New York: Viking Press (First German edition, 1925); Bowlby, J. (1946). *Forty-Four Juvenile Thieves*. London: Balliere, Tindall & Cox; Werner, E.E. & Smith, R.S. (1992). *Overcoming the Odds—High Risk Children from Birth to Adulthood*. Ithaca NY: Cornell University Press; McCord, W., McCord, J., & Zola, I. K. (1959). *Origins of Crime*. New York: Columbia University Press; Gilligan, J. (1997). *Violence: Reflections on a National Epidemic*. New York: Vintage Books (G. P. Putnam's Sons, 1996).

15. Sroufe, A., Egeland, B., Carlson, E.A., Collins, W.A. (2005). *The Development of the Person*. New York: The Guilford Press.

16. Brazelton, B. (1981). Affective reactivity in mother-child interaction. Presented at the 12th Annual M. S. Mahler Symposium on Child Development, May, Philadelphia, PA.

17. Beebe, B. (2005). Infant research and implications for adult treatment. Video presentation to the Psychoanalytic Center of Philadelphia Scientific Meeting, March 4, Philadelphia, PA.

18. In my original aggression model design (see *The Development of Aggression in Early Childhood* [1979]), I proposed that the trend I here call *hostile aggression* be labeled *hostile destructiveness*. In a further effort to sharpen the clarity of the model, I am here limiting the sub-trend *hostile destructiveness* specifically to aggression feelings we all commonly link with destructiveness, namely, *hostility, hate, rage* and more complex feeling-laden motivations that include hostility and destructiveness, like *revenge*. I need this further clarification because as I define them in chapter 2, more benign negative feelings like *annoyance, irritability,* and *anger* do not lead to the wish *to harm, to inflict pain* and certainly not *to destroy*. Aggression is a complex phenomenon; it has defied scientists' efforts to fully understand it and explain it.

19. I explain how this comes about in chapter 2.

20. Detailed in chapters 2, 5, and 16 of *The Future of Prejudice: Psychoanalysis and the Prevention of Prejudice*, ed. H. Parens, A. Mahfouz, S.W. Twemlow & D.E. Scharff (2007). Lanham, MD: Rowman & Littlefield Publishers, Inc.

21. While the major English dictionaries define prejudice as being both negative and positive pre-judgments, i.e., negative and positive views held without basis in facts, it is most commonly understood in its negative bias. I will focus in this book only on negative prejudice.

22. Spitz, R. (1946). The smiling response: A contribution to the ontogenesis of social relations. *Genetic Psychology Monographs* 34:57–125; Spitz, R. (1965). *The First Year of Life*. New York: International Universities Press.

23. Piaget, J. (1937). *La Construction du Réel Chez l'Enfant*. Neuchâtel: Delachaux et Niestle; Piaget, J. (1963). The Child's Conception of the World. Paterson, N.J.: Littlefield, Adams.

24. I proposed this in chapters 2 and 16 in *The Future of Prejudice*, edited by H. Parens, A. Mahfouz, S.W. Twemlow & D.E. Scharff, published in 2007 by Rowman & Littlefield Publishers, Inc.

25. Chapters 2 and 16 in *The Future of Prejudice*.

26. Parens, H. (2008). *The Urgent Need for Universal Parenting Education: A Documentary*. A DVD Produced by Parens, H. & Gilligan, P., Director, Thomas Jefferson University, Medical School Media Division, Philadelphia, PA.

27. Chapters 2 and 16 in *The Future of Prejudice*.

28. Chapters 2 and 16 in *The Future of Prejudice*.

29. Chapters 2 and 16 in *The Future of Prejudice*.

30. Gilligan, J. (1997). *Violence: Reflections on a National Epidemic.* New York: Vintage Books.

31. Volkan, V.D. (1988). *The Need to Have Enemies and Allies: From Clinical Practice to International Relationships.* Northvale, NJ: Jason Aronson.

32. Kandel, E.R. (1979). Psychotherapy and the single synapse. *The New England Journal of Medicine,* 301(19):1028–37; Kandel, E R., Schwartz, J.H., & Jessell, T.M. (1991). *Principles of Neural Science,* Third Edition. New York: Elsevier.

33. Chapters 2 and 16 in *The Future of Prejudice.*

34. Parens, H. (2004). *Renewal of Life—Healing from the Holocaust.* Rockville, MD: Schreiber Publishing, Inc.

# 2

# WHAT IS AGGRESSION?

- We believe we know what aggression is. [1] What more do we really need to know about it?
- First, we're not born with it like it turns out in us. It's shaped by our experiences.
- Aggression is not all "bad"; in fact, some of it is "good," really good!
- Our research-based model explains what is "bad" in it which needs to be contained; and what is "good" in it which needs to be fostered.
- Understanding this facilitates handling your child's aggression constructively.
- In the chapters that follow we'll talk about how to avoid generating "bad" aggression in everyday parent-child interactions.
- It's all about how you can optimize your child's aggression profile.

## WHY WE NEED TO KNOW WHAT AGGRESSION REALLY IS

There would be no point in trying to understand what aggression is, where it comes from, or what causes its various manifestations, were it not for the fact that dealing with our children's hostility—toward us, others, and themselves—is among the most troublesome tasks of parenting. Difficult and unpleasant as it is, it is unavoidable that our children—little ones, grade-school ones, and adolescents—will often be angry with us, even at times hate us, wish they could be rid of us, and then dread the thought ever after.

30-month-old Joey, upset because Mother prohibits his taking a toy from another child, half shouts at her, "I hate you!" Troubled, Mother—who knows that children are less able than adults to control their feelings—tells him, "Oh, I know you don't mean that."

Unfortunately, not a helpful comeback! We'll talk about why it is not helpful.

Ted, a bright fifteen-year-old, has been searching to buy a guitar. He's never tried his hand at it. His father asks whether the one he is considering buying, one offered for sale by a friend, is as good a deal as he might get in a well-known instrument store in town. Convinced by his friend that "it's a good deal," he angrily blurts out as he walks away from his father: "You always mess things up!" Stunned, upset, his father backs off.

It is equally unavoidable that we, as parents, will at times be furious with our children and, because we love them, feel terrible about it after. Few experiences produce more guilt and shame in good parents than those moments when we feel, "I'd like to be rid of that little . . . "

Ambivalence—being angry with, feeling hostile toward, and even hating a person we love—is experienced in all primary relationships. These are the relationships most meaningful to us: between parents and children, between siblings, between boyfriend and girlfriend, between husband and wife. Of course, being angry with or hating those we love causes much difficulty in our close relationships.

## WHEN SHOULD PARENTS START TO DEAL WITH THEIR CHILDREN'S AGGRESSIVE BEHAVIORS?

People have asked me: When should I start to set limits with my child? I answer: When limits are needed. When a teething 7-month-old bites mother's breast while suckling, it's reasonable for the mother to react with "Ouch! Don't do that!" This informs the baby that she hurt you and you want her to not do that. You then gently verbally set limits that are appropriate even with a 7-month-old. Obviously no harshness is needed to let the baby learn that biting mother—or anyone for that matter—is not acceptable behavior.

The child's aggression profile develops from the first days of life on. Parents often tell me that their young children won't understand; that it makes no sense to them to tell them to not do something. Children understand our communications much earlier than many parents believe. It is not that a 7-month-old already understands mother's words. It's she also hear the sounds Mother made in reaction to something she did. Infants hear our tone, see our gestures and facial expressions that tell much even if we say nothing. A mother's or father's look can cast sunshine into the child's life or terrify the child. We all know the look of joy that opens the skies; and we know "the look that kills!" This understanding begins in the early weeks of life.

*Most basic in child rearing is this. When growth-promoting[2] childrearing efforts are made to optimize a child's development, including his/her aggression profile, the earlier in the child's life such growth promoting strategies are put into play, the healthier will the development be of the foundation of the child's personality. The healthier their foundation, the more likely the child's further developing personality and aggression profile will be healthy.*

Equally expectable, the poorer the young child's foundation and developing aggression profile, the more difficult will it be to restructure the aggression profile into a healthy one as years pass. It is a mistake to assume that "I can wait till my child is old enough," say 5 or 6, or older, to institute child rearing strategies regarding any aspect of the child's behaviors, especially so with respect to aggression and relatedness. Some parents make the gross mistake of thinking that they'll "talk to their kids when they are teenagers, because what good is it talking to young kids when you can't *really* talk to them. After all kids don't really understand and they don't remember!" This is totally wrong; children understand and remember only too well.

It is well known now, that with an adolescent whose aggression profile has developed into one leading to antisocial behavior, delinquency, or criminality, it will be difficult to convert that teenager's aggression profile into a healthy one. It can be done. But it will require much work to undo such established unhealthy trends in aggression. For this reason, the parent who picks up this book, and books like it, and tries to apply to a conduct-troubled teenager some of the principles I and others talk about is very likely to find it a struggle to undo the teenager's troubled beginnings and to change his/her established patterns of coping with life. Working with conduct disturbed teenagers has taught us how difficult it is to change their view of others, adults and peers, and of the society in which they live.

## UNDERSTANDING OUR CHILDREN'S BEHAVIORS HELPS US DEVISE GROWTH-PROMOTING STRATEGIES FOR CHILD REARING

When we understand a problem, we are more likely to know how to solve it. When we understand what our child's behavior is about, toddler or teenager, we can parent more constructively and with more confidence; our child-rearing strategies are more likely to work. There is much that parents understand, and much they do well, without recourse to the help of others or books. Much of what we do that is based on what we feel, understand, and believe is best will, most likely, be best for our children. But, we may at times not be as right about what we understand and what to do as we believe. And, even the best of parents at times find themselves in a quandary about what to do, particularly with respect to their children's aggressive behavior.

As noted in chapter 1, I have had the privilege to study and work clinically and educationally for nearly four decades with parents and their children. From these decades of work and from our personal experiences as parents, my colleagues and I have gained much respect for parents, for their devotion, ingenuity, and all-consuming efforts to rear their children well. We have learned well what a taxing and challenging job parenting is!

## HOW A CHILD'S AGGRESSION CAN CREATE PROBLEMS FOR HIMSELF AND HIS PARENTS

13-month-old Mary was very angry with her mother. Outraged, she raised her arm visibly intending to hit her; but she stopped her motion, her arm upright, stopped in mid-air. She *inhibited* her action to strike the Mommy to whom she was already so well attached.

We are all very clever at protecting ourselves against knowing what we feel when what we feel causes us much anxiety, fear, distress, and/or pain. Freud and many psychoanalysts who followed him have talked about this now for a century.

But these psychic "defense mechanisms," while they protect us now, can also have maladaptive effects at the time the defense is erected and, if these defense mechanisms become part of our customary coping strategies, may also be maladaptive later. What mental health professionals have long known is that, when children and adolescents (and adults) do all they can to hold back their intense hostile and hate feelings they also tend to *inhibit* that "good" aggression which we use in the service of learning in school and in achieving our goals. Years before I started the project I described in chapter 1, a colleague and I found[3] in the psychotherapeutic treatment of a cluster of elementary and high school kids that, when we could help them understand what made them so angry and helped them tolerate these feelings and deal with them constructively, they began to do better in school, at home, and with their peers. We believed that dealing better with their hostility and hate, they were able to free up their "good" aggressive energies and apply these to learning. This finding was in the back of my mind when I started the study of aggression I described in chapter 1.

## SO, WHAT IS AGGRESSION?

Let's establish what we mean by *aggression*. Aggression is not uniformly defined. One reason for this is that behaviors of very different kinds can and have plausibly been catalogued under the heading of aggression. For example, *hostility* is a form of aggression we know to be very troublesome. *Assertiveness*, on the other hand, is a form of aggression that can serve us well in achieving our goals; in fact, we cannot cope well without it. Most problematic is that we do not all mean the same thing when we call some behavior *aggressive*.

Here is the model of aggression I developed out of our research and clinical findings. Over four decades of study, it has held up and served me well. A number of my colleagues have let me know that it has also served them well.

## A WORKING MODEL FOR UNDERSTANDING AGGRESSION

Aggression shows itself in different forms that are evident even in very young children. All these forms of aggressive behaviors have one common feature: Each is

*An attempt to control, act upon, and master* **oneself** *and* **one's environment**, *including the people within it.*

These aggressive behaviors seem to be propelled by inborn adaptive mechanisms and by an "inner force" that motivates them.

## CATEGORIES OF AGGRESSIVE BEHAVIORS

Observing our infants twice weekly for two-hour sessions (see chapter 1) allowed us to catalogue most of the aggressive behaviors we saw during their first 15 months of life into *four categories:*

1. Unpleasure-related destructiveness[4] (rage reaction of infancy);
2. Nondestructive aggression (pressured exploratory/learning activity);
3. Nonaffective destructiveness (feeding activity); and
4. Pleasure-related destructiveness (teasing and taunting activity).

1. The easiest behaviors to catalogue were those that look like *rage. Rage* is a built-in reaction evident from birth on. In its purest form in early childhood, it seems automatic and looks like a reflex to unbearable pain. Experiencing pain may start with the infant whining and then crying, but if the pain that triggers it is not tended to or does not spontaneously stop, the crying will become more intense and at some point will explode into a rage reaction. Since this is the clearest evidence of the type of aggression we all know, I used *the rage reaction of infancy* as the best example of what I called *unpleasure-related destructiveness,* the technical term for pain-triggered behavior which in an older individual might lead to destructive behavior. In quality a rage reaction is clearly *hostile;* but we do not believe that it requires "an idea" associated with pain. I'll say more about that shortly.

2. The behavior in category 2 pushed me to research aggression. In 1973, I described in detail[5] how a 15-week-old baby demonstrated the type of "aggressive" activity which I believe, by virtue of the pressure on the child's face and in her entire body as well as the persistence of her 25-minutes-long "work" I labeled, *nondestructive aggression.*

After a 25-minute nap 15-week-old Jane woke up. Out of nowhere, her mother put a set of plastic rings on a string in front of her—perhaps to give her something "to play with." We filmed her "play," one continuous 30-minute period of activity during which she was amazingly occupied with these rings. After staring at them, she began to pull them apart and mouth them; her facial expression and the vocal sounds she was making gave clear evidence of much pressure and effort. She moved the rings back and forth while she stared at them, a serious look on her face; she looked like she was "working." Was she trying to discover what these "things" are? She'd not seen such things before? Notable was her intense, work-like seriousness, the constancy of her efforts, the inner-drivenness of that activity. After about 15 minutes she became frustrated, burped up a bit of milk, returned to the rings and after yet more effort, she stopped, lay her head on the floor, I thought, really tired out. All in all Jane had been "busy" for about 25 minutes.

We observed this kind of pressured, driven, "exploratory" activity in 8 or our (then) 9 infants from the ages of 8 to 16 weeks on, during periods of wakefulness and physiologic and emotional comfort. In Jane, the strong pressure and duration of this exploratory activity was impressive. Its persistence was compelling; Jane did not elect to look; she seemed driven from within to look, to explore, I thought, to gratify the push from within to learn about, to control, to master this new world into which she was born! More below.

3. The third type of aggressive behavior category, *nonaffective destructiveness,* is evident day in and day out. When we eat, we do so by destroying animal and vegetable life. Sure, in infancy, the feeding activity of the human young is principally one of taking in liquids. But it is not long before solids are introduced. If we are to understand aggression in our universe, we must also consider this form of aggression. This aggressive behavior too is destructive. But this destruction is not driven by the wish to harm what we have destroyed and are chewing to bits and enjoy. We're not angry; we do this to survive! I therefore labeled this aggressive behavior, nonaffective destructiveness, nonaffective meaning without feeling hostility, hate, or rage. This fact distinguishes this type of aggression from the type where the destruction is driven by those negative feelings which lead to wanting to cause harm.

4. The fourth category of aggressive behaviors, *pleasure-related destructiveness*, took us by surprise. We began to see this type of aggression when the infants were just turning one year of age. Two examples stand out. The first took place between two 11-month-old kids.

Jane seemed to be pleasantly busy exploring the environment in her usual way. She came to Tammy, also 11 months old, standing there, pacifier in her mouth as was her wont at this time. Jane paused a moment standing in front of Tammy, both looking at each other, when Jane just reached for and plucked Tammy's pacifier from her mouth! Jane's mother reacted immediately, got up and returned the pacifier to Tammy while telling Jane not to do that. Jane didn't seem particularly troubled by her mother's reaction. She just walked away. She circled back to Tammy and looking at her, reached for Tammy's pacifier and again pulled it from her mouth. Jane seemed to look a bit more intently now. Tammy got upset, turned to her mother for help which she got as both her mother and Jane's mother reacted to the event; each mother tending to her own kid. Jane's mother's tone was more troubled and firm this time. Jane walked away seemingly not too dismayed about all this, a bit of a smirk on her face. After a few moments, there she was again, in front of Tammy and again, pulled the pacifier from her mouth. This time Jane smiled as she did this; Tammy now started to cry! Both mothers were there in an instant. Jane's mother scolded her, which did not seem to surprise Jane.

What was this behavior about? Was it 11-month-old Jane's wish to hurt Tammy? Was it her experiencing pleasure at having an impact on her universe? Was it real pleasure at seeing someone react with distress and cry? Clearly it felt nasty to Tammy. Was this Jane's intention? It certainly was not an act of friendliness. Was it aggressive? Yes, it was acting upon her universe; to have an effect on it. Where do we categorize this type of aggression? I was not sure in what category to put it. The second event was more complex but helped me see and understand a well-known but extremely important dynamic of hostile aggression.

18-month-old Candy and her twin sister were playing among the other children and their mothers as we carried out our usual observations (see chapter 1). For no reason visible to us, 2½ year-old Donnie approached Candy and thrust his arm around her neck and grabbed her head—in wrestling it's "a half-Nelson." We were all startled! Especially so, Candy and Donnie's mothers; they intervened immediately. Candy didn't retaliate against Donnie. She moped; and she disrupted her sister's play with toys. Though upset, her mother calmed her sympathetically.

At our next group session three days later, Candy, her sister, and her mother came as usual. Candy seemed subdued. Some 20 minutes later, I saw Candy's face come to attention as she focused across our Children's Unit's Day Room where we met. Donnie, his younger sister (who was our research subject), and their mother had just walked in. Directly, Candy walked up to him and without a sound, raised her fist and struck him in the arm! With this she smiled softly, Mona Lisa–like. Donnie was startled but interestingly, did not strike back. Candy's mother readied to get up but saw that the event was over.

It made clear sense to me; it might have to Candy's mother as well. In fact, I commented to the mothers that it seemed as though Candy had been planning how to let Donnie know that she was very angry with him for what he had done to her 3 days before. I wondered if Donnie reacted by doing nothing when Candy hit him because he too understood that this was retribution for what he had done to her.

And then here is another example. This time the hostile behavior is expressed with pleasure and the overt wish to cause emotional pain. This kind of behavior becomes evident in children from about 1 year of age on, in behavior we would identify as taunting.

Two-and-a-half-year-old Susan seemed rather restless as she went from one toy to another. She noted with interest a toy 1½-year-old Tommy was exploring. With a half smile on her face, she reached for that toy and pulled it from Tommy's hand. Her mother was looking elsewhere and did not see this. Within moments, Susan—again smiling—grabbed the next toy Tommy picked up. Again, she watched Tommy's reaction with seeming satisfaction. Tommy fussed. He picked up yet another toy, and in a moment, Susan grabbed it. Her smile now conveyed a feeling of getting pleasure out of being nasty to Tommy. Now Tommy was heard, and Susan's mother, tuned in to what was going on, intervened.

We felt that most of the aggressive behaviors we saw in the young children could be classified in these four categories. To be sure some behaviors are more complex and fall through the cracks, such as a 6-month-old tearing a page out of a book. It best falls under the category of exploring, that is, nondestructive aggression. But clearly, it is destructive although the infant is totally unaware that it is. Having these categories of behavior, what could we say about aggression as a whole? Being researchers, we had to come up with some explanatory ideas, with hypotheses about aggression. Here's what I came up with.

## THERE ARE THREE TRENDS OF AGGRESSION

I proposed that these 4 categories of aggressive behavior show us evidence of *three* **trends** *of aggression*, or 3 psychologically and functionally different kinds of aggression:

1. *Hostile aggression* (categories 1 and 4)
2. *Nondestructive aggression* (category 2), and
3. *Non-affective destructiveness* (category 3).

**1. The trend *hostile aggression*** is what we see in angry, nasty behavior, and especially in hurtful behavior that is driven by hate and rage as we find in bullying, torturing, vengefulness, and the like. As I detail below, hostile aggression is generated in us to try by force to remove any thing, alive or not, that we believe, rightly or wrongly, threatens to harm or injure us. But, while in essence it is self-protective, we all know that it often causes many individual and collective problems and much human suffering.

We use different words: anger, hostility, hate, rage, to express the different degrees of this type of aggression. We know that the level of intensity of this aggression gives the aggressive feelings we then have very different qualities. It's not the same to be angry with someone and to hate that someone. Therefore, the trend hostile aggression represents a wide range of "hostile" feelings. I use the concept hostile aggression as an umbrella term that includes this well-known range of hostile feelings that span varying levels of intensity: from irritability to anger, then, to hostility, hate, and rage and all the increasingly more destructive thoughts and behaviors these feelings give rise to.

And we all know that these various intensities of hostile aggression tend to lead to very different outcomes. I should define these terms, familiar as they are, because we often use them differently—in fact, it's at times difficult to know just what level of hostility a given person means—and because there are important distinctions between them that call for different handling strategies by caregivers.

**Anger** is an unpleasant and troubling feeling we have when someone causes us distress of any sort, but it is moderate distress. In anger, our negative feelings toward the one or the thing that causes us distress, does not lead us to the point of wanting to cause that person or thing harm; we are satisfied by telling that person to stop causing us distress or stop the thing that does so, and if it stops, we can go about our way. In contrast to rage, which is a reflex-like reaction, anger as well as hostility and hate, are always associated with an idea. That is, true feelings of anger require the child's ability to think, such as: "She is bothering me; she is annoying me; that makes me angry with her."

**Hostility** per se, the noun, is what we feel when the distress caused us reaches a level of emotional pain that leads us to want to inflict pain on that source, person or thing, in order to be rid of it, to make the source stop doing what it's doing. Whereas in anger we don't want to inflict pain, in hostility we do. A critical step has taken place: hostility is experienced when one feels, "this pain is too much!" Or, "I can't take it!" The intensity of emotional (psychic) pain has crossed a line of tolerance. This line of tolerance, how much emotional pain one can take at a given moment, is critical for what the emotional pain leads us to want to do. With anger one just wants the pain to be stopped. With hostility one wants to cause the person pain and then some more. With rage one may want to tear them to bits. With hate one may want to do a variety of hurtful things or never see that person again. Each word has an individualized meaning determined by the intensity of the emotional pain experienced.

I said that hostile aggression is generated in us to try by force to remove any thing, alive or not, that we believe, rightly or wrongly, threatens to harm or injure us. While I am speaking of psychological behavior, it is based on the biological reactivity within us which drives this behavior. Our reaction to emotional pain has a physical, bodily root: that fundamental principle in biology which in Medicine we call "irritability of the protoplasm." A cell, the smallest building block of all tissues in our body, stated simply consists of a nucleus, protoplasm in which the nucleus lies, and a surrounding membrane that contains both. Just like an egg—yolk, white, and shell. By virtue of the "irritability of the protoplasm," when a toxic agent or substance accumulates in the cell, an alarm reactivity occurs within the protoplasm to protect against the destruction of the cell. This alarm reaction acts primarily to rid the cell of that which threatens its existence.

Drawing a parallel between this single cell and a multi-celled single organism, when the organism is threatened with harm or injury, a bio-psychological force is set in motion to rid the organism of the toxic agent. In psychological life, this bio-psychological force is "aggression." Therefore, I say "aggression is generated by psychic pain" which is activated by the biological mandate to preserve life.

A critical psychological factor in our experience of psychic (emotional) pain is that physical pain caused us by someone may make us angry. But the degree of psychic pain that comes with it will be mostly determined by whether the pain experienced was caused accidently or intentionally. If someone accidently steps on my foot; I don't like it; but accidents happen. If he intentionally stomps on my foot; that hurts me but in addition, I take it as a serious offense. *Intentionally caused physical pain* causes much more *emotional pain* than accidental pain.

**Rage** is an intense reaction of hostile aggression caused by a painful event that brings with it unbearable emotional pain. A rage reaction is physiologically driven, automatic, and may occur even before an infant can put into thought or understand what the source of the pain is, whether accidental or intentional. Rage, in fact, is the most primitive form of hostile aggression. While anger and hostility do not appear until about 6 months of age, rage can appear at birth.

**Hate** is the most complex of the hostile aggression feelings. Those who have studied it hold that hate is not experienced until the child is about 18 months of age. In contrast to anger, hostility, and rage, hate endures well beyond the event that gives rise to it and tends to be difficult to reverse. Even a series of apologies may not do it.

One more critical thought about hostile aggression. It will be of much value to caregivers to consider the fact that when the emotional pain one experiences crosses the line of tolerance, "I can't take this! It's too much!" *hostile aggression* undergoes a qualitative change that has led me to speak of this aggression as *hostile destructiveness*.[6] I have done this to emphasize that in reaction to *excessive emotional pain*, the aggression carries with it the wish to harm or even destroy. Milder levels of hostile aggression, as when we feel annoyance, irritation, or even anger do not lead to the wish to harm or destroy. This makes it useful for caregivers to try to evaluate the level of emotional pain the child they care for is experiencing.

So, given all these explanations, what do we make of Jane's behavior with Tammy? I could not be sure into which category of aggression to put it. While Jane's intention may not have been to hurt Tammy—which I think is the case—Tammy was hurt. This example fell between categories. If it was Jane's intention to upset Tammy then it had to be categorized as hurtful, *as in teasing*.

But I learned something critical from the example of Candy and Donnie, in that Candy dished out hostile feelings with a smile on her face; it seemed to be a pleasurable discharge of hostility toward another. My grasp of her behavior, however, was that Candy's seemingly pleasurable "attack" on Donnie was not really driven primarily by pleasure, but rather, by a quietly planned, perhaps unconscious, belated retribution for Donnie's startling, painful, and hurtful attack on her 3 days before.

> *This then was not driven in origin by pleasure but by a prior experi-*
> *ence of emotional pain: Donnie's intentional "attack" on her. So, when*
> *someone enjoys hurting another, while the attacker is experiencing*
> *pleasure, this hurting of another probably owes its origin to having*
> *oneself been subjected to experiences of excessive emotional pain that*
> *occurred before, perhaps even long before.*

I therefore put this type of aggression into the trend hostile aggression, assuming that this is the trend of aggression that drives this kind of behavior. This can account for the hostility in teasing, taunting, and bullying—even if the hostility is only mild in teasing, more than little in taunting, and surely even more in bullying. So the pleasure-related destructiveness category of behaviors really belongs in the trend of hostile aggression.

**2. The trend *nondestructive aggression*** is well represented in the activity I described in 15-week-old Jane. This example, which I use as an example for nondestructive aggression, is simply considered by some theorists to be assertiveness. Based on the psychodynamics (the meaning of the action, its quality and character) of this behavior, I consider assertiveness to be a manifestation of nondestructive aggression. Furthermore, I hold that nondestructive aggression is the engine of "autonomy." The child's sense of autonomy,[7] of "I want to do this or that; I can do this or that!" is a critical element in the development of a "sense of self," of the mental construction we call one's "Self" (see chapter 3).

I called it nondestructive aggression because this aggressive behavior is not used to destroy something; and it is aggressive because of the quality and character of its inherent pressure. It is the energy that drives us to pursue our goals, to gain control over things, including oneself and those around us. By "control" here I don't mean to make oneself into an automaton, but to have some influence on how one reacts to events, what one does with ones' feelings, how one drives oneself. So far as "to control others" it is not to make them automatons either, nor to just make them do what we want, but to be able to accommodate ourselves to the others and have them act toward us in ways that we would like, surely in ways that do not harm us. When the need to control others becomes restrictive of others, in human interactions it is driven by anxiety or it is in the service of achieving goals that may or may not be in the interest of others. As I detailed in 1979[8] I held and still hold that the aim of nondestructive aggression is "the exploration, asserting oneself upon, control, assimilation, and mastery of the self and environment" (p. 101). This I then held and still do is the primary aim of all aggression, including that of hostile destructiveness.

**3. The trend *non-affective destructiveness,*** whether or not it is so labeled, must be included in any general theory of aggression. I believe that to understand the nature of human aggression, we must take into account all aggression evident in the Animal Kingdom. Yes, our greatest concern is what I call hostile aggression and especially its subcategory hostile destructiveness. True, during wartime, in times when "terrorism" in on our minds, hostile destructiveness preoccupies us from morning till night. But overall, the most common animal aggression is what ethnologists have called prey aggression, the aggression brought into action when a lioness chases a gazelle and once she catches it, kills it and now gratified, tears it piece by piece. The lioness uses sheer destructiveness to achieve her end, which is to provide herself with the food she needs. The fact is that self-preservation requires us to destroy animate organisms, animal or plant, to meet the needs of our body. To do so we destroy, we break down magnificently formed tissues, meat or vegetable. But clearly, we do not do so out of anger, hostility, or hate.

For our purposes in this book, to help parents and other caregivers deal constructively with their children's aggression we do not need to concern ourselves with helping them deal with their children's nonaffective destructiveness. Our challenge is to help parents optimize the way they help their children cope with their hostile aggression and with their nondestructive aggression. Here I want to distill what I already said about them.

## WHAT IS *NONDESTRUCTIVE AGGRESSION?*

- *Nondestructive aggression* is essential for constructive adaptation.
- It is present and functioning at birth.
- It is the clearest example of the inherent nature of aggression.
- Its aim is to assert oneself upon, control, and master oneself and one's environment.
- It propels and sustains self-determination and
- It drives us in the achievement of personal wishes and aims.
- This type of aggression is inherent in becoming competent and self-reliant.
- It motivates self-fulfilling competitiveness without being hostile and destructive.
- It serves to secure one's needs and to protect one's self, property, and rights.
- MOST IMPORTANT: *Nondestructive aggression* is the product of an inborn system that, as its primary function, serves survival. Some have called it a "life force."

## WHAT ARE *HOSTILE AGGRESSION* AND *HOSTILE DESTRUCTIVENESS?*

- *Hostile aggression* is a reaction of "wanting to rid oneself of something bad."
- It consists of the range of feelings from *irritability* to *annoyance, anger, hostility, rage,* and *hate.* These feelings lead to hostile behaviors as bullying, cruelty, revenge, etc.
- *Hostile aggression* is *not inborn.* This is one of its most critical features.[9]
- *Hostile aggression* is *not spontaneously activated.*
- But, there is a *mechanism* in our brain that can be activated to generate (produce) in us those hostile feelings of *hostile aggression. This mechanism is inborn.*
- This mechanism is activated by an experience of *emotional (psychic) pain.*

Therefore,

- An experience of psychic pain is *required* for generating in us hostile aggression.
- Psychic pain gives to aggression the *emotional* quality of anger, hostility, and hate.
- This *hostile aggression* changes into *hostile destructiveness* when the *psychic pain* felt crosses one's tolerance for it: "*I can't take this, it's too much!*"
- Pain that crosses one's tolerance-line changes the quality of hostile feelings from just wanting it stopped to *wanting to harm or destroy* the person causing such emotional pain.
- MOST IMPORTANT: *The degree to which hostile destructiveness is generated in us can be lessened or can be heightened by the degree to which one is subjected to psychic pain.*

## IMPLICATIONS FOR PARENTING

This model of aggression has large implications for avoiding the development of trouble-makers.

These trends in aggression are determined by the interplay of the child's *biologic make-up* and his/her real life *experiences* from birth on. On the side of their biological make-up for example, an infant born with a disturbance of any of her/his vital body systems such as the digestive system (as with colic), or the respiratory system (as with asthma), or the skin (as with eczema) commonly suffers much distress which the infant experiences both physically and *emotionally*. Also, infants born with immaturities of their central nervous system may find it difficult to tolerate the rhythms of daily life. For instance, an infant who *reacts rapidly* to any event (a "quick-reactor") when beginning to feel hungry may feel much distress when mother cannot be there immediately to feed the baby. Or an infant with a low threshold for irritability or some physiological intolerance is likely to react intensely to being too hot or too cold or tired. Some infants react with distress to what they experience as unbearable sounds, like loud noises. Of course, infants with allergies will react with irritability to items to which they are allergic. All these kids experience various kinds of pain which will also cause them "emotional pain."

Fortunately, most babies are not burdened with such biological vulnerabilities. In fact, most are born with remarkable tolerances, patience and resilience. They can wait reasonably to be fed, diapered, and tended to in the varied ways caregivers do 24 hours a day, 7 days a week.

*Experience* is the largest factor that determines the formation of the child's aggression profile. Decades of research and clinical work has documented the fact that, in development and in adaptation, *nondestructive aggression tends to be more favorable, when the level of hostile aggression in the child/adolescent's aggression profile is low.* We find in clinical work that when an individual struggles to contain a high-pressured accumulation of *hostile* destructiveness he/she experiences intense anxiety, and unconsciously feeling helpless, puts up defenses to self-protect by inhibiting the discharge of all expressions of aggression, both hostile and nondestructive. While blocking the discharge of intense feelings of hostility and hate in human interaction is desirable, it is undesirable that nondestructive aggression be inhibited given that it fuels assertiveness, persistence in pursuing goals, self-containment, regulation of action, and morally responsible compliance.

Note that the key hostile destructiveness generating factor is *excessive* psychic pain. But while excessive psychic pain causes no end of problems, unavoidable experiences of benign or moderate psychic pain often lead to efforts to master these and improve one's life situation. For instance, even infants have built-in adaptive mechanisms that become activated when they experience pain or discomfort, such as by putting their thumb or pacifier in their mouths. In doing so they are adapting, they are learning to soothe themselves; they are learning to be self-reliant (independent, some would say). Therefore, we do not want our children to never experience psychic pain—not that we could ever achieve this—we just want it to be in doses they can cope, even struggle some with.

And there are ways of enhancing a child's capability to cope and to modify the hostility generated within the child. This capability, in large part, depends on the child's having a good relationship with his or her parents. Each child has the capability to lessen the amount and the intensity of hostility that life circumstances generate within him or her. A sufficiently positive relationship to mother or father is necessary for the development of that potential capability. A good emotional relationship with our children has far-reaching implications, not only in the area of aggression but in all dimensions of emotional life (see chapters 1 and 10).

In the course of our studies in aggression and in education for parenting (see chapter 1), we have identified common areas of parent-child interaction where the child's aggression profile is shaped—where, (1) *nondestructive aggression* can be enhanced and *hostile aggression* be lessened; or the reverse, (2) *nondestructive aggression* can be weakened and *hostile aggression* intensified. These are:

- Expecting *obedience* is loaded with problems of hostility; *compliance* is not.
- How do we achieve *compliance?* By *setting limits and punishing constructively.*
- Teaching the child *how to discharge anger and hostility in acceptable ways.*
- Growth-promoting handling of the child's *rage reactions* and *temper tantrums.*
- Helping the child *cope with painful emotional feelings.*

In the chapters that follow we'll talk about optimizing parents' handling of these areas of parent-child interaction. In the process of exploring these everyday parent–child interactions, parents will find strategies that can also be applied in other circumstances. And we'll conclude the book with a chapter on the fact that *optimizing the parent-child relationship optimizes the child's aggression profile.*

## NOTES

1. "Aggression" is defined so variably that, among professionals and in the vernacular, one often cannot be sure what the user of the term means. I have addressed this dilemma in detail in H. Parens (1979 [2008]). *The Development of Aggression in Early Childhood.* Lanham, MD: Jason Aronson/Roman & Littlefield Publishers, Inc.

2. In our parenting education work we devised a 10-point scale of the quality of the parent's child rearing efforts which we described as *"from growth-disturbing to growth-promoting,"* meaning childrearing that interferes with or optimizes the child's developing emotional health. The more growth-promoting the parenting, the better the child's developing emotional health (see Parens, H. (1993), "Toward preventing experience-derived emotional disorders: Education for Parenting," in: *Prevention in Mental Health,* H. Parens & S. Kramer, eds., pp. 121–148. Northvale, NJ: Jason Aronson, Inc. as well as the DVD, *The Urgent Need for Universal Parenting Education: A Documentary* written and produced by H. Parens with media production by P. Gilligan, from the Thomas Jefferson University, Medical School Media Division, Philadelphia, PA., 2008.

3. Parens, H. & Weech, A.A., Jr. (1966). Accelerated Learning Responses in Young Patients with School Problems. *J. Amer. Acad. Child Psychiatry,* 5:75–92.

4. I am here using the technical terms I used in our original study, first reported in H. Parens (1979), *The Development of Aggression in Early Childhood.* Lanham, MD: Jason Aronson/Rowman & Littlefield Publishers, Inc. Revised Edition, 2008.

The term "unpleasure" technically means a negative feeling. It is equivalent to "psychic pain," i.e., the emotional experience of pain.

5. Parens, H. (1973). Aggression: A Reconsideration. *J. Amer. Psychoanalytic Assn.*, 21:34–60. Also shown in Parens, H., Pollock, L., & Prall, R.C. (1974). Film #2: *Toward an Epigenesis of Aggression in Early Childhood.* Audio-Visual Medical Section, Eastern Pennsylvania Psychiatric Institute, Philadelphia, PA.

6. It's not just humans who can run amuck with *hostile aggression*, with *hostile destructiveness.* In 2003, J.A. Thompson in an (unpublished) article entitled "Killer apes on American Airlines or how religion was the main hijacker on September 11" wrote: "In 1974, in Jane Goodall's preserve in Africa, one of the field workers watched as a group of male chimpanzees came together and with coordination, stealth, and surprise moved through a neighboring community, sought out a lone victim, and murdered him. Over the course of the next few weeks, they watched the same group repeatedly attack the neighboring community until they had destroyed all the males. Since then, this violent raiding has been observed repeatedly in chimpanzees" (p. 4).

7. An adaptive behavioral thrust inherent in the biology of living organisms.

8. Henri Parens (1979 [2008]). *The Development of Aggression in Early Childhood.* Lanham, MD: Jason Aronson/Rowman & Littlefield Publishers, Inc.

9. Oh yes, you say, "So why does the newborn come out of the birth-canal screaming at you?" Just think of it. The newborn has just gone through a "being squeezed to life" experience! Just imagine being squeezed out like toothpaste, pushed through a very tight flesh-canal, out of that wonderful warm chamber! Your head is gripped and squeezed—documented by how it's often misshapen at birth— your shoulders are squashed and squeezed, first one . . . then your trunk, followed by the other . . . then you're grabbed by some rough or gentle hands that tug at you to get the hell out, and you're lunged into a void, half gasping, half choking, suddenly in dire need of oxygen and you scream for air! It's a harrowing experience, for both the baby and the mother. And we all jump for joy; at least most of us. Nonetheless, for the totally uninformed and innocent newborn, it was a rough voyage . . . and it caused the infant much *unpleasure* which is why the newborn is screaming—and not because the newborn is angry to begin with.

**❸**

# ON COMPLIANCE

- We can get children to live up to our expectations by *demanding that they obey us, whatever we say,* or that they *comply with what we tell them we expect of them.*[1]
- What's the difference between getting them to *obey* and getting them to *comply?*
- What is *compliance* and what is *obedience?*
- "What kind of adults do we want our children to become?"
- What makes achieving *compliance* with our expectations so difficult a challenge?
- How do *compliance* and *obedience* impact on the child's personality formation?
- *Compliance* challenges but it also develops the child's sense of self.
- Demanding *obedience* (excessive compliance) dwarfs the development of self.
- From obedience (excessive compliance) to insufficient compliance.
- The problems with *insufficient compliance.*
- Should we expect, is it desirable, that children comply with all our expectations?
- Are all our expectations important? What are growth-enhancing expectations?
- The development of the ability to comply.
- How can we best achieve growth-promoting compliance?

## COMPLIANCE VERSUS OBEDIENCE

**O**ne of the most challenging tasks to achieve with our children and adolescents is that of obtaining compliance from them in growth promoting ways.

What do I mean by compliance? Let me first note that in some corners of the world, in their child rearing, parents aim for and demand obedience. On this question, the central concern I have is that the two, compliance and obedience, are vastly different concepts that have vastly different consequences for the individual child and for society. Given that we do not all use these concepts, compliance as well as obedience, similarly, I must define how I use them. And, because of the relevance compliance and obedience bear on "what kind of adults do we want our children to become," a question crucial to ourselves and society, I have turned to the *Oxford English Dictionary (OED)* for the authoritative definitions I use for these concepts.

> **Compliance** is "acting in accordance with, or the yielding to a desire, request, condition" stated by another. This dictionary says that it is "a consenting to act in conformity with, an acceding to, practical consent." The dictionary defines "Comply" as "to be accommodating, . . . do the civil or polite [thing], . . . to make oneself agreeable" (pp. 492–93). This is what I have in mind in my use of the word "compliance."[2]

I use compliance to mean *the child's accepting and conforming, even if against initial or continuing resistance, to the parent's expressed wish that he or she behave in accordance with the parent's expectations of the child. In this, the child yields, but also chooses, to do what the parent wishes.*

And here is the *OED's* definition of "obedience":

> **Obedience** is "submission to the rule or authority of another; compliance with a command, law, or the like." [Important, the Oxford includes] Passive obedience: [to let oneself] to be treated according to the will of another in which [one] suffers without remonstrance or resistance. . . . Unqualified obedience or submission to authority, whether the commands be reasonable or unreasonable, lawful or unlawful." (p. 1962)

This definition too conforms to my grasp of the word, and highlights my concern with the concept "obedience." Here, I propose that *to obey is to yield to authority; to do as ordered or commanded; it allows no question and requires no explanation. "Don't even think; do it!" It is authoritarian.*

## WHAT KIND OF CHILDREN DO WE WANT?

The principles by which we rear our children determine what kind of children and then adults they are likely to become. In chapter 1, I spoke of the fact that social scientists have documented the correlation between harsh handling of children and delinquent and criminal behaviors. It is well known that human beings with large loads of accumulated hostility and hate are likely to turn it against others. Such persons can readily be mobilized to discharge their hate against a designated chosen victim—as happens in malignant prejudice.

Some anthropological studies[3] have documented that where fathers are harshly authoritarian and strict, even brutal disciplinarians, correlates strongly with their children becoming more hostile, hating, and destructive over time. These anthropologists found that the harsh treatment of children is programmed in societies that more than others rear their children to engage in warfare. According to some German mental health colleagues, this seemed to have been at the core of the Nazi ideology which ruled Germany from 1933 to 1945.

Whether we expect *compliance* or *obedience* in our children bears on the question: what kind of kids, and later adults, do we want our children to become? We do have choices:

> 1. *Do we want them to grow into self-reliant, respectful, and responsible members of society, raising their children like this as well; but also, when convinced of its necessity and morality, to be ready to fight for their home and country?*

Or,

> 2. *Do we want them to become well-regulated, obedient and predictable members of society who never challenge authority, and who will raise their children strictly to execute unquestioningly whatever order they are given by authority—irrespective of the order's moral character—to do whatever they are told is for the benefit of their home and country?*

## WHAT MAKES ACHIEVING COMPLIANCE IN OUR CHILDREN SO LARGE A CHALLENGE?

Achieving *obedience* in children is not difficult: just crush their emerging sense of self and their strivings for autonomy. According to psychoanalysts

L. Koehler and W. Bohleber, some have even declared that to achieve obedience, "the child's will or stubbornness must be broken."[4] Threaten them and punish them harshly; they will obey!

Achieving compliance is more difficult. Here is why.

In development and adaptation, there is a direct but complex relation between the child's nondestructive aggression and the development of *his sense of self* and his relationship to others. The development of the sense of self—"I am Joseph/Josephine"—is essential to not only adapt but also, specifically, to develop a sense of "I can do this or that!" or "I can make this happen!," to setting up goals for oneself, to feeling reasonably self-confident, to persevere, to take on responsibility, to be a contributing member of society, and more. We all think about this; we even ask our children, "What are you gonna be/do when you grow up?" We want them to feel: "I am capable of doing this or that; I don't need someone to do it for me." We all want our children to become competent individuals, which means that each must have a sufficiently stable sense of autonomy, the sense of "I am able to do; I can do it" or "I am able to make this happen."

There is a powerful inborn factor at work in developing a sense of self and of autonomy; and this powerful factor creates a problem! It's what we call "primary narcissism," a term that means that infants come into the world with an inborn sense of being valued, of being meaningful. Where, you might ask, does *primary narcissism* come from? It comes from the biological imperative Mother Nature built into all living organisms, which is to maintain life, to stay alive. I suggest that primary narcissism is the psychological counterpart of this biological imperative to maintain life, to survive, because of the organism's inherent self-value. This inherent self-value is the biological imperative that leads living organisms to "fight to the death" or to take flight in the face of deadly force. Living substance fights to stay alive.

In 1979 I detailed the bio-psychological link between the self's primary narcissism and aggression.[5] I have said that the child's primary narcissism uses the force of nondestructive aggression to fuel the child's developing sense of autonomy, the sense that leads the toddler to say "me do it!" when he/she wants to do something the mother is trying to do for the child. When the parent allows it, many a toddler will want to "me do it!" While we all like to have things done for us, to be served in various normal settings, this does not take away from our need to feel competent to do whatever we decide we need to do.

So, once the young child is able to move about—usually from about 4 to 6 months of age on when he/she begins to crawl—developing his/her sense of self and the sense of autonomy, the child begins to orient to the universe in which she/he lives. While the infant's familiarity with this universe is already rich, it is nonetheless very sparse: the infant is really only beginning to know his/her mother and father and those who buzz around him/her taking care of the baby. But once able to move around, his/her now increasingly accessible surroundings become enticing, exciting, and the infant often feels he must explore it. Just as "nature abhors a vacuum" we say in medicine, so too the infant "abhors living in a universe he/she does not know." Enticed, excited, the infant starts to actively explore his surroundings. And if it has not yet been necessary, now it will become necessary for the primary caregiver to set limits. And this is where the challenge to comply begins, for both child and mother.

The challenge emerges when, seeing the child is doing or is about to do something that will put him/her or something the mother values at risk, Mother tells the child "You can't do that!" But as the child's behavior suggests, to him/her this means, "You can't do what you want to do!" The challenge lies in the fact that the mother's task and the child's wish/aim/goal are in conflict with one another.

The mother's experience is, "I need to protect my child from doing something that may cause him, or me, or something I value, harm." Or "I have to insist, for his own good, that he has to do what I am telling him to do. As a responsible mother, I have to do this."

The child's experience is something like, "My mother won't let me do what my sense of autonomy drives me to need to do! I didn't choose to do what I'm doing; something inside me makes me feel I've got to do it!" And the child feels, "She is stepping on my sense of self!" And this, the child experiences as an injury to her/his sense of self and to her/his healthy narcissism, which causes him more or less intense emotional pain and thereby generates hostility in the child toward the mother (or father) who is setting limits. The conflict between young child and mother is real. To be a responsible mother she must at times step on her child's emerging sense of self and of autonomy. Where these conflicts between child and parent are too frequent and/or too intense, the level of hostility generated in the child and in the mother/father will be high.

## COMPLIANCE

*Compliance* plays a major part in preparing children for a productive life, in organizing groups into societies and in making these societies functional and able to secure their survival. But in Behavioral Science we have found that expecting compliance can carry with it an undesirable price if it is either excessive or if it is insufficient.

As a member of a society, the individual cannot function at his/her best, be confident, self-reliant, or use rational morality-based judgment, if that society disallows excessively the individual's sense of self and healthy narcissism. Humans are "pack animals." Well or not, we collaborate in packs to survive; each member of the group makes his/her individual society-surviving contribution. In time of war, when it is recognized to be for the good of the community and of one's family, compliance may take on the color of *obedience*. War-contingent compliance, even under conditions of war, does not demand abdication of the sense of self; it engages the self to safeguard the common good. In obedience, the sense of self is more or less abdicated: the self submits to authority without asking a question. And in *passive obedience*, the self submits in "unqualified obedience . . . [even when] the commands [are] unreasonable . . . or unlawful" (the *OED*, p. 1962), as was adopted by many who embraced the Nazi ideology.

The abdication of the self can only be compelled by disallowing, suppressing, or even crushing the child's inborn primary narcissism and thrust to autonomy.

If these are "disallowed," it leads to a lesser or greater degree of narcissistic injury, which causes psychic (emotional) pain and generates in the child hostile aggression.

If these are "suppressed," it will lead to a greater narcissistic injury which will generate in the child more intense negative feelings of hostile destructiveness.

If they are "crushed" it will further intensify the narcissistic injury which will generate high-level hostile destructiveness, possibly in the form of rage, that generally cannot be discharged against the crushing authority due to dread of strong punishment. When a child is enraged he in turn dreads that he will be destroyed.[6] The intense hostility, hate, or rage remains internalized in the child creating internal turmoil and anxiety.

To cope with these intense feelings of hostility, hate, and rage, defense mechanisms are activated to reduce the anxiety they stir within the child, within any of us. Among the mechanisms commonly activated which are most troublesome for family life and society are the (1) *displacement* of these unwanted feelings, and (2) *identification with the aggressor*. Both of these invoke subsidiary mechanisms I have called (3) *reality-distorting defenses* which include *"reductionism, caricaturing, depreciation, vilification . . . and generalization"* of the "other(s)."

In displacement, we direct our accumulated feelings of hate and rage onto "others," rather than to those who caused the feelings in the first place. Innocent "others" then become victimized. In identification with the aggressor, we act toward others like the harsh abusive parent/authority acted toward us. In reality-distorting defenses we falsify the characteristics of innocent "other(s)," in order to give oneself reason for maltreating, even killing him/them.

To harshly control and rigorously regulate children's inborn dispositions to need to do what they seem driven to do—which is viewed by some as the child's "will"—has been a guiding principle in some even highly civilized societies. What has not been recognized is that such efforts to make the child obedient for the purpose of making the child civilized will predictably bring with it heightened levels of accumulating hostile destructiveness in the child. This is because when children are reared harshly to make them obedient, the same basic reactive process is triggered in them as when children are harshly abused and/or neglected at home: repeated, prolonged excessive psychic pain → high-level hostile destructiveness.[7]

But, you may ask, doesn't obedience make us better workers and citizens? The history of civilization has demonstrated that the formation of very productive students, workers, and citizens can be achieved with the discipline obtained by constructively instilling compliance.

Compliance with parents' wishes is highly facilitated when the child trusts them. Trust comes not from a show of power, but from the child's feeling that the parent values the child's inherent sense of self, that the parent (authority) has the child's best interest at heart. As I detail later in this chapter, the child's developing ability to judge will be applied not only to his/her own behavior but also to that of others; in fact judging others is easier than judging oneself. If the parent's behavior is believed not to be reasonable given the circumstances, the child's trust in the parent will be challenged. When the parent's behavior continues to challenge trust, this trust will erode. Compliance is unlikely where there is little or no trust in authority, parent or other.

What then leads children to be obedient, to be even passively obedient? Obedience results from

1. In earliest childhood, fear of rejection and abandonment which leads to intense anxiety, even dread. Or,
2. From about 2 on, fear of the loss of love from his/her parents which, when basic trust is not secure, the child feels can happen anytime. This is felt by children whose emotional attachment to their parents is insecure, feels to the child to be in jeopardy. Or,

3. Fear of parental (or other) authority, usually because the threat of punishment is perceived to be large. For instance during the Nazi era, many Germans who did not accept the laws instituted in 1935 by the Nazi regime complied with these due to their fear of well-established threats to life and freedom; being sent to a concentration camp for noncompliance with this authoritarian rule was then a well-known reality. Or

4. Unquestioning (often unreasoned) obedience due to passivity. This may result from the "crushing" of one's inborn strivings for autonomy, to do what one feels compelled to do. Or it may come from having been taught and learned that "I can't trust my judgment; if I listen to myself I'll get into deep trouble." This may result from identifying with parents who hold dogmatic views or who are "always right and always know what's best." Or,

5. It may come from fundamentalist education that fosters the conviction that one's own group—racial, ethnic, national, or religious—is superior to others'. We saw this in Stalinist Communism when children reported their own parents to authorities for not complying with communist dogma. This compliance was *rationalized*, that is, it was based on falsified reasoning that was fortified by *self-righteousness*. In fact *passive obedience* is usually *rationalized*.

## THE PROBLEM WITH *OBEDIENCE* (OR *EXCESSIVE COMPLIANCE*)

*Obedience (excessive compliance)* to authority has played a central role in the history of Civilization. Remarkable yet not strange, major religions' Holy Scriptures and liturgies affirm very similar views on what is right and what is wrong. Problems arise when what we know to be right and wrong is applied only to one's own or selected societies and not to that of others. As Ben Kiernan's History of Genocide[8] and studies of prejudice hold, since Biblical times humans have shown again and again, often with reason, that we discriminate against members outside our own ethnic, religious, or national community. In this, obedience (excessive compliance) to authority has played a central role. In fact, Kiernan observes that

> In the first book of Samuel (15:1-16:1), God recalled Amalekites had "lain in wait" for the Israelites on their journey from Egypt, and he told Saul: "Now go and smite Amalek, and utterly destroy all that they have, and spare them

not; but slay both man and woman, infant and suckling, ox and sheep." But Saul spared Agag, king of Amalek and his kingdom's best stock. When God found that Saul "hath not followed my commandments," Samuel "hewed Agag in pieces before the Lord." God punished Saul for refusing to "utterly destroy the sinners the Amalekites" by denying Saul's descendants the throne of Israel. [And Kiernan tells us that] Demands for obedience and genocide recur in Judeo-Christian (and Islamic) scripture, [while at the same time] so do models of dissent and nonviolence. (2007, pp. 6–7)

I noted before that anthropological studies as well as that more recently reported by Bohleber and powerfully portrayed by film director Michael Haneke,[9] all have found that where fathers are harshly authoritarian and are strict, even brutal disciplinarians, correlates strongly with their children becoming hostile and destructive over time, and that harshness in rearing children has even been programmed in societies that put a high priority on surviving by and engaging in warfare. Evidence for this quite well documented assumption comes from many corners.

And, let's not underestimate the degree to which, in trying to achieve obedience by harsh limit setting and punishment, these strategies are often highly emotional and subjective or cold and removed, and that the border between harshly strict discipline and child abuse is well known to be a steep slippery slope. Here are tragic examples of this problem in early childhood:

In November 1993, a major American newspaper[10] carried the front page, headline report from which a few sentences follow: "L.M. was only 23 months old when he died after a beating . . . in July. . . . M.L. was 3 when [he was found in June] in the basement [of his home], battered, naked, dehydrated and suffering from a broken leg. S.S. was 2 when he died of massive head injuries received during a beating . . . in September 1991. . . . And . . . R.T. still bears the scars from being dunked, at the age of 2, into a tub so hot that it seared off her skin. . . . All four tragedies, prosecutors contend, had something in common: The violence was triggered by a toilet-training accident."

"Getting children out of diapers is one of the most frustrating and time-consuming hurdles that all parents face. But for some it is so frustrating that researchers now are linking toilet-training accidents with many of the most serious—sometimes deadly—cases of child abuse." (p. 1)[11]

The challenge to parents of getting their children to comply is only too well known. Of themselves, harsh limit setting and punishment do not tend to work as well as parents hope. These are often equated by the child or adolescent as maltreatment and abuse. No matter how often Father may say, "I'm doing this for your own good," children feel, "If my father really loved

me he would never do this to me!" When they accept the parent's rationalization, it is generally because they cope with the harshness of the parent by
identification with the aggressor. Two facts then follow from being harshly
disciplined and punished.

1. The harshness is perpetuated from generation to generation by identification with the aggressor which through identification with the
   harsh parent tends to bring with it the rationalization that "proof that
   my Father was right is that it worked for me, and it'll work for my
   children." And
2. It tends to develop children who are harsh in their personal relationships and in whom harshness toward unknown others is seen as justi-
   fied and righteous given that it is condoned by their parents and, the
   child then deduces, by the society of which her or his parents are the
   representatives. This documents what researchers in Behavioral Science have found in warrior cultures where children are treated sadis-
   tically to make them "good (sadistic) warriors," even if at the expense
   of their family and other social relationships.

Decades of research and clinical work on child development, parenting, and
aggression, have led me to conclude that harshness in interaction with our
children is not the most successful strategy for getting healthy compliance
from them. But while harshly achieved obedience has played a disastrous
role in the enactment of dictates of militant fundamentalism—a driving factor in both Nazism and Stalinist Communism where individual rights, even
life were threatened by noncompliance, we also know that when compliance is blatantly insufficient it may equally lead to delinquency, prejudice,
and crime. Let's look at the problem of insufficient compliance.

## FROM EXCESSIVE COMPLIANCE (PASSIVE OBEDIENCE) TO INSUFFICIENT COMPLIANCE

A phenomenon of notable consequence to German society has followed
from harsh rearing that demanded *passive obedience* of its children. The
crimes against humanity unleashed in Germany but committed by European Nazis[12] from 1935 to 1945 created all kinds of problems now recorded
for three generations among those who, during the first generation were
victims and those who were perpetrators, and their respective descendent
second and third generations.

W. Bohleber[13] speaks to an issue directly pertinent to this chapter's aim which is to explain why achieving compliance in our children is far more advantageous to children and to society than demanding unquestioning obedience from them. German psychoanalysts L. Koehler and W. Bohleber, independently, hold that those who were reared strictly to be obedient became well suited for carrying out Nazi ideology.

Bohleber tells us that the guilt and shame the Nazi generation's crimes caused many Germans led them while raising their own children to remain silent about what happened and what they did during the Nazi years. The second generation reacted in what Koehler speaks of as the "revolution of 1967," by rejecting authoritarian means of raising and educating their own children. The guilt and shame borne by the Nazi generation parents, and the consequent antiauthoritarian position taken by some second generation parents led many among them to fail to guide their own children, the third generation, to compliance with universally accepted mores.

Bohleber speaks to this failure of some second generation parents. He tells us that during some xenophobic riots in Rostock,[14] 14- to 15-year-olds who threw stones and Molotov cocktails at a home of asylum-seekers were astounded that nobody stopped them: "It can't be true that I can simply throw a Molly and the police does nothing . . . it's a lot of shit that they just let you do it" (p. 14). And Bohleber writes, "with the best of intentions, children were allowed to do as they pleased, parents . . . communicated almost no rules and set no limits" (p. 12). He adds, "It seems there was nobody . . . who would confront them with the gravity of their offence" (p. 14). Thus, some German mental health professionals observe that from strict, stern demands for unquestioning obedience the pendulum swung too far into antiauthoritarianism and insufficient *compliance* with societal expectations.

## THE PROBLEM OF INSUFFICIENT COMPLIANCE

*Insufficient compliance* had led to problems long present in all societies including bullying, delinquency, and crime, individual and collective, such as racial and ethnic mob crimes like lynching in the United States, pogroms in Russia and Poland, and more recently against migrant "asylum-seekers" as occurred in Germany and other "developed countries."

By insufficient compliance I mean *the child or adolescent's obstinate disregard for the parents' (or other authority's) clearly and frequently stated expectations*—assuming that these expectations are age-appropriate, reasonable, and morality-adherent.

As I said earlier, as children develop and confront new challenges, it is quite common for them to challenge the compliance hoped for by their parents. Children vary from birth on in their degree of malleability; some infants find it very difficult to abandon their own inner driven behaviors, which then requires of the parents greater efforts to achieve compliance from them. We'll address this aspect of the issue in the next chapter, on limit setting. And below, we'll consider growth-promoting expectable categories and levels of compliance, as well as the developmental line for the ability to comply, that is, when can a child be expected to understand the implications of not complying?

For now let me note that when a normally developing child does not more or less sufficiently comply with age-appropriate expectations this often arises from the child's not trusting sufficiently the parent's commitment to love, protect, and respect the child. Not trusting authority to be caring and benevolent, the child does not acquire a positive regard for the parent's authority and, self-protectively, disregards it. This negative experience of authority eventually tends to be replicated with other adult authority—even when this authority is benevolent. Kids like this, feeling that relationships with adults will not be in their best interest, in time may turn for mutual love, protection, and respect to peers whose feelings toward authority correspond with their own; some among them end up in gangs. There, interestingly, these noncompliant youth must and are willing to adhere with the gang's own usually rigorous rules of conduct.

But another problem of large consequence to society seems to have emerged in the last several decades, which comes directly from insufficient compliance. It is that, in many countries in the Western world, much disruption in our educational systems arises from a level of insufficient compliance, even total noncompliance, on the part of many students in our schools.

Sure, teachers have always had to deal with some insufficiently compliant students; but never to this degree. This large increase in insufficient compliance is especially marked at middle and high school levels but is seen even earlier. The consequences that follow from student noncompliance in classes seriously compromise their education and their future. For many kids, it jeopardizes life-improving opportunities which compulsory education brings. Noncompliance, leading to poor learning and school performance, leads to painful self-disappointment and discourages many a youngster from continuing in school. Many adults are not aware of the fact that some 25 percent of teenagers in the United States, and in some sectors of our society about 50 percent of them, do not graduate from high school.

Part of the problem lies in the fact that insufficient compliance often leads to teacher-student as well as student-student problems of unprecedented dimensions.[15] Insufficient or noncompliance leads many teachers to use coercive and shaming strategies to enforce compliance, strategies that are driven not just by their expectation that the students learn but also, by their anger and even rage toward seriously defiant students. While the teacher's intention may start as a wish to help students learn, under these conditions it ends up causing such youngsters much harm. Among students and between teachers and students, this has led to increased levels of bullying, with escalations into violence and bullying-induced suicides. And, there have also been occasional horrific crimes as happened in Columbine.

Among the factors that contribute to this upsurge in noncompliance in schools, one of central concern for parents is the following. Very troubling is that not all insufficient compliance and arises in children's being maltreated—abused or severely neglected. Many, in fact, come from families that are quite well off and with quite healthy and loving parents. Let's look at this.

A number of factors contribute to this high level of noncompliance in kids including, in addition to child abuse and neglect, much highly stimulating media—movies, television, computer games—that are heavily weighted toward violence and defiance, the notable decrease in three-generation families with grandparents to help, as well as the increase in nuclear family breakdowns, and other factors that are highly resistant to mental health efforts for change.

But there is one other factor often not taken into account where, I believe, the voice of mental health may impact positively. A number of Child Mental Health professionals assume that this new level of insufficient compliance on the part of our youth may have arisen with the advent of a social development that reflects a highly desirable advance in civilization, namely, the Women's Liberation Movement. A central part of the Human Rights movement, the demand for equal rights by women[16] progressively opened the way for many women to attain higher education and enter the work force on all fronts and levels of performance, professional, business, industry, etc. It is a long-awaited advance in civilization that to this day is continuing to spread over the globe—some, still against harsh resistance. The benefit of this movement to the well-being of women just cannot be doubted. But it may have brought with it unanticipated problems, among them the one I want to address now.

Let me first say, with much appreciation, that many women do not "choose" to work outside the home; being the only parent, they do so to feed, shelter, and care for their children.

I cannot speak on this topic with statistical support nor with strong authority. But I want to put forward an explanatory hypothesis to which much professional and nonprofessional anecdotal evidence points. *While so many women are at work outside their home, who is taking care of and bringing up their children?* And, I put forward this question as an hypothesis: Might this phenomenon in one way or another have led to the level of *insufficient* or even *noncompliance* we see in our youth? Two problems come with this question.

The first is that efforts to deal with this question have led to the development of day-care and preschools programs that have multiplied into a new industry. But, have we done enough to secure day-care and preschool programs that meet sufficiently the needs of young children? I believe, in fact I know that we have not!

Having now for decades been privileged to help train women who have chosen the fields of child psychiatry and of child psychoanalysis, while teaching them child development, I have witnessed great distress some have expressed when made aware of the needs young children have for familial, personalized emotional nurturance and care, packaged in with their physical care. These mental health graduate students recognized that physical care could securely be provided by others than themselves; but could "others" also provide the kind of emotional nurturance which generally only parents give their children, that kind of emotionally invested nurturance on which children's emotional health depends?

One mother of our original research group (see chapter 1) put the issue in sensitive words. She told us that she realized while she was taking care of her neighbor's children for several days now that, while she really likes these kids, she realized that she couldn't let herself feel about them the way she feels about her own kids. She couldn't, she said, because if she did, she would find it very difficult to send them back to their own parents at the end of the day. She couldn't invest them emotionally to the level that she did her own kids. Only biological or adoptive parents do that.

Studies of child development and attachment all document the critical need for emotional engagement in human relationships from infancy on and throughout life. While physical care is essential for health and well-being, it is not what makes humans thrive! Profound emotional engagement is what brings with it a child's eventual self-valuation and inner-emotional sustainment, optimizing childhood physical and emotional development and sustaining lifelong physical and mental health. "Parental quality" emotional engagement is essential to making our children thrive. Unfortunately this does not often come from others than the child's own emotionally invested and emotionally investing parents.

Many efforts have and continue to be made, to deal with the problem brought about by the fact that now both mothers and fathers have joined the work force in large numbers. *The problem is not insurmountable.* But it must be recognized for us to deal with it effectively.

Many men, sympathetic to the rights of their wives to become who they wish to be, have more and more engaged in the care of the children, even very young ones, from their infancy on. Those fathers who do so become closer to their children from even the first days of the child's life, forging a stronger attachment between themselves and their young children, to the benefit of the child, the father, and the mother. Of course, families vary; couples vary in their willingness and ability to care for their young children. Some men are wonderful baby holders; others seem at first to have no clue that reciprocal molding is necessary for a baby to feel comfortably held; but they learn. In parenting education classes, teachers have been amazed at many teenage boys' showing surprising gentleness and pleasure in interacting with young children.

Following on my work and research in child development and parenting, I have been asked by health professionals: How should we deal with women's rights and this newly created dilemma? Study of the question led me during the last three decades to lecture to professional audiences about the need for "an individualized prescription for each family." Each family has to determine what would best serve the entire family and the individual members of the family, mother, father, and child(ren). The challenge is large. But retreating to coercive dictation that women must chose to have babies or join the work force is unacceptable and unworkable.

I am not advocating a universe filled with self-centered individuals who clamor only for their rights. Rather, what can we do to see to it that each of us has the right to make the best we can of our individual and our collective life? But, given the advantages of it, we must do so without sacrificing our children's learning to comply with reasonable authority.

The second problem is this: what happens at home in families where both parents have joined the work force? How, you might ask, has this dilemma led to so much *noncompliance* in students in school?

Many child psychiatrists and psychologists who have treated children of such two-working-outside-the-home-parent families have found that a number of these children feel they come second to their parents' outside-home work commitments. Their parents most likely do not feel this way, and while it may in some instances be true, in most it certainly is not. Nonetheless, this is the way many children feel. Parents are troubled by this, either because they don't feel this way, or because they do but they feel that their kid is only a selfish "spoiled brat!" For those who do not feel their work is more important than their child, this text can help. Those who feel their child is a "spoiled brat," the problem requires more than what I am about to address here.[17]

Those who do not feel that their work is more important than their kids tend to feel guilty because they do love them; but their children in one way or another have let them know that they feel "neglected." Some parents, often coming home tired, unconsciously try to quiet or lessen the guilt they feel by backing off in the face of their children's protests from reasonable demands and expectations Mom or Dad have of them. While the children may feel rewarded that they don't have to do what other kids do, they are unaware of the eventual cost to them of not learning to comply with their parents' expectations. In a short time, sensing their parents' inability (out of guilt) to stand up to their resistance to compliance, some children tend to intensify and even assert their noncompliance, feeling then an enlarged sense of power which heightens the child's narcissism. This narcissism, however, now threatens to become the narcissism of the "spoiled kid" who has increasing difficulty dealing with the disappointment and the anger of not getting what he wants.

Negative consequences follow from this dynamic. Let me mention just a couple of them. First, having difficulty being able to cope with not getting everything one wants creates pain each time such a disappointment occurs. But disappointments are unavoidable in life. Learning to cope reasonably with them makes life much more pleasant; one protects oneself against repeatedly feeling painfully injured and pouting or having a blooming fit. All parents who have a child whose narcissism is that of a "spoiled kid" know this well. The child feels miserable; the parent gets very angry with the child, all of which further burdens their relationship.

A second result follows from a child who, in defying his parents' reasonable-enough expectations, develops an inflated "sense of power." No doubt, this child will at times find, as do all kids, that he or she can't deal with a frightening situation and experience much anxiety. Since the child feels more powerful than his parents, he will not turn to them for protection when frightened as most children automatically do. After all, his parents are weaker than he; so how can they help him! To cope with the anxiety, the child will then use psychological defense mechanisms that are likely to interfere with sound and positive adaptation. And there are more problems as well, but let's get back to the question of insufficient or noncompliance.

Many children who defy their parents' reasonable-enough expectations will, when they go to school, feel that they do not have to comply with the teachers' expectations that they listen in class and do their homework; nor eventually of the policemen's expectations that they obey laws. The path to school failure and to delinquency is facilitated.

I have stated my hypothesis simply. But we all know that *compliance/noncompliance*, like any psychological character trait, is governed by multiple factors and cannot be stated to derive from just one. In addition, children vary in their coping with whatever their real-life condition or situation. For example, children of single-parent families tend to not react as negatively to Mom's working outside the home, because they grasp the fact that Mom has to do this to put food on the table and buy they all need. In fact, many will pitch in with home chores, some even without being asked to do so. So often, in spite of their complaining about Mom's not being at home, we see an older sibling become the temporary caregiver for his or her younger siblings when Mom is at work. Kids are well known to surprise adults with what they can do when the conditions require it. The reader can see that I cannot assert my hypothesis with no reservations.

Then add this. Where the parent-child relationship is quite good, but when Mom goes to work, the child may nonetheless feel that Mom's work is more important to her than the child and the child feels "neglected"; but this child may with the passage of time, especially as a teenager, feel proud that Mom, through her work, is recognized by society as a productive citizen, whether Mom's a doctor, or lawyer, or a CEO of a company, or runs a store, or is a seamstress, or whatever.

In short, I put this hypothesis forward not to weigh against the advancing tide of the rights of women but to facilitate its achievement, while at the same time seeing to it that we secure our children's well-being and optimize their development and their ability to comply with reasonable and well-intentioned authority—because we all know that growth-promoting guidance can enormously better their lives.

Given the miscarriages of excessive compliance and the unacceptability of insufficient compliance, as standards of human rights have evolved, so must the standards of healthy compliance we expect from our children. We assert that children must learn to comply with their parents and society's reasonable and growth-promoting expectations.

Several questions arise from this assertion.

1. What are reasonable and growth-promoting expectations?
2. At what age can we expect compliance; what is its development time-table? And
3. How do we best achieve *compliance* with the expectations we have of our children?

## WHAT ARE REASONABLE AND GROWTH-PROMOTING EXPECTATIONS?

We all have expectations of our children. We all want them to make us proud of them, to have society's approval of them and of us. We all have a program to achieve this even before they are born; some of us more firmly so than others.

In years of work with kids and their parents, like others, I have discovered that kids come into the world with a mind of their own. All parents find that their infants don't seem to have the same program for themselves in mind that we do—some babies more than others; in fact, some don't like our program at all. This is so with wake-sleep cycles, with eating, with a number of things even from the very beginning. How do we get them to accept our program?

Mental health professionals know that both parent and child have to compromise. Unfortunately, some parents, in an authoritarian way, assume that the child must accept their program. This works in some cases; in most, it does not. Many built-in individual factors in both the baby and the parents create this program dilemma. Most common in these is rigidity of adaptability in the parent (resulting from her or his genetic make-up and life experiences) or in the child (generally in-born factor). Some parents and some babies are quite a bit more malleable than others. Margaret Mahler, renowned child psychoanalyst, held that the mother is the one who most often yields to the child's needs which, given the mother's greater resources, Dr. Mahler felt is the way it should be. But mother also has to hold the line on the child's complying reasonably.

To be sure, we all know that it is undesirable to **not** have expectations of our children. They know that having expectations of them is part of our valuing them and wanting what's best for them, even when at times they argue that our expectations show that we don't care about their well-being. In turn, they have expectations of us, their parents. Consider Bohleber's comment that the Rostock 14- to 15-year-olds, who threw stones and Molotov cocktails at a home of asylum-seekers, were astounded that nobody stopped them: "It can't be true that I can simply throw a Molly and the police does nothing . . . it's a lot of shit that they just let you do it" (1995, p. 14). Sure, most kids, most of the time, want to be allowed to do whatever they want. But, like the Rostock youth, they also expect us to protect them and guide them and this often means that we cannot let them do what they want. So, what expectations should we have of them?

Our expectations cannot all have equal weight. We should have categories based on degree of obligation such as (1) "This you must do" or, "This you cannot do"; and (2) "This I expect you to do or to not do. If you don't comply you will lose a privilege"; and (3) "I really wish you would do this, or that you would not do this."

Before expecting that the child can grasp the notion of "obligatory," "this you must do" and "this you cannot do," we have to recognize that the young child has not yet developed the ability to anticipate or to judge what the consequences of her or his behaviors and actions truly might be. We'll look at this in the next section on the timetable for the development of the ability to comply. But before we get to the timetable, here are a few key examples of categories of expectations.

## CATEGORIES OF EXPECTATIONS WITH DEGREES OF OBLIGATION

### Obligatory Expectations

"This you must do" and "This you cannot do"; you have no choice; you can complain, but no arguments are accepted. Here are a couple of examples:

1. Unless you are truly sick, you have to go to school every school day.
2. You have to do your homework; if you need help, ask for it. We'll be glad to help. If we can't help we'll get someone who can.
3. We all have to obey the law. You do too! In the neighborhood and at school. For instance, you don't mess with other people's mail.

These examples obviously cannot apply to young kids. Each family has to determine what is "obligatory" for their family, be it going to religious services every week, never hitting your little sister (or brother), keeping your room sanitary (i.e., all food or liquid leftovers are to be cleaned out before the day is over), or whatever. One cannot make all expectations obligatory because it diminishes the child's recognition that some expectations matter more than others.

## Desirable Expectations

"This I expect you to do or to not do. If you don't comply you will lose a privilege." With this, the parent does not feel the behavior is totally unacceptable; but it does run counter what you feel is so important for your child to comply with.

1. Some families of teenagers insist on knowing where the kid is when not in school or at home, or on getting home by a certain time on weekend nights. Not complying earns a scolding and may lead to the loss of a privilege. In chapter 4, we talk about how to weigh in on limit setting and punishment and that the child's age and personality traits have to be taken into account.
2. You live in this house. Chores need to be done. As a responsible member of the family, you are expected to help clear the dinner table, put the dishes in the dishwasher or help to wash them, or empty the dishwasher or dry the dishes. Again, age is determining of what we can expect our kids to help with. Kids who feel respected, loved, and valued are willing to help at home, some even as young as 5 years of age. In fact, they feel good about helping. If the child does not comply, withdraw a privilege.

Here the child has some choice. Not complying earns him a degree of disappointment by the parents and the loss of a privilege. We talk about this in chapter 4.

## Wished-for Expectations

"I really wish you would do this, or you would not do this." It's a hoped-for expectation. The parent has to deal with this disappointment, but care must be exercised in letting the child know she/he is disappointed. For instance,

1. A child of average intelligence works well enough in school to make B's. The reasonable enough parent wishes for the child to try harder to get A's. Some children will respond to such wishes, knowing that this is what Mom and/or Dad really want. Children can read us pretty well; they read our facial and vocal reactions to their announcing they

got another B in math. "That's good, John; do the best you can, that's what counts."

2. "It would be very nice if you could share some of your toys with your sister; I wish it wasn't so hard to do!" Most parents wish their children would treat each other well. This tends to be difficult for kids given that we don't, nor should we, ask them if it's OK to have another baby. What first-borns see is that now they have to share their Mom and Dad and everything else.

So, our expectations have to have variable weight; some are not negotiable; others are. Our children have a right to have a voice in these matters. But it is the parents' responsibility to decide on which expectation they do, and on which they do not.

## THE DEVELOPMENT OF THE ABILITY TO COMPLY

The ability to comply with parental expectations requires mental abilities not yet present at birth. The child's ability to control her inner push to do what she wants and to get what she wants requires the development of *adaptive functions* such as being able to put the brakes on the inner pressure and delay getting what she wants, even to tolerate not getting what she wants. And it requires the development of *cognitive (thinking) functions* to be able to think at a level where the parent's expectations can be assessed by and make sense to the child.

Getting children to obey parents when they use coercive training methods can be achieved earlier than when children achieve the ability to comply. Threat of punishment in young children is very efficient in getting obedience even when the child cannot yet think. But we have and will continue to consider the risks attached to harsh rearing strategies.

We now know from psychological and brain studies of child development that soon after birth, two types of experiences are registered in the brain: (1) experiences that occur frequently and (2) occasional experiences that are intensely painful. Registered in the brain, they become part of our memory bank. But near birth, infants can't yet put their experiences into ideas or thoughts. What is foremost recorded of experiences that give rise to early memory formation is *what is felt physically and emotionally.* These feeling-experiences, now recorded in *implicit memory,*[18] will resonate with, and be reactivated by the kinds of experiences that gave rise to these feelings in the first place. And such repeated feeling-experiences then amplify and stabilize those that are already recorded in *implicit memory*. Critical is that even though implicit memories *cannot be recalled on demand,* from their unconscious recesses of the mind, these feelings will play a large role in the person's baseline personality and moods for years to come.

Erik Erikson taught us that by 6 months an infant will be able to sufficiently predict whether or not when he cries, mother (or other usual caregiver) will or will not come to help the baby, and will react caringly or hurtfully to the baby's appeal for care. These experiences over time lead to the development of "basic trust" or "basic mistrust" which, in turn, brings with it the infant's feeling that he is deserving of trust, i.e., is "trustworthy," or that he is not deserving of trust and is not a good enough baby. This early learning is based on classical conditioning,[19] and the feelings and moods recorded in primitive centers of the brain will stabilize very early in life.

The classical conditioning mode of learning predominates during the first two years, registering experiences as these are felt and perceived by the infant. Thus prior to the third year, one can coerce an infant to be obedient. If you don't do what I say, I will stop taking care of you! Or I'll hurt you! But one cannot yet expect the less than 3 years old to choose to comply, because he is not yet able to weigh the consequences of not meeting parents' expectations when he is not threatened with the loss of care or of pain. Infants may comply with parents' expectations but this is on the basis of wanting to please the parent, not on the basis of weighing the meaning and merits of complying.

The period from 2 to 8 years of age is one during which basic adaptive and a number of critical cognitive abilities develop. Kagan and Herschkowitz[20] tell us that, during the 2 to 6 years period, five thinking (cognitive) abilities progressively develop on which the ability to comply depends. These include:

(a) *"The reliable integration of past and present"*: from 4 years of age on, children begin to progressively use thinking of past experiences in order to understand and interpret what they are currently experiencing (p. 190).

(b) *"Anticipating the future:* . . . the ability to relate the present to . . . the future also matures during [the] four- and seven-year old [period]" (p. 190).

(c) *The "appreciation of causality:* . . . a 5- or 6-year-old who makes an error reflects on the possible reasons for the mistake, and, on occasion, corrects herself. . . . 6- to 7-year-olds are usually reflective following a mistake; that is, they take more time studying [the next time the task needs to be done]" (pp. 193–94).

(d) *Enhanced "semantic [recognition of the meaning of words, phrases, ideas] categories":* Most of us can remember experiences from about 5 or 6 years of age on. The reason is that we then began to record experiences in word concepts, in stories about or narratives of events. At about 6 we begin to be able to link and delink *events* from the *feelings* they generated in us. A child then "might remember the fact that he was mad at a parent a week earlier and [do something annoying to the parent now] without any feeling of anger" (p. 198).

(e) *Recognition of the relations or differences between what they expect and others expect:* By 7, a child tends to compare the standards of behavior others expect of him with those he holds for himself. He is able to compare his behavior with what parents expect. Generally, well cared for children tend to make efforts to avoid criticism from parents and teachers (p. 206).

Correlating these findings with what we see in observing children's behaviors,

*the 2 to 8 years period is the critical period for establishing a well-developed* **foundation** *for the ability to comply with parental expectations.*

We also know from psychoanalytic child development that the **foundation** for conscience formation and the development of morality, a significant contributor to achieving compliance, organizes during the 3 to 6 years period. Then, learning to abide by rules of play and fairness reaches a new level of organization during the 6 to 12 years period which most children under 6 do not yet have and therefore, less than 6-year-olds can't play games governed by rules and consequences as is required in playing checkers and cards games (beyond "War" and "Go Fish!"). The 9- to 12-year-old can, and his progressively developing moral judgment and guidelines for conduct begin to significantly influence his behavior in human interactions.

Then as the 12- to 18-year-old progressively shifts the foremost center of influence in his life from his family to his peer group, that peer group increasingly dictates and modifies his beliefs and behavior, and with it the adolescent's conscience undergoes some revisions. Generally, the better the relationships in the adolescent's core family, the more will her conscience retain its original basic structure but will now add to, and begin to integrate the old with the new elements of conscience. The poorer the family relationships, the more will her peer group influence her conscience revisions, perhaps even leading to its overall re-formation, to correspond with the peer group's beliefs and behaviors.

## A TIMETABLE FOR THE ABILITY TO COMPLY

What do we make of these notes on adaptive, cognitive, and emotional development? Adding 4 decades of research (see chapter 1) and of clinical work with children and adolescence, I come up with the following time-table, as a guide, for understanding when a normal-average child may be expected to comply with parents' expectations.

**Before 2 years of age,** parents begin to tell the infant what expectations they have of the child with regard to eating, sleeping, not biting, not hitting, not taking other kids' toys, and the like. Limit setting will increasingly be needed as the 8- to 24-month-old child is driven to explore his environment, to check out and test his newly emerging abilities, as well as many things and encounters novel to him. Given that the child's ability to learn will be based on classical conditioning, and the need to hold on to the mother's (and father's) good feelings toward the toddler, some simple but meaningful expectations of the child's behavior will be feasible. Simple cause and effect can be explained and may be grasped by the child, such as "You can't throw your sippy-cup, it could make a big mess!" When the caregiver expresses feelings of disapproval, the less than two year old will get the message, but verbal explanations should be given along with the parent's demanding compliance (see chapter 4 on limit setting). Because feelings are understood even by infants, words at this early age carry their meaning by the feeling-tone we put into using them. This "how to behave" starts to be conveyed by parents to the child during the first year of life even when the baby can't yet understand words.

**During the second and third year of life,** the child is more or less responsive to the parent's demand for *compliance* because he doesn't want to lose mother's love and care; but also, if the child's basic trust is secure, then it is because he feels that mother means to help him as well. In this, the child will put the brakes on his *strivings for autonomy,* which by their inherent healthy aggressive nature push against the demands for compliance made by the caring parent.

*The period between 2 and 8 years of life is the era when compliance is most easily and most favorably developed.* Again: the better the child's basic trust, the more favorable the parent-child relationship (already well-established during the first two years of life), the more likely will compliance be achieved. Where basic mistrust predominates, where there is much parent-child conflict in the relationship, compliance will be more difficult to achieve, although all reasonable efforts to achieve it are strongly recommended.

*If a good degree of compliance is not established during the 2 to 8 years period, achieving compliance in the years that follow will be more difficult.*

**During this 2 to 8 years** golden era for compliance, the child will progressively develop the cluster of abilities required to grasp and assess the merits of complying with the parent's expectations. While limit setting has already been required, from 2 years of age on, given the young child's increasing efforts to test and master the environment and himself, the need for limit-setting will increase. Of course, the degree to which limit setting is needed will depend on the child's inborn dispositions, including the child's energy level, the intensity of her curiosity, and the degree of aggressive pressure of her strivings for autonomy. Testable explanations and reasons for the demands made will generally facilitate compliance. We detail strategies for this challenge in chapter 4.

**From 4 to 8 years,** that remarkable period when most children begin to learn to recognize and write letters, then words, then eventually to read and write, demonstrates the child's growing ability to read meaning into symbols. This extends into the child's progressively grasping the meaning of parents' intentions and expectations. And then beyond 6 or 7 years, the child will grasp meaning whether it is stated simply or with humor, with patience or with annoyance, or even with sarcasm—that undesirable tendency some parents have. Parents can increasingly expect compliance from 6- to 8-year-olds. In some well-put-together kids who have already demonstrated a strong need to have their own way, the challenge of setting limits that continues for some years to come will require greater patience and persistence on the part of the parents. Encouragement and reasonable praise for good performance are likely to go farther and faster than harsh demands and punishment. More on this in chapter 4.

When a good, healthy, level of *compliance* is achieved by 8 or so years of age, the way to achieving *compliance* with school and social expectations is well-paved. "Healthy compliance" is based on a willing acceptance of parents' expectations, on an unconscious agreement to adopt the parents' beliefs and codes of behavior, all essentially based on a positively valued identification with the parents. The converse holds as well. When an insufficient level of *compliance* by age 8 years prevails, most commonly due to basic mistrust of their parents' care and intentions—although one occasionally finds a child whose uncertain sense of self and of autonomy makes compliance very difficult[21]—compliance with school and society is likely to be insufficient.

What is achieved by age 8 years, we might say "the foundation years for compliance," does not close the door on further possibility of its development. The continuing development **during the 8 to 14 years period** of adaptive, cognitive, and emotional functioning allows for the acquisition of new skills and abilities that may bring about a new trend in compliance. The challenge, however, of establishing compliance where a good foundation of it was not achieved by 8 years, is that patterns of reactivity that led to insufficient compliance will have to be undone, before patterns of compliance take sufficient hold to become predictable. Much more work will now have to go into achieving healthy compliance.

Dramatic life events with much meaning for an elementary-school-age child, say the role of a loved teacher who has won the child's trust, may bring about a significant reversal of old patterns of noncompliance-reactivity. The sudden loss of such a teacher, by the child's internalizing the teacher's expectations, can virtually overnight transform the child into one who will comply. Or, the influence of newly acquired friends who convey the merits of compliance may have a beneficial effect.

**During the 14 to 19 years period,** we cannot predict achieving compliance in adolescents whose compliance profile up to now has been weak, even less so with those who largely have been noncompliant. In adolescents of this age, the hope of instilling sufficient compliance with societal mores and rules of conduct can only be achieved by remedial educational, therapeutic, or dramatic means—the latter for instance, as being influenced by a former noncompliant person who has paid a heavy price for past delinquent or even criminal behavior. Some adolescents whose upbringing have been replete with neglect, or over-restrictive or harsh handling, may go through a period of rebellion from which, with the help of better adjusted friends or benevolent adults, they may modify their tendency from noncompliance to sufficient compliance.

We will talk about the question of how we can best achieve compliance in our children in the next chapter.


## NOTES

1. Like with the rest of this book, much of the documentation of the ideas presented in this chapter have been eliminated in this more reader-friendly version of the "for professionals" version of this book, *Handling Children's Aggression Constructively—Toward Taming Human Destructiveness,* which was published in 2011 by Jason Aronson/Rowman & Littlefield Publishers, Inc.

2. I want to note as a psychiatrist-psychoanalyst that I have found that patients and colleagues sometimes confound me with the fact that we don't always mean the same thing when we use certain words. The word aggression, for instance, one of the key words of this book is a fine example; amazing, the different meanings we give to the word. It makes me appreciate Lewis Carroll's complaint through Alice's voice in *Through the Looking Glass*, paraphrasing what Alice says, "How can you make words mean so many different things!"

3. West, M.M. and Konner, M.J. (1976). The role of the father: an anthropological perspective. In: *The Role of the Father in Child Development*, ed. M.E. Lamb, pp. 192–207. New York: John Wiley & Sons, Inc.

4. Psychoanalyst Lotte Koehler, who grew up in Nazi Germany, tells me that some child rearing books in Europe—such as *"The German mother and her first child* [which had] already appeared before Hitler took power in 1933"— have as much as declared this to be desirable. Also, Werner Bohleber remarks in "The children of the perpetrators—the after-effects of National Socialism on the following generations" which he presented in Toronto, May 4, 1995, that "according to Nazi ideology . . . the boy's will was to be broken" to make him obedient, but also "hard and manly" (p. 10).

5. In *The Development of Aggression in Early Childhood*, chapter 3 (Parens, H., 1979 [2008]).

6. Psychoanalytic developmental theory holds that in early life, the experience of feelings of intense hostility and rage (*hostile destructiveness*) are experienced by the young child as enormously powerful while the child's adaptive capabilities are still weak. As a result the young child fears that his own destructiveness may destroy him too.

7. It is very likely that harsh rearing, or intense abuse or neglect in childhood prior to World War II played their part in there being highly sadistic Nazis in Germany, equally sadistic Jewish "Kapos" in the death camps, and sadistic French special police, *la Milice*, who, like such hostile individuals in most European countries, brutally pursued Jews, Gypsies, and other "undesirables," to incarcerate them in concentration camps where many died of starvation and disease or by being sent East to the Nazi death camps.

8. Ben Kiernan's *Blood and Soil—A World History of Genocide and Extermination from Sparta to Darfur*, published in 2007 by Yale University Press.

9. See Bohleber reference above. Michael Haneke's German film *The White Ribbon*.

10. The *Philadelphia Inquirer*, November 9, 1993. Front page, feature story by Martha Woodall, *Inquirer* staff writer.

11. This reference comes from Parens, Scattergood, Duff & Singletary's *Parenting for Emotional Growth: The Textbook, Unit 2*, (p. 109). (See footnote 1 for complete reference.)

12. I first applied the term "Nazis" to include European perpetrators as well as the Germans, who collaborated to carry out the Holocaust, in 2004 (in my mem-

oirs, *Renewal of Life—Healing from the Holocaust*). In doing so I assert that, while Germany's Nazi (National Socialist) regime, by instituting its 1935 Nuremberg Laws—which stripped specified minorities of citizenship and all kinds of other human rights—initiated, engineered, and carried out the largest crime against humanity in recorded history, all but two countries in Europe—Denmark and Bulgaria—collaborated in carrying out this monstrous crime. It is moral dishonesty to hold only Germany of the Third Reich responsible for it; the German Nazis could not have carried this crime out without the collaboration of many non-German Europeans. Historians have recorded these facts. See Michael R. Marrus & Robert O. Paxton (1983). *Vichy France and the Jews*. New York: Schocken Books; as well as Saul Friedlander (2007). *The Years of Extermination: Nazi Germany and the Jews, 1939–1945*. New York: HarperCollins.

13. Bohleber 1995.

14. A German colleague has a different explanation that may have merit as well. She believes that the Rostock youth in question had in fact continued to be overly controlled given that they were in what was formerly East Germany, which in effect was itself under Communist rule, and therefore equally totalitarian as had been Nazi Germany. These youth then, had not been raised in an antiauthoritarian way. They would thus further document the result of strict, harsh rearing that demands obedience, rather than being reared under conditions of insufficient compliance.

15. Twemlow, Fonagy & Sacco, a team of psychoanalyst psychiatrist and psychologists, have done and continue to do extensive work in schools that points to this problem.

16. In the United States, the world's first women's rights convention was held in 1848. The movement persisted during the first half of the twentieth century with an increasingly demanding voice that led to the launching of the Women's Liberation Movement at its Chicago convention in 1968. http://www.ibiblio.org/prism/mar98/path.html.

17. The child may be a "spoiled brat"; this may require more parental guidance than I am discussing in this text. If it is not that the child is a "spoiled brat," but rather that the average-expectable emotional needs of rearing a particular child demands more of the parents than the parents assumed when they decided to have a child, the resulting problems may be large and the parents might find it enormously helpful to seek help from a child-trained mental health professional to sort things out and institute a psychotherapeutic process to help both parents and child find more constructive and adaptive ways of dealing with what has already developed in the child and how to proceed henceforth. The consequences of not resolving such a situation positively may have life-lasting consequences for all concerned, parents and child.

18. Memory researchers tell us and there is agreement among them that there are two types of memory that conform well with what we find in intense psychotherapies: 1. *Implicit memory*, also called *procedural memory*, is the first form of memory which becomes recorded in the brain. It is not retrievable at will; it seems

to reside in the person's unconscious mind and may emerge, after much effort, not as fully developed ideas but as images of experience. For example, in the course of a clinical psychoanalysis, a painfully traumatized patient while putting into words what came to her mind, suddenly crying and in anguish, put into words a fantasy of a child crying bitterly and who is trying to cling to her caregiver who pushes her away. This opened a series of spontaneous powerful fantasies of an infant, who, crying and pleading for comforting is pushed away repeatedly; and finally the infant quiets, is curled up in the corner of her crib, her cover over her head, hopeless.

2. *Explicit memory*, also called *declarative memory*, is the second type of memory, which we generally are able to remember at will or with minor effort. *Explicit memory* generally carries with it the ability to remember an experience in words, in ideas, in time, as well as with feelings. By 5 to 6 years of age, the capacity for *explicit memory* is sufficiently developed that most people can remember their past to about those years.

19. Classical conditioning has been shown to already occur in the unborn child, during the third trimester of fetal life. This intrauterine learning Kagan and Herschkowitz (2005) tell us "can be preserved through the early postnatal months. [These authors go on to describe a study of] a chimpanzee fetus [who was subjected to] a 500 Hz tone CS [as a Conditioning Stimulus] followed by a vibroacoustic US [unconditioned stimulus] that provoked physical movement [in the fetus], over 150 trials over a 30-day period. Presentation of the CS alone 58 days after birth provoked a conditioned [physical movement in the infant ape]" (pp. 57–58).

20. Kagan, Jerome & Herschkowitz, Norbert (2005). *A Young Mind in a Growing Child*. Mahwah, NJ: Lawrence Erlbaum Associates.

21. Some children with harsh obsessive-compulsive disorders, or with autistic spectrum disorders as Asperger's Syndrome, may find it difficult to comply with even quite reasonable parental expectations due to excessive, disorganizing anxiety, and not due to basic mistrust of their parents.

# 4

# ACHIEVING COMPLIANCE THROUGH DISCIPLINE, LIMIT SETTING, AND PUNISHMENT

**F**oremost, our children comply with our expectations of them because, knowing we love them and want what's best for them, they want to (1) show they love us, (2) please us, and (3) be like us. But when our children do not live up to our reasonable expectations, we achieve the *discipline to comply* by means of *limit setting* and *punishment*.

Here is how I use these terms.

*Discipline* is a state of functioning that has two applications and definitions. *From the parent's position, it is the parent's efforts to help the child develop the ability to behave in ways that are acceptable to them and to the social group in which they live; and, for the child, it is the progressive ability to do what is expected of him and to do what the child demands of himself—which means to develop "self-discipline."*

Note then, that discipline (1) requires collaborative action between child and parents and (2) is an undertaking that fosters the development in the child of a sense of competence and self-reliance. *Discipline* is usually brought about when the child's behavior continues to challenge the parent's expectations of what the child's conduct should be.

*Limit setting* is the parent's restriction of some activity the parent feels is harmful—to the child, to the parent, to someone else, to something *valued—or which is not socially acceptable.* In this, *the parent acts as an agent of the child's adaptive functioning at a time when these functions are not sufficiently developed within or are resisted by the child.*

In other words, the parent does for the child what the child himself cannot yet do or will not do that is in his best interest, whether it is because of insufficient ability or lack of understanding, or the unwillingness to recognize, or in defiance of, the consequences of his actions.

**Punishment** *is a strategy in which—as a sign of substantial disapproval and to enforce one's limit setting—the parent withdraws a privilege or inflicts pain upon the child.*

I want to point out that *competent limit setting reduces and may even eliminate the need for punishment.*

## GENERALLY, ACCEPTING PARENTAL AUTHORITY IS IN THE CHILD'S BEST INTEREST

As I said in chapter 3, the rejection of authoritarianism and the rising awareness of human rights now prevalent in many parts of the world, lead to the need to correspondingly program our strategies for developing compliance in our children. Rather than by strict, harsh measures that deny the child's sense of self and of autonomy, we have to find ways to obtain compliance with authority in our children while allowing their sense of self and their healthy narcissism to make of their life what they want and can, while based on reasonable principles and a human rights–based sense of morality. It is well known that children, young and teenagers, don't always know what's best for them, and that they may one day regret having done what they did, or not having done what we expected of them. Nonetheless our conviction that "we know best" needs to be weighed honestly against the learning that comes from making mistakes—or from not listening to Mom or Dad. We're not always right and our children are not always wrong. How do you feel when someone else is convinced they know what's best for you when what they think is best is at odds with what you think is best?

It is well established that we do not achieve free-will compliance in our child by always being sweet, or by always giving in to what the child wants, or by making no demands on the child that counter the child's will. It is reasonable and realistic to hold that when it's time to go to bed, it's time to go to bed! When it's time to get up to go to school, it's time to get up! If you have homework, you must do it; and it's best to not wait till the last minute! A protesting child should be taken seriously; her complaints should be listened to; but this does not carry with it a promise that her wish will be met. Limit setting, to which we turn now, is needed to get there.

## RATIONALE

Achieving compliance is so large a challenge because limit setting encroaches on the child's developing sense of self and his strivings for autonomy. Given their psychobiological role in securing that the self becomes productive and self-reliant and adapts competently, strivings for autonomy have to be rigorous—life is just full of challenges from the moment the baby starts the journey out of the birth canal. These strivings for autonomy are pre-wired (pre-birth brain development) and, therefore, are driven from within. When the parent attempts to restrict the activities of a young child driven by that inner pressure, the child is frustrated—which causes him psychic pain. Like all experiences that cause psychic pain, when frustration becomes intense it generates hostility within the child. This hostility is experienced toward the person who is causing the psychic pain, the one setting the limit. But this person is most commonly one who is highly emotionally valued by the child, be it Mother or Father; the hostility experienced is toward someone the child loves! In this way, setting limits often creates an internal conflict in the child.

But when the child resists the demand made by the parent, limit setting becomes challenging for the parent too. It causes the parent psychic pain when, setting limits that are in the child's or teenager's best interest, the child feels hostility toward the parent instead of appreciation. What thanks for trying to help your kid! Consider the difficulty your 13-year-old daughter might encounter, were she allowed on a date with an 18-year-old boy she likes but who does not know she is only thirteen! Mother sets limits. The 13-year-old becomes furious and stomps upstairs, shouting at her mother, "I hate you; you never trust me, and you never want me to be happy!" It cannot be avoided; it must be done. But we parents do need to think of how we might best meet this challenge.

- We don't get appreciation for protecting the child. More difficult is that the child's reaction often evokes in the parent a counter-reaction of anger, which troubles the parent further and often, makes the parent uncertain about insisting on compliance. Feeling hostility toward one's child produces guilt, self-doubt, and even, in some of us, feeling that one is a hurtful parent.[1]

- Second, a child's resisting the parent's limit setting often leads the parent to set limits angrily, at times even destructively (as by shaming or insulting) and punish before it is necessary.
- Third, parents may set limits but not consistently follow through. Feeling conflicted over setting limits the parent may do so in an unclear manner, conveying her uncertain feelings about it. This may lead some children to increasingly defy limits and expectations.

In summary,

- As the child experiences it, difficulties arise because his strivings for autonomy, essential for a healthy sense of self, are being interfered with.
- If limit setting is done in the context of increasing hostility in both child and parent, it is likely to lead to problems in the child's developing a competent sense of autonomy, self-reliance, and a responsibility-accepting sense of self.
- Limit setting commonly stirs up feelings of hostility toward the parent the child loves, thereby producing a conflict of ambivalence within the child. Ambivalence creates an internal conflict that is produced by experiencing coexisting or alternating feelings of love and hate toward a loved person. Important is that conflicts due to ambivalence in early childhood have a tendency to stabilize, and then become part of the parent-child relationship. *While ambivalence is unavoidable in human relationships, it is important that it not get too intense.*

But there is a caveat with regard to the child. This conflict due to *ambivalence* holds the potential for creating problems within the child when the ambivalence is intense. But when the ambivalence is *moderate*, it can produce significant healthy growth. It will cause a moderate conflict in the child that will trigger accommodative reactions to resolve it; this will lead to his:

- Learning to deal constructively with his hostility given that he will feel "Nice kids don't hate their mother; it feels lousy; it's not nice!" No one needs to tell the child; he feels it.
- This leads to mild guilt which fosters internalizing the parents' expectation.

- This in turn will forge reasonable compliance to parents and authority. And
- It will mold healthy assertiveness: "I know when to say no and when not to."

*This will not be achieved if the ambivalence experienced toward the parent is too intense.*

So setting limits, the bugaboo of parenting, is necessary. Being firm with the child is fine. Being angry with the child is unavoidable. Being hateful toward and mean-spirited with the child is very problematic and should be avoided. This is one large reason why avoiding overly strict, harsh limits and punishment are crucial. Then, once the conflict in setting limits subsides, it is enormously helpful to talk about what happened, to try to help the child learn from the distress experienced by both parent and child; and, when necessary, to talk about and lessen whatever hurt feelings were experienced and repair whatever emotional wounds were caused. One does so by apologies, explanations, and talking about what happened that went awry, *not* by gifts of candy or toys. This applies to kids at all ages, early childhood and adolescence.

Now let's talk about effective and constructive ways to set limits.

## SETTING LIMITS CONSTRUCTIVELY

*Competent, constructive limit setting not only fosters compliance; it also reduces and may even eliminate the need for punishment.*

It is important to reduce as best we can the need for punishment for two reasons. First, when limit setting fails it generates anger and often hostility, in both child and parent; punishment, then, is commonly dished out with anger, even hostility between child and parent. Second, as all parents know, because punishment often brings with it the discharge of the parent's own hostility toward the child, it tends to cloud its aim of being in the child's best interest—even when the parent insists that it is for the child's good!

Growing up is difficult. Large demands are made on kids: by their environment, the occasionally excessive demands they make on themselves, and by the significant frustrations and pains that often come from their interactions with peers and others, children are at times at wits' end and may push even the best of parents to the point where the parents behave in ways they subsequently wish they had not done. Parents need to recognize that when a child feels secure enough at home, it's at home that he or she may let loose, even be onerous, because it's the safest place in the world to let off steam, the place where he will get least hurt and most easily forgiven. There is no way out of it: it will be necessary for parents to discipline their children, to set limits, and from time to time to punish them.

Every parent who has more than one child knows that children vary in how they respond to limits. Inborn dispositions play a large part. So do the child's prior experiences. Some children are more malleable than others; some tend to resist guidance and direction more than others. As a result, some children will be easier than others to set limits with, and some will challenge the parents' wits, love, and fortitude. I am speaking of children who fall within the wide range of normal behaviors. The "more difficult child" at the far end of the spectrum of irritability may require more specifically tailored strategies. There are good books[2] that address this type of child.

## WHEN TO SET LIMITS

I am asked, "When should I start setting limits?" I answer, "When limits are needed."

> When Candy was 5 months old, she crawled toward her twin Cindy. In her exploratory push, Candy grabbed the toy that Cindy held. Even though we could not infer that Candy was intentionally taking something from Cindy, in contrast to her simply being attracted to the toy Cindy was holding, the group of mothers uniformly reacted with the feeling that this should not be permitted. Candy's mother immediately went to Candy, took the toy from her, returned it to Cindy, and told her 5-month-old daughter that she was not allowed to take the toy from Cindy.

Some parents are taken aback by the thought that it is reasonable to set limits with a 5-month-old child. I point out that if the child is doing something the parent does not approve of, then the parent ought to convey this to the child and set an age-appropriate and situation-appropriate limit. The setting of this limit was not done with anger or even annoyance. It was done with the awareness that this 5-month-old had transgressed in a social situation, and since Mother felt this is not desirable behavior, she conveyed this to her child by her action. Certainly, a 5-month-old is too young for an explanation—although it causes no harm to say a few words—but she is not too young to get the message conveyed by Mother's emotional tone and action that she is not allowed to take another kid's toy.

Thirteen months of age, Jane seemed to constantly be propelled—as are most children at this age—to want what others have. When she wanted my coffee, I did not allow her to take it, telling her that it was hot and might hurt her and that coffee is not for children. After that, she turned to her mother and conveyed to her that she wanted some juice.

At this age, Jane was not so easy with peers. She would demand, pull, hold onto things, and she would become angry. This particular morning, she screamed twice and shouted in anger at two of her young peers. She was tenaciously pursuing the purse that Temmy was holding. Temmy held on for about a minute, but Jane persisted in her demand, kept pulling, and angrily scolded Temmy, who let go of her end and began to cry.

Jane's mother intervened. Prior to her physical intervention, Jane's mother had been giving Jane instructions from a distance, telling her not to behave as she was with Temmy and raising her voice as time went by. Ultimately, when Jane pulled the purse from Temmy, Mother got up, went to Jane, retrieved the purse from her, and returned it to Temmy. As she did so, she told Jane—with mild anger and a scolding tone—that Jane is not allowed to take things from others.

I have found in years of observation that most children begin to require limits from about 6 months of age on. Our studies show that the requirement for limits from this time on is largely the product of a biological upsurge in aggressiveness (in the form of assertiveness) in children that is part and parcel of a maturational change occurring around this time period.

Parents are often frustrated by the fact that when they set limits—even with a child as young as 6 or 13 months old—they need to repeat the limits more often than they like. Thirteen-month-old Jane's mother was annoyed by the fact that (as had been happening for about five months now) Jane did not respond easily to Mother's expectations and Mother had to repeat them a number of times. Furthermore, Mother was quite annoyed when it became necessary for her to go to Jane and put some force behind the behavioral expectation she had of her lovely, feisty daughter.

My impression is that parents seem to recognize that while the child seems driven by an inner pressure to do what she is doing, the child does not have built-in controls over it. The development of such controls occurs only over time as the child makes conscious efforts to put on the brakes. As I explained in chapter 3, the child is pushed from within to do what most parents believe she "wants" to do; but the fact is that the child is driven and often seems compelled to do it. This is at the basis of that fact that generally none of us likes to be told what to do. This is so from the very beginning of life. Therefore, the mother's expectations often run against not only the child's endowment and inability to know how to control her inner pressures, but also against the child's wishes, healthy narcissism, and strivings toward autonomy (see chapter 3 for more detail on this point). For these reasons, limit setting is a long process, one that requires repetition and is often tedious for both child and parents.

One more point on when to set limits: it behooves parents *to set limits only when they are truly needed.*

## PRINCIPLES OF LIMIT-SETTING

I said in chapter 3,

> To get compliance from our kids, the expectations we have must have meaning, be reasonable; they can't all be equally obligatory.

A few paragraphs back, I said that limits should be set in ways that are "age-appropriate" and "situation-appropriate." They should also be "state-appropriate" and "history-appropriate."

- Regarding *age-appropriate*: One can't have the same expectations for a child when he is 7 months, 7 years, or 14 years of age. We'll take this up more extensively below.
- Regarding *state-appropriate*: A 7-month-old who bites Mother's nipple while falling asleep requires a different tone and approach to biting than the wide-awake 3-year-old who, much distressed and angry, bites her playmate.
- Regarding *situation-appropriate*: A different tone and approach is warranted when an 18-month-old takes a toy from another child than when that 18-month-old tries to pull an air-conditioner plug or walks into the street.
- And regarding *history-appropriate*: What is your child's history of reacting to your limit setting?
  1. If the child readily complies when limits are set, or limits are not often required, a freer hand can be allowed in setting limits—more casualness, less firmness, more time.
  2. If from early life on, the child, like Jane, tends to resist limits, and setting limits often becomes a mini-battle of wills, a more structured and predictable pattern of limit setting would be very helpful. It's also likely that more firmness and a greater conveyance of disapproval will be needed.

3. If the child from quite early on not only resists but puts up a struggle when Mom sets limits, battles of wills are common and at times difficult, a well structured, clearly defined pattern of limit setting will be necessary. There is a greater likelihood that limits may fail and punishment will be needed with this child more than with the other two.

Parental readiness for setting limits is highly facilitating of the entire enterprise, for both parent and child. Explain to the child why the limit is needed; have a strategy or structured pattern of limit setting, be reasonable, and be firm. For parents, be lovingly firm.

Why explain? So that your child/adolescent will know your reason for stepping on his sense of self. "Because I said so" will not impress your child! "Because I'm the boss," he'll think you're a bully and will likely lose respect for you. If you feel you've already amply explained and your child keeps resisting with "why?," "Because I said so" is OK.

Pattern your limit setting so that your child will learn what to expect from you. Take a set number of steps before you feel you have failed and go to punishment.

It is great to avoid punishment; but, not by giving in to the child who is stubbornly refusing to comply with the limits. When you do, you both lose.

## THE BASIC LIMIT SETTING MODEL

**Step 1:** Tell your child what to do or not do. Don't ask! "Will you take your coat off?" That's a question. The child may not want to. Tell him to do so! Use a tone of expectation.

If your child does not comply, take

**Step 2:** Repeat what you said a bit more firmly, and a bit louder. Tell him why you are telling him to do whatever it is. "Take your coat off, it's cold outside but not in here [which of course the child know]; you'll start to sweat and be uncomfortable." Or, "Get to your homework; yesterday you didn't have it finished when it was time for you to go to bed."

If your child still does not comply, go to

**Step 3:** Now tell your child this is the third time you're telling her to do what you said, and you don't like that. Remind your child how unpleasant things turned out the last time you went through this with her. Your tone is still more firm than before. *Don't plead!* It may make your child feel guilty and, if he/she enjoys your pleading, he/she is on the way to developing a streak of meanness; then, look out for his/her eventual way of relating to others, peers and adults (including teachers).

If you still get no compliance, go to

**Step 4:** Now go to your child, with firmness and moderate anger tell her you really don't like her behavior! If she does not do what you said now, there will be a punishment. *This is a **warning** of things to come, it is **not a threat.*** Be clear: your child should know where you stand.

You can present it as the child's choice: she/he can do what you say or she/he can choose the punishment—no "favorite" activity (whatever recreational activity the child likes) today or the next day or on the weekend. This heightens the child's awareness that she/he is in fact choosing: "I comply or I take punishment." This heightens the child's sense of having a say in how this potentially miserable event turns out. The child is made aware that these are the conditions and he/she has to weigh the consequences of making a decision. You explained the reason for the limit; he/she has the responsibility of choosing. Even before thinking ability is developed well enough, the task of choosing and taking responsibility for his/her actions is set in motion.

If you still get no compliance, the child in fact is choosing that you go to

**Step 5:** You now tell the child she/he will not be allowed to do her/his favorite activity tonight, or tomorrow, or on the weekend (we'll talk about punishment below). And, with the young child and the preteen, you press her/him to do what you told her/him to do 4 steps before.

Establish this limit-setting pattern from as early on as the occasion presents itself. This is best achieved from about 2 years of age on to 6. With 6- to 10-year-olds you should not need that many steps to get compliance; 4 or even 3 may be enough. With non-difficult adolescents, you should not need more than 3 steps.

Consider the following:

- Let's assume that you set a limit and soon come to recognize that the limit is not really necessary. Tell your child/teenager you've thought it over; it's OK to do what he's doing.
  I have never heard of a child/teenager turn to his/her mother or father and ridicule the parent for having changed her/his mind. Quite invariably, the child/teenager appreciates his/her parent's thoughtfulness and flexibility. In fact, it is a good model for the child, and it is likely the

child will adopt thoughtfulness and flexibility in his interactions with others. Some parents think that changing one's mind is a sign of weakness. But the child and certainly the teenager will recognize when the parent's change of mind is due to reasonableness; and, the parent who never changes his mind when reasonable to do so will soon be experienced by the child as rigid—and with this, in the eyes of the child/teenager, the parent's authority and reliability diminishes.

• Vary your pattern according to the kind of child you have.
That is, if you have a child who is shy and timid, slow the pace of limit-setting down, go easy; if your child is quite vigorous and even a bit hyperactive, move into limit setting more quickly and take two or three steps instead of five. If you have a hyperactive child, you and your child would very likely benefit from professional help. If you have a difficult adolescent, more rigorous behavioral strategies will be needed and again professional help may be wise.

## A CRITICAL POINT IN SETTING LIMITS

Two-year-old Harry once again stood up on the chair from which his mother had just taken him. Pushed to anger, Mother pulled him off the chair somewhat harshly. Harry, now upset and crying, stretched his arms up to his mother, conveying that he wanted her to pick him up. She turned away from him with, "I told you not to stand on the chair. You're a bad boy!" Rejected by Mother, Harry shuffled across the room to his father and leaned on him. Father said, "Don't come to me. You're being bad." Harry's crying intensified; he hid his head in the sofa, and I learned that for hours later he seemed upset.

We all operate biologically and psychologically under the general principle that we want to hold on to what feels good and get rid of what feels bad; we all want to take in, to internalize, that which feels good, and to reject, deny, and throw out that which feels bad. For this reason, setting limits under favorable emotional conditions tends to favor the child's internalizing the parents' expectations. The reverse—not internalizing parental expectations—is likely to occur when limits are set with hostility and in a mean-spirited interaction.

A critical point occurs when the parent has scolded the child and the child becomes upset and turns to the parent for comforting. If the parent has gotten to the point of scolding the child—and the child has gotten to the point of being upset enough to cry, fuss, and want comforting—it is understandable that the parent is going to be angry with the child. When the child is upset, however, who do we expect the child will turn to for comforting? Of course, he'll turn to the caregiver to whom she/he is attached; and that usually is the parent—even when at this moment that parent is angry with the distressed child.

I have often found that some angry mothers will reject the child's appeal for comfort under these circumstances. I have been told, "He's trying to get his way," or, "He's trying to butter me up." I think that is wrong. What I see is that when a child is scolded by his mother, he feels threatened that his world is falling apart. Made very anxious then, he turns to his mother for comforting. Who else would he turn to for protection and safety? And, the mother (or father) should accept the plea and comfort the child. The reason for this is twofold—and this applies not only to kids of all ages but also adults.

In terms of young children, first, given the principle that we all want to retain what feels good and try to eject from ourselves what feels bad, consider the following. The mother who picks up the child who is making a plea for comforting has the opportunity to repeat her limit setting under conditions when the child is experiencing her as the comforting, loving, soothing, good mother.

Upset because Mother told her she could not take Betty's ball, 3-year-old Lucy was on her mother's lap. Mother was quietly saying, "I know it upsets you that you can't have Betty's ball. But, it's hers. She doesn't want to let you play with it right now. You can't just take it from her. I can't let you do that. I wouldn't let her take your things." Mother hugged Lucy gently. Lucy still looked a bit sad. But she slowly nodded just once and stayed, comfortable, in Mother's lap for a few minutes. Then she was off, playing with Betty again.

Given how Harry's parents rejected his plea for comforting, repeated the limit in anger and told him he's a bad child, this in fact undermined their efforts to set limits and intensified Harry's emerging feelings of hate toward them. And, at the same time they were intensifying their own feelings of anger toward their own child. But the principle is this:

What Lucy's mother is doing will lead to Lucy's internalizing Mother's expectation because it is stated under conditions of comforting and soothing in the hands of a good mother. It comes from the "good mother" and will be experienced as being done for the child's well-being. By contrast, the handling of Harry by his parents makes him wish to eject what, as he then perceives her, his "bad mother" is telling him; he does not to hear what she is saying, and he therefore is likely to reject internalizing his mother's expectation.

Of course this is a simple model; nothing in psychic life is that simple. Yes, Harry will eventually internalize the "bad mother's" actions and her hostility-laden stated expectation. It will, however, be internalized with an overload of anger, a wish to resist it and to be rid of it, with the full play of hostility still attached to the experience. Lucy on the other hand, comforted by her sympathetic mother, is helped to lessen and perhaps even eliminate the angry feelings her mother's limit setting generated within her.

The second reason for responding positively to the scolded child's appeal for comfort is this. In the course of development, we all start out with feelings about ourselves and others—especially our family members, most particularly our mothers and fathers. Some of these feelings are good, and some are bad. These feelings become part of the images we have of ourselves and those to whom we are close.

Mental health professionals speak of the "good self" and the "bad self," the "good mother" and the "bad mother." We assume that we all form images of ourselves, which we retain in our minds and which play a large part in our emotional life. The larger the feelings we have of love for ourselves and our mothers, fathers, and siblings, the less our feelings of anger and hate toward others and ourselves. The larger the load of generated hostility within us—the larger our feelings of self-hate, of hate toward our mothers and fathers, the larger our negative feelings of ambivalence that stabilize within us over time.

The more hostile our feelings toward others and ourselves, the greater the difficulties we encounter in life. The development of our relationships, our self-esteem, and the character of our conscience, our ability to cope, to work, and to derive gratification from all of these, all are determined by the balance of the feelings of love and hate toward others and ourselves we carry within us. Taking this into account, trying to lessen the degree of hostility we feel in setting limits becomes crucial.

*It is exactly at the point where a child who has been scolded and now wants to be comforted that ambivalence can be significantly lessened or intensified.*

## PRINCIPLES OF PUNISHMENT

Of course, you want to avoid it. The negative consequences of needing to punish often are large. Too frequent punishment erodes parent-child relationships.

When we punish our child, we do so in the child's best interest. Regrettably, as all parents know, punishment often occurs when a parent is angry, sometimes in fact feels hostility toward her/his child. This regrettably may override the parent's genuine aim to punish in the child's best interest. Even the best parents are at times driven to actions they regret by what they feel to be their children's unacceptable behavior.

There are two basic forms of punishment: the *withdrawal of a privilege* and the *inflicting of pain*. The withdrawal of privilege is much safer and generally much better than inflicting pain—kids have enough pain just meeting the demands of everyday life. Unfortunately, too many parents forget that their growing up years were full of anxiety-producing challenges and even outright psychic pain.

In punishing by the withdrawal of a privilege, let me make a rather obvious comment. When choosing the withdrawal of a privilege, it is well to choose a privilege the child enjoys. A child may say that she doesn't care that she can't play with her new toy, or can't watch that (her favorite) program on TV! Children will often say they don't care in order to lessen the sting of having a privilege withdrawn. Sometimes a child may say this to retaliate against the parent, to try to make the parent feel ineffectual. In withdrawing a privilege rely more on what you know your child has enjoyed in the past and is likely to enjoy now, rather than on the child's response when a heated battle of wills is going on between the two of you.

The mildest effective withdrawal of privilege is the "time out."

For the young child, the child has to sit or be in some limited space and stay there for a limited number of minutes. When carried out properly (see below), this can work very well with children from 18 months to 6 years. Beyond that age including into adolescence, it takes the form of "grounding," which works well too. And of course there are other privileges that matter to kids, TV, computer, cell-phone, etc.

When withdrawing a privilege, be reasonable; dose the amount of punishment to the degree of unacceptability of noncompliance. For instance, don't take the TV, or the computer or cell-phone, away for more than one program at a time, or for more than one evening or day at a time.

Don't withdraw things that are needed for your child's well-being such as securing a good relationship with you, or food or sleep. Don't disallow a TV program recommended by a teacher as an assignment. If your child has some difficulty making friends, don't punish by disallowing a peer from coming to the house.

Use your judgment: the older the child, the more difficult he/she is to set limits with, the more you up the punishment, etc. The younger

the child, the more shy or timid, the more slowly you move into punishment.

Inflicting pain is loaded with problems. Unfortunately, some energetic
young children younger than 5 just will not comply with limits even when
privilege withdrawal would seem reasonably dosed. Likely raising an eye-
brow in the reader, I have found that many of these younger kids tend to
not stop until they get a swat on the bottom.

But, I hold to strict rules and limits on "a swat on the bottom":

- Never swat a less-than-2-year-old child.
- Never use anything other than your open hand. A fist is out of order.
  Belts, sticks, paddles, and all else are out of order too.
- Give no more than *one moderate swat* on the bottom of the less-than-
  6-year-old.
- Always swat on the clothed bottom. Do not make the child take off
  her/his pants! A *moderate* swat on the back of a shoulder too can put
  emphasis on the need for compliance.
- If you have to physically transport your 4- to 6-year-old child to his
  room—you do not send a less-than-4-year-old to his room because
  it may create more problems than it solves (see below)—be firm but
  exert the least force needed. There's a good chance that your child will
  say that you're hurting him; you have to make sure that your hold is
  not, in fact, hurtful.
- Physical modes of punishment too easily run into becoming child
  abuse, and parents *must* avoid child abuse. Child abuse cripples—
  child, parent, and their relationship.

I'll comment below about physical punishment in the 6- to 10-year-old and
adolescent age ranges.

## LIMIT-SETTING AND PUNISHMENT OVER THE YEARS

It's critical, of course, to consider the child's age when setting limits. This
is because, as I detailed in chapter 3, the state of self and the self's ability
to understand, predict, know, judge, and adapt, are not present during the
first 2 years and develop only gradually thereafter. We can assume that
these abilities become sufficiently developed by 6 to 8 years. Note that the
timetable I, or any developmentalists, suggest is not intended to give exact
ages at which all children will have developed a given ability. This is because

children vary in their development schedules—due to both their biological endowment and their experiences. So the numbers given are "at about this (given) age."

Mental health research and clinical work this past century has taught us that it is in the best interest of the child and the parents for children to be permitted and helped to express their feelings and thoughts. We expect these expressions to be made, however, with reasonableness, appropriateness, and good judgment. It is the task of each family to determine what constitutes expressions that are reasonable, appropriate, and expressed with good judgment.

Let's look briefly at limit setting and punishment over the years.

## Infancy (0 to 12 months)

Taking what we have learned about brain development and the development of intelligence (see chapter 3), we cannot expect the less-than-two-year-old to process the parent's expectations, to understand why the parent is having such expectations. But, the child will resonate with the parent's feelings about what the child is doing and what the mother expects. Finding again and again that mother reacts unpleasantly, in tones alarming to the baby/toddler when the baby/toddler does a given thing or acts a given way, the less-than-two-year-old can learn to comply with mother's age-appropriate expectations. One can explain to the infant why one makes the given demand; it is a very good habit to get into—that is, to talk to one's baby[3]—but at this age, it's the feeling tone that will be well "understood."

It's rather common that babies will bite Mother's breast and bite others, or grab another baby's hair and not yet be able to let go, or reach for a cup of hot coffee, or hit (playfully or not). Infant limits begin to be needed.

**What to do?** **Limit Setting:** Because the child cannot yet anticipate the effects of his actions, or judge their consequences, caregivers must take over what the child should do, act in the child's behalf, as the child's representative. Mildly toned limit setting has to be predominantly instructive: the infant needs to learn what he can't do and why he can't do it. Again, while the mother's tone will convey the expectation, it is advantageous to explain in words even before the child can speak.

**Punishment:** Compliance at this age can only be hoped for; it cannot yet be expected.

There is no plausible justification for, or potential usefulness in punishing the less-than-one-year-old infant—given that he cannot and will not yet for many months be able to "anticipate the effects of his actions, nor judge their potential consequences." In fact, punishment is never reasonable with infants less than 1 year of age.

## Toddlerhood (12 to 24 Months)

Strivings for autonomy and the first upsurge of aggression (see chapter 2) will emerge at about 6 months or so. From then to about 24 months, due to the toddler's emerging ability to move about, the need for limit setting will mushroom. Depending on the child's inborn energy level, the intensity of her strivings for autonomy, and her malleability (degree of flexibility[4] in her reactions to demands for compliance), the degree of limit setting needed will vary. Low-energy-type mothers will have their hands full with a high-energy[5] child due to their respective different inborn energy styles. A calm-reactor, slower-moving mother or father is likely to experience her or his child's brisk and energetic reactivity to be annoying and challenging because it will be a mismatch for the parent's own reactivity style.

During this age period, the basic limit-setting model begins to be frequently needed. It will feel natural to the parent. But, still, the parent's tone will play a larger role than the child's word and thought-based understanding. And then, there will be times when a limit has to be set quickly; there will be no time for the step-wise progression of the basic model. For instance,

Thirteen-month-old Louis reaches for an air conditioner plug engaged in an electrical outlet. What does Mother or Father do? We have seen varying reactions. One mother firmly prohibits Louis's touching the plug or outlet, getting up quickly and telling him it's a dangerous thing. He persists, and, with Mother's further prohibition, he becomes angry. She holds his hands firmly but without hurting him as he pulls against her effort to inhibit his reaching for the plug, and, with seriousness in her voice, she tells him he is not allowed to touch the plug/outlet because doing this might hurt him. She tells him she doesn't want him to get hurt. He gets angrier and begins to cry. When he then reaches for her to be picked up, she does so. While comforting him, she repeats her prohibition and the reason for it. She also tells him that she knows it's hard to not be able to do what he wants.

Another mother seeing this type of behavior at first says nothing. But as her young child persists in touching the plug, she shouts from across the room that he'd better get away from there or she'll smack him. Because he does not comply with Mother's distance communication, she goes to him, yanks his arm angrily, and loudly proclaims that he is determined to kill himself. Now frightened, he stretches his arms out to Mother. She ignores him and returns to her seat.

Limit setting will more and more be needed; battles of wills will heat up; ambivalence will wax and wane. With children who are easily upset (they have a low threshold of irritability), temper tantrums may emerge (we talk about these in chapter 6).

**What to do?** *Limit Setting:* For young children, as Ben Spock recommended years ago, "baby-proof" the house! Make it safe for the toddler to move about in the space available to him. Put your favorite pottery, breakable valued things, knickknacks, out of the toddler's reach.

The increase in limit setting now required will help the toddler learn basic rules of care for himself and valued things. Select and put out of reach the books you don't want your toddler to inadvertently damage. Get the toddler her/his own collection of books—and read them to the toddler; most of them love being read to; and there are wonderful books for toddlers. The added benefit of using reading as a means of interacting with him is that it will make him value reading.

Even though the toddler will not yet grasp the reasons for the limits, start the process of making limit setting instructive; the toddler is about to begin to learn what is reasonable and what is not, what is not permitted and why it is not, basic information the toddler will eventually need to know for his well-being. When appropriate, clarification of what is permitted coupled with what is not permitted can be very helpful even before thought-based understanding is developed.

Caution: do not assume that the toddler can't understand you at all! The patterning of limit setting now guides both child and parent. Both will be able to guess what will happen if the toddler does not comply. Compliance that comes at this age will be based on learning what you mean from understanding the tone of what you say more than your words.

Do be careful. Both excessive and insufficient limit setting during this toddler period are major concerns. *Excessive limit setting* may interfere with *the inner push to learn* what the world is made of, that is, to explore—which is where learning begins. It will interfere with the child's need to learn what happens if I do this or that. Learning does not begin in school; *it begins at home.* The child's strivings for autonomy require that the toddler begin to learn all she can about, and how to solve problems in, the world into which she was born. If this learning by means of exploration is too interfered with and discouraged, it may make learning a negative experience and set up a conflict about learning, which the child may then carry into school. It may then discourage the spontaneous and natural drive to learn.

*Insufficient limit setting* will fail to guide the child well enough in determining what behavior is reasonable and what is not. And it can bring the problem I talked about in chapter 3: *insufficient compliance.* The child will then learn the hard way and may pay a heavy price for not learning to comply reasonably.

**Punishment:** When setting limits fails, "time outs" are perfect for toddlers. Given the toddler's push to do things and move about, "1 minute 'time out' per age in years" is a good formula: one minute time out for a one-year-old; two minutes time out for a two-year-old, etc.

*I am in total agreement with Dr. Karl-Heinz Brisch who holds that there are risks in "time outs."[6] This generally is because the "time out" is mal-handled or abused. The formula of "1 minute . . . per age in years" is essential to adhere to. The "time out" should occur in the same room where Mother or Father (the one who administered the "time out") is. The child should not be sent to another room. The reason is that, in keeping with the principle that "punishment should not bring with it the withdrawal of things vital to the child's well-being," separating the young child from the parent under conditions of anger and distress undermines the crucial development of the child's attachment to the parent—a development most vital to the child's well-being. This principle should hold for children **under the age of 4 years**.*

"Time outs" that are too long are experienced as harsh and threatening; they are too punitive. But the "time out" decided on must be held: no talking to Mom or anyone, no playing with toys, no reading a book; just sit and learn what Mom or other caregiver said.

Physical punishment, even with our rules, is generally inferior to a "time out." But a swat on the bottom may be needed with some quite challenging very driven and determined toddlers. I'll say more about this in the next section (the preschool child).

## Preschool years (2 to 5 years)

The 2- to 5-year period enters the "golden era for learning to comply" (see chapter 3). It is the first stage of thought-based rather than just conditional and emotional-based learning the whys and how to comply; the parent's word-explanations begin to be understood intellectually.

From 2 to 5 years, propelled by the child's increasing adaptive, cognitive, and emotional abilities and skills, the child's exploratory behaviors will become more complex and will increasingly require guidance, and increasingly compel and challenge the parents to set limits. But it is important for parents to realize that, while setting limits is unpleasant, these years are the start of the optimal period during which setting limits impacts most favorably on the child's learning to comply with their expectations. It's also a good time to help the child increase her/his ability to adapt constructively which will be facilitated by the parent's being able to persist while also being able to make compromises depending on the "obligatory level" of the expectation.

Early self-discipline starts. This of course is the period for toilet training which is challenging for both child and parents (see chapter 3 for a news report of overly harsh toilet training). Moderate-level expectations as brushing teeth, washing hands and eventually the rest of one's body; bedtime; and eating well will for many kids no doubt require more or less firm limits. Challenging but requiring more encouragement than limit setting are: learning colors, reading letters, and then reading words. Each child will require her or his own program, depending on her or his developing abilities, talents, and skills.

Preschool experience is critical in that it establishes a baseline for the child's school years that will follow. Is the preschool experience positive or negative? If it is negative, what needs to be done? Does the child have much pain on separating from the parent when taken to school? When it is too difficult, this problem needs to be solved because the pain the child experiences will become linked with school itself and set a pattern of disliking school which may then dampen the gratification that comes with studying and learning. In addition, it will generate hostility in the child—as well as in the parent. In the chapters that follow we discuss handling the various reactions that often come with such childhood distress: expressing anger, hostility, and hate; tantrums; experiencing anxiety, sadness, and depression. We have learned over the last 8 decades that early separation problems need to be taken seriously. If these persist during the 2 to 5 years period, professional consultation may be very helpful—for both child and parents.

Learning to play with peers, not just side by side, but rather with one another begins during the 2 to 5 years period. Playing wildly, taking things from others, having difficulty sharing reasonably, hitting, teasing, all require limit setting and guidance. Here specifically, these limit-setting challenges are valuable occasions for helping one's child find ways to interact with peers that will pave the way to their being able to make and retain friends for years to come.

For most kids, the first peer relations occur at home. Sibling relationships are crucial in that we all live most of our active life with our peers. And, except for one-child families, it's at home that we first learn to live with peers. And it's up to parents to mediate, to see to it that their children learn to live together in some reasonable degree of harmony. Having to mediate conflict between their kids are opportunities for parents to help kids learn to live with peers.

It makes parents' task easier when they see that these unpleasant events are occasions to teach our kids to cope constructively. Sure, parents experience these episodes of maladaptive behavior in their kids as a burden. But in fact, in dealing with these maladaptive behaviors, we help kids to better govern their reactivity, improve their problem-solving skills, increase their self-discipline, and grow into more confident kids who have success in relating to others. I understand that the Chinese writing symbol for "danger" (or "crisis," some say) is the same as that for "opportunity." We also find in clinical work that "crises" in parent-child life are "opportunities" to teach kids to cope better. In addition, these preschool years also are the time, according to Erikson, when the child develops a sense of initiative. This sense of initiative molds the developing self into a self that can make things happen, fostering "self-reliance."

**What to do?**     **Setting Limits:** With children 2 to 5 years of age, the parents' use of the basic limit-setting model should increasingly become automatic and be predictable by the preschooler. By now parents know quite well the limit-setting pattern that works best for their particular child. Limit setting continues to be instructional but now more and more aims at the child's consolidating self-discipline: to internalize parental and preschool teachers' expectations.

> *Parents should allow the child to protest their limit setting to a reasonable degree; they should not muzzle the child; but at the same time, parents should hold the line depending on the "obligatory level" of the expectation. And there is much to be gained by having a heart-to-heart talk with the 2- to 5-year-old after such unpleasant episodes have cooled a bit.*

**Punishment:** The punishment of choice for the 2- to 5-year-old continues to be the "time out." In addition, where more than a time out is needed, withdrawal of privilege can now include choice activities the child especially likes, such as being excluded from a family game or a young child TV program. Just because the child is getting older does not mean the punishment should multiply. Excessive punishment puzzles the child, may intensify his/her sense of having done something really wrong, and it may challenge the child's judgment of what is reasonable. Once the child develops the ability

to judge, the excessively punishing parent will be experienced more negatively by the child than most parents wish for.

But here is another punishment issue of much concern.

> When Jane was about 3 years old she and her mother got into an unpleasant
> interchange. Quite aware that she was now irritating her mother, Jane per-
> sisted in stepping "playfully" (to Jane) on her mother's foot! But, it bothered
> Mother. Mother set limits with her, quite well. Jane persisted in stepping on
> Mother's foot, teasing her with it, blatantly defying Mother's demand that she
> stop it. As Jane was about to yet again step on her mother's foot, Mother got
> hold of Jane's arm and gave her one swat on the bottom. Jane immediately
> stopped stepping on her mother's foot.

To Jane, it was a game; to Mother, it was annoying. Jane disregarded not
only her mother's telling her to stop; she also disregarded the distress she
was progressively causing her mother. My impression is that Mother's aim
was not to hurt Jane physically; it seemed more to tell Jane "Look at what
you're doing to both of us! Look at what you're bringing onto yourself!"
Mother was insisting on reasonable toddler behavior.

I have found that during this age period when all reasonable parents
are appalled at and aware of the highly negative consequences of physical
child abuse, many parents automatically reject the notion of "a swat on the
clothed bottom." I know why they do. Physical punishment is a slippery
slope. But I ask, to what degree was the "swat on the bottom" this mother
gave her daughter damaging to her child's body or her psyche? I ask this
question to engage the reader's thinking about this controversial issue: is a
swat on the young child's padded bottom child abuse? This issue is, I believe, more complicated than many well-intentioned people assume. I too,
among many, raise my voice strongly against abuses and neglect of children,
in fact, abuses of all people. Child abuse and neglect should be outlawed everywhere. As I have quoted more than once, "a United Nations Children's
Fund (UNICEF) report [holds] 'that an estimated 40 million children glob-
ally under the age of 15, suffer from violence, abuse, and neglect (according
to a UN-sponsored study led by Paulo S. Pinheiro, in what is deemed to
be) the first detailed look at how children experience violence all over the
world, and what must be done to prevent and end this scourge' (*United
Nations News 2005*). I should note that 40 million is probably an underes-
timation."[7] While this report does not specify that the "violence, abuse, and
neglect" occur at home, my decades of clinical work and research lead me
to say that abuse and neglect that are experienced at home are more psychologically damaging than when these occur elsewhere. And while I do not

know where these occur most—given terrible events as genocides—that which happens at home far outnumbers that which happens in schools and the neighborhood, including the recruiting of children as soldiers.

The serious negative consequences of abusing children physically (as well as sexually), today are well-known. Many studies have traced their lifelong-lasting consequences (see chapter 1). None of those among us who are concerned with the ravages these create and the rise these give to emotional disorders in our children, to bullying, delinquency, and crime, individual and collective, can condone any abuse or neglect of children.

I want to highlight here, however, as I have elsewhere[8] that equal to the harsh consequences to a child's emotional life of physical abuses (physical and sexual) and neglect, *emotional abuse* has for too long been left in the shadow of our awareness and concern. While, not as blatant as physical abuses, *emotional abuse* too has serious harmful consequences. In fact,

*Much more* **emotional abuse** *occurs at home, in school, and in the neighborhood than physical abuse.*

Acts of rejecting, depreciating, shaming, and humiliating their children by parents and teachers occur everywhere. These acts of emotional abuse, by injuring a child's healthy narcissism, especially and foremost when experienced at home, tend to bring with them a poor sense of self and a diminished sense of autonomy and initiative; they also lead to insecurity, low self-esteem, poor self-confidence, as well as rage toward others. And these painful factors of self-experiencing, especially rage toward others, pave the way to bullying, delinquency, and crime. A child's emotional scars may not be as visible as his physical scars, but psychological scars are often less reversible than physical ones.

Over my years of infant and young child observation, I have seen on many an occasion a distraught mother of a young child who, abiding by our reasonable constrictions against child abuse, will glare or show disdain at her 3- or 4-year-old who is defying her expectation at a given moment. Close observation of the child's face suggests a painful psychological threat. As an infant observer, I assure the reader, *such reactions are amply visible; but they do require tuning in on the child's reaction.* I am speaking of Moms especially because between 2 and 5, they tend to be the limit setter more frequently than Dads. To be sure, Dads do similar things; many of them more harshly than Moms.

My clinical data (verbalized by kids in psychotherapy) too, affirm that many young children, and even older ones than 2- to 5-year-olds, wish their mother would hit them rather than give them a dirty look or say any one of the hurtful things many Moms and Dads say. The idea of "the evil eye" has long existed; so has "the look that kills!" Our understanding of its chilling effect, especially when it comes from one's mother or father, does not require education. Or, consider the feelings of the child whose mother explodes, "You brat, you'll be the death of me!" Such verbal explosions run wild and, psychologically, they wound deeply.

Children can take Mom's or Dad's "angry look"; that's bearable. Parents' hostility, hate, and rage, with their unconscious intention to hurt (see chapter 2) their own child, kids find unbearable; "it's too much!" and it generates hostility in them toward the parent. In fact, Jane could no doubt see her mother's angry look; I saw it. At the moment it did not stop Jane's teasing Mom. What would Mother have done next? Jane was intensifying the challenge to Mom.

I learned much from seeing such interactions among mother-child pairs whose relationships, according to current mental health attachment measures, were quite secure. Is all physical punitive contact abuse? What is? What is not? Was Jane's mother's action child abuse? Was it sadistic; did she derive pleasure from striking her daughter? Was Jane's mother's aim to bully her, tease her, mock her, or humiliate her? My impression is, No. She wanted her feisty 3-year-old daughter to stop disregarding her own Mom's expression of distress and to comply!

*I think that the concept "child abuse" is at risk of losing its specified and valuable meaning if we call all physical punitive contact child abuse, a meaning that can guide us to clearly declare what is harmful and should not happen!*

## Early Elementary School years (5 to 8 years)

From 5 to 8 years of age, the child's abilities to think and express himself verbally continue to develop. So does his beginning to evaluate where he stands in the family and to others in school. He/she is developing a sense of right and wrong, not just of good and bad or approval and disapproval, but of right and wrong based on rules and regulations in all aspects of her/his behavior and interactions with others. This age period is a high point when rather common lying and cheating in good kids can be dealt with constructively. With these, the child's ability to judge his/her own actions and those of others is developing and she/he can now really begin to intellectually grasp what her/his parents' and teachers' expectations are and why they stand for them. For the 5- to 8-year-old, explanations for and discussions of reasons and principles behind expectations begin to be meaningful things to think about. Developing the ability to comply is increasingly based on both cognitive and emotional understanding the whys and wherefores of expectations.

The child between 5 and 8 years takes a large step in further developing his/her becoming a learner and a doer. She wants to be shown what to do and try to learn to do it herself. Many challenges loom.

- The early school years begin to demand of kids that they come to school on time, sit in their seats, follow instructions, as well as restrain their movements and behaviors.
- Compliance with others than mother and father, while already expected in preschool, now becomes a daily, more taxing challenge.
- Most kids learn to meet these challenges satisfactorily—if by virtue of their relationships with their parents they have already learned to comply with their parents' expectations.
- When they have not, the challenge of complying in school will generally be more difficult. Limit-setting efforts by teachers will increase with those kids who resist demands for compliance with school expectations.

Children whose parents are engaged in their child's school experience, by asking their kids, and listening with interest to what they say about their school day, by checking the work their child brings home—what they've done in school and what homework they have—by going to parent-teacher conferences, will feel supported and encouraged to engage in their schoolwork. This is when the child's brain and cognitive (intelligence) functions are developing sufficiently to make learning to work—to learn, study, and do homework—possible.

Where school compliance is good, and when the child's school efforts are appreciated by his/her parents, the child's self-esteem is boosted, which encourages the child to continue in his efforts to do well. Where school compliance is poor, parents' efforts to encourage it will be best achieved by guidance—explanations of the importance of complying with teachers' expectations that ultimately will benefit the child—and by setting limits. Having been in school for about 7 hours, most second and third graders, if not also first graders, will have some homework to do. "I was in school all day, and now more work to do!" Yes, and when kids don't comply with the teacher's demand, it becomes the parents' responsibility at home to get their child to comply with those demands.

In addition, all kinds of additional daily events will require encouragement and even limits: such as getting up in time and doing all the things needed to get ready for and be in school on time; to be at dinner with the family; to get ready for bed in due time; and more.

Limit setting for the 5- to 8-year-old will become most focused on:

- Peer-related activities both at home (between siblings) and outside, such as, learning to play by rules,
- Breaking rules, cheating and lying. It's not just bad kids who lie; most kids do!
- School affiliated responsibilities, book bags preparation, homework,
- Home affiliated responsibilities, such as, beginning to help with chores, keeping one's own or shared room in reasonable condition, and
- Self-care responsibilities, health and hygiene, etc. are large challenges for the child. They must increasingly be mastered, and limit setting must aim at facilitating the child's developing competence.
- Sibling conflict resolution will continue to be required; the same principles apply as were suggested for the 2- to 5-year-olds.

**What to do?** *Limit Setting*: The same basic model of setting limits constructively works well. By this age period, parents know their child well and know the type of limit setting that seems to work best with him/her. Because the demands of everyday life continue to demand much effort from them, and many frustrations and disappointments occur to all 5- to 8-year-olds (and at all ages), irritability, anger, even hostility will be part of every child's experience. The fortunate ones will most express this at home, the safest place on earth to lose one's cool and temper. Those who don't feel secure enough at home to risk being angry there will have to find other places to let loose. If this is done in school, optimal school functioning and learning may suffer; if it's done in the community, the cost to friendship, to respect by neighbors, to peer approval (which is difficult to achieve well) will no doubt be substantial.

Look at the section on the Principles of Limit Setting above to energize and support your efforts when you feel some doubt about what to do. Tailor these principles to your child's age and temperament.

*Punishment:* Punishment is quite likely to be required. Compliance with parental expectations is not fully achieved with any 5-year-old; much is yet to be developed cognitively, emotionally, and adaptively to further establish the sought-after degree of meeting the parents' expectations. Limits will be required, will be set, and with all normal enough 5- to 8-year-olds, will at times fail. The withdrawal of privileges, which now means even more to the child than it did before, always the punishment of choice, can work well. Time outs are not as likely to be onerous to the 6-year-old as they were earlier, and therefore are not likely to be as effective. Withdrawing a favorite TV program, or computer privileges, especially computer games devised for those young ones who just take to computers like fish to water, will work better than time outs.

*Physical punishment should now be totally avoided.*

Even a swat on any part of the body can now cause more problems than it can solve. Insults, shaming, humiliating, hurtful statements, all should be avoided; all of which comes down to:

*Avoid emotional abuse!*

If the parent is about to give his or her kid the evil eye, the parent needs to call a time out (like is done in sports) and come back to the problem with the 5- to 8-year-old (and older kid) when somewhat cooled down and in better control.

Here are a few further notes concerning 5- to 8-year-olds. Some well-behaved, lovable kids seem to become more expectation-resistant during this 5 to 8 years era. As they get bigger they want more autonomy and become more insistent on wanting to do things their own way; it is more difficult for them to tame their own resistance than it is for others. But with parents holding the line and explaining the reasons for needing to comply, they do come around and progressively improve their compliance.

Some kids may resist complying with expectations because of difficulties that have shown to a degree from very early on in life, but these difficulties were not yet leading to worrisome challenges for parents. Some of these kids have already shown a recognizable stubborn streak (usually due to a greater inborn tendency for obsessive-compulsive ways of coping with challenges) which may now present more difficulty in complying with expectations.

In some, it may become evident now that they have some learning dysfunction which up-to-now has not been clearly recognized; they may perhaps even have some degree of dyslexia (difficulty in recognizing and processing what they read). They are likely to resist doing homework, perhaps even dislike going to school. When such resistances persist, given that they may ultimately affect the child's learning capability, consultation with school psychologists or child psychiatrists can be enormously guiding in optimizing that child's development. Not complying with doing homework and not liking to go to school may not be due to being a kid who just wants to play; it may hide some underlying problem that causes the child to feel disappointed in himself when he tries to learn. This calls for professional attention.

Some energetic, constantly in motion kids will now show evidence of being unable to sit still in school, or to not be able to pay attention over a span of time. Teachers are likely to be the first to tell parents that their child seems to have such a problem. Again, consultation with a Child Psychiatrist or Psychologist can clear the picture and lead to their prescribing some helpful programs for handling these difficulties or, where needed, recommend specific forms of treatment. As a general principle, it behooves parents to seek consultation with professionals when they are troubled by their children's too persistent noncompliance with their expectations. Generally, it's wise for parents to ask themselves, "Is something going on that needs attention I'm not specifically educated to understand?" Mental health professionals and child development experts have learned more about how to optimize a child's physical and psychological development during the 20th century than we had known during the entire history of civilization. Regrettably, being a good parent does not make one an expert in how to optimize one's child's psychological and emotional development.

## Later Elementary School Years (Ages 8–12)

From 8 to 12 years of age all that has been set in motion between 5 to 8 years of age continues. School demands continue with expectations increasing commensurate with the child's further developing cognitive and adaptive capabilities. So too, home chores are now added for which the child this age is adequately developed that will commonly require encouragement and even some limit setting, such as keeping their room or their shared room space in reasonable order, help set the table, clear the table, take out the garbage, etc. Most kids this age can facilitate Mom and Dad's homemaking responsibilities—there's always more than enough to do for everyone to pitch in. Homework is critical and for many kids whose sense of autonomy and self-discipline has not developed sufficiently, parents staying on top of their kids' performance can keep them continue to grow in these abilities.

*What to do? Limit Setting:* Limit setting to further enhance the child's self-discipline where it is weak is much needed in order to prepare the child adequately for further education and the greater life challenges that lay ahead. The same general limit-setting measures apply as they did for the 5 to 8 years period.

**Punishment:** Privilege withdrawal is by far the preferred strategy. The privileges we give our kids are more and more cherished by them. Computers and for some of our internet whizzes, internet contacts, chats, Facebook and the like, games, and TV are high priority privileges. Withdrawing these sting but do no harm; use them when needed. Again, it's important to withdraw privileges that are not essential for your 8- to 12-year-old's education and well-being. For instance, with a child who has some difficulty making friends, don't take away the privilege of his asking a kid over after school. For those of us who are fortunate enough, kids should never be punished by being sent to bed without having had dinner.

*Physical punishment and emotional abuse should be avoided!*

## Adolescence (12 to 18 years)

Mental health professionals recognize adolescence as the critical stage it is, during which humans evolve from the child into the young adult. In my own work,[9] I have suggested that adolescence be considered as extending from 12 to 21 or so years. While the 18 to 21 years period transitions into young adulthood, for many who go on to college, some developmentalists hold that the protective conditions of college prolong the experience of being an adolescent which may then, for many of them, carry over into these years.

Given the large challenge their child's adolescence brings with it for parents, it may serve parents well to have a grasp of the psychological developmental challenges their teenager faces during this era. Erik Erikson, pre-eminent psychoanalyst, proposed[10]—and it has stood the test of time—that in the course of the child's development, adolescence is the developmental period during which the young person's "identity" becomes definitively structured for all to see and as well as for the adolescent herself/himself. While self-identity will continue to develop over the years, this is the period when one's "self-identity" most fully consolidates. A metamorphosis of the self takes place that is especially influenced by the following dramatic developmental tasks[11] that challenge the adolescent:

1. There is an acceleration of the process of becoming an individual able to govern all aspects of oneself in one's world including beginning to consider the direction one's life will take; essentially thinking about "Who am I; who do I want to become?" In contrast to the 6-year-old wanting to be a fireman when he grows up, this "who do I want to become?" is "for real."

2. There is a gradual reduction of the nuclear family being at the center of the adolescent's universe, with a progressive turning toward the peer world, given that this is the universe where during the rest of life the self's personal life will most take place, including eventually finding a mate with whom to take on the biological mandate to "preserve the species" and establish a new generation to continue community life.

3. There is further detailing and specification of one's gender-self and of one's aggressive-self. One's ultimate gender determination progressively stabilizes during adolescence; so does the sense of oneself as someone with a defined aggression profile—including both nondestructive and hostility-laden aggressive self. Both the gender and aggressive aspects of self-experience create much anxiety, and both strongly co-determine the self's ultimate—though not unmodifiable—character and personality.

4. There is a striking evolution of one's adaptive capabilities, including one's defining body growth, size, form, features, attributes, etc, which much contribute to one's self-image and personality.

5. There is a dramatic evolving of one's cognitive and emotional capabilities which serve to master the enormous volume of school learning and socialization expected by peers, family, and society (see third paragraph below).

6. There is a continuing defining of one's enlarging skills and talents, such as in sports, art, music, dance, theater, etc. which in essence are creative ways of using one's energies, what in psychology we call "sublimation." These sublimations, when further developed in adolescence, become pathways for creatively channeling psychological energies that may when not harnessed lead teenagers into trouble. It's well known that when teenagers are involved in sports or the arts, they tend to get into less trouble and it also enhances their positive self-development.

7. Critical as well is that with the process of becoming an individual, *shifting the center of one's universe from the family to the peer group leads to the family's values and mores being tested against those of the selected peer group and with this, there may be some revisions of one's mores and values, that is, some revisions in one's conscience.* Here again, the better the family relations have been over the years, the less the revisions of conscience and conduct; the poorer the relationships at home, the greater the influence of the peer group over these revisions.

These adolescent developmental tasks and the remarkable changes they bring about, magnificent as they are, still leave the need for parental guidance and help. In a recent newspaper piece, journalist Elizabeth Cooney[12] reported on an interview with Frances Jensen, a neurologist at Harvard Medical School and Children's Hospital Boston. Cooney writes that Dr. Jensen points out "We all know [the cognitive functions that take place in] the frontal lobe. . . . It's insight, judgment, inhibition [of action], self-awareness, [recognition of] cause and effect, acknowledgment of cause and effect. And big surprise: [Its development is] not done in [the] teen years. Hence [teens'] impulsiveness, their unpredictable behavior, their lack of ability to acknowledge cause and effect, despite the fact they are getting 800s on the SATs and can be cognitively highly functional and memorize at a much more impressive rate that we as adults do later." So, as all parents know, intelligent as they may be, adolescents at times absolutely need to be told to abide by our guidelines, mores, and wishes! And then, no bargaining! In families where teens and their parents have a good, secure relationship, they'll heed, mmh, 80 percent of the time—that's not a B, that's an A+ for parenting. Where the relationship is troubled from early childhood on, parents' wishes will not go far.

Limit setting now occurs everywhere, at home, in school, in the peer group, in individual peer relations, in society. And limit setting continues to be needed, but so is the protection of the integrity of the adolescent's developing self. And, adolescents will now become more than ever protective of their dramatically developing self. Their progressively growing emotional and physical power and aggression will be well mobilized in the service of this self-protection.

*What to do?* *Limit Setting:* Adolescence is a long period of complex development and so, we have to consider "what to do" in terms of the sub-period of adolescence we are talking about.

Above all, parents must *respect* the adolescent's developing sense of self. How, *really, honestly,* would you, the parent, when you were an adolescent, have wanted to be treated? That's the best guideline, if the parent really thinks of how he or she felt then. To think, "My Dad was right to be harsh and mean-spirited to prevent me from getting in trouble" is in all likelihood not true, it is rationalizing how it felt to be an adolescent. Reasonable limits based on well-reasoned and explainable expectations, administered with loving firmness, will usually eventually work well with the adolescent.

*During the 12 to 15 year period* the need for limit setting takes a very challenging turn. First of all, the challenges of school, homework, home chores, health self-care and hygiene often demand encouragement if not outright limit setting. With regard to school and homework, where kids have developed a good degree of self-discipline, parents showing interest in the state of their adolescents' activities and encouraging them are not only very supportive but also tend to diminish the need for limit setting. "How did the homework go?" "How's school?" "How did your project go over?" etc. demonstrate your interest. Of course, the parents' interest has to be genuine to be meaningful and encouraging to the developing student-worker.

As self-discipline expands and further stabilizes, an interesting phenomenon occurs in some very bright kids when they enter the middle to high school years. Being very bright, they have breezed through elementary school with only moderate exertion. They seem to expect, not altogether wrongly, that learning will continue to be achievable with moderate effort. Now a test comes back, not with the expected A, but with a C! The C wounds the kid's healthy narcissism and she rationalized: "Oh; that was a fluke!" Since this happens even to many good students, Mom and Dad don't get upset; "Hey, you just have to study more; you're in 7th (or 8th, or 9th) grade now." Then the next test comes back, not with an A but, again with a C! Now the wound is deeper and doesn't yield as well to the rationalization that it's a fluke. Now Mom is worried and Dad gets heated! Now Mom and maybe Dad too, gives her a bit of a lecture! And then yet the next, the third time, the expected A turns out to be a C! Mom and Dad are furious: "Take away her computer, her iPhone!"

Dad, a professional with a good reputation having talked to a work friend whose daughter went through a similar experience explains to him that this is an opportunity for his daughter to learn that being smart is great, but it isn't enough to be successful in life. She also has to apply her intelligence to the challenge at hand, in his daughter's case, the challenge of learning increasingly more difficult materials, by studying, that is, by working! Intelligence is no longer enough to learn complex problem solving strategies like algebra for instance, or to sort out the dynamics of two countries in conflict. Now, rather than yelling and taking away privileges, Mom and Dad have a heart to heart talk with her—and explain to her just what Dad learned from his friend. This was actually not strange to Dad given that he went through a similar experience at her age.

The 12- to 15-year-old who has relied more on his intelligence than on applying that intelligence with self-discipline now has to be encouraged to further develop his self-discipline: "You have to study long enough and well enough to really learn this more complicated material." This 12- to 15-year-old really had not yet learned *that she has to learn to work!* Now "the problem" was "an opportunity" to help their daughter develop further, in a better adaptive way.

With regard to home chores, resistance to helping is common. An eager-to-help-at-home 13-year-old is not often to be found in normal homes. Prodding is often needed. Where resistance is too frequent or high, limits will be needed.

Interestingly, self-care and hygiene problems are not uncommon in this age group. The reason is that the struggle with bodily changes that come with maturation and the development of their sexual body creates much anxiety in most kids. With these hormone-driven bodily changes comes heightened sexual interest and fantasies that at times, in normal kids, create much of the anxiety this age kids have. This anxiety at times leads to defending against making these bodily changes attractive by over-eating, unconsciously driven to make these bodily changes less visible; or by, again unconsciously, making oneself smell bad by not washing or bathing, so as to keep interested others away. Limit setting with youngsters so affected are often needed; focusing on hygiene is preferable to focusing on looking more attractive—which may be just what the 13-year-old who smells bad wants very much, but the anxiety it causes her leads her to avoid.

On the other hand, just as challenging if not more, are the kids who at this time, seeing the effect they have on other peers, generally peers of the other sex, are excited by this and search now for ways to deal with these changes in themselves. But the experience is new; the pressures have never been dealt with before; "Girls are saying and doing this; guys are saying and doing that; what should I do or should I not do?"

These days, electronic media and channels of communication greatly facilitate activity between kids this age that they would not engage in directly, at least not immediately. Pictures on wireless phones are easily communicated; texting flows like water; what gets written would not dare be said directly. Pressure coming from all sides among peers is unavoidable. Parents soon get hints that such activity is going on by intercepting computer, internet, cell-phones, messaging, or pictures. Many react in alarm at finding some of what is being shared among their kid and his or her peers. Limit setting is thrust into action, sometimes with alarm. Privilege withdrawal commonly is activated, particularly about the cell-phone and the computer.

Among some 12- to 15-year-olds, alcohol and drugs begin to be experimented with. Limit setting is again invoked. But peer pressure may make compliance with parents' expectations difficult and to enforce the limits set, privilege withdrawal is then often necessary.

**What to do?** **Limit Setting:** The principles of limit setting spelled out before apply throughout the years. We put emphasis on parents' respecting their young adolescent's developing self, on their using *loving firmness,* and on their using reasonable measures.

> *Limit setting now continues to predominantly be self-discipline consolidating.*

By now, limit setting is well patterned. The 12- to 15-year-old knows only too well what Mom and Dad will do. They also quickly learn what particular teachers will do; of course they may pretend to not know. Don't be fooled: 12- to 15-year-olds can know and can predict.

Now even a bit more than before, let the adolescent argue the reason you give for the limit, let him talk and you listen. If the reasoning is pretty well done, say so. If you agree with it, you may elect to change your mind about the limit. If you don't agree with it, or if you do but still see more merit in the limit, tell him his reasoning is good, but it doesn't weigh as much as your reason for the limit, and hold to it.

But we all know that where the history of battles of wills has been hard and long, and relationships are overburdened with ambivalence and troubled, setting limits may become a very challenging task. The development of compliance and of self-discipline may be less optimal than is desirable—based on now for years having needed to reject parents' expectations. If problems have not gone for too long and are not too harsh, professional help may be what could set good development back on track—and probably also improve parent-child relationships.

**Punishment:** Privilege withdrawal is becoming the only option. But care must be exercised to not withhold what will benefit the adolescent's well-being. For instance, grounding can be used—but not if the 12- to 15-year-old's well-being depends on it. "You can't go to John's house" is not going to benefit a kid who has difficulty socializing. TV withdrawal is now feeble with the 12- to 15-year-old, if it works at all. Computer for an evening or cell-phone withdrawal for a day works. We value a heart to heart talk with the adolescent after such episodes have cooled a bit.

> *Physical punishment now is highly problematic and potentially destructive.*

Physical punishment and punishments that carry with them shaming, depreciation, and humiliation of young adolescents—emotional abuse—will mobilize much hostility and hate and may eventually lead to bullying, even delinquency, and in some cases even crime (see chapter 5).

*From 15 to 18 years of age,* the same challenges listed for the 12- to 15-year-olds continue. But to these, the further challenge now lies in how and when parents set limits with their mid- to late-adolescent. From about 15 to 18, and then into the 18 to 21-or-so age group, as the offspring is well on the way to making his peer group the center of his social life, a greater or lesser degree of distancing himself from his family of origin and abiding by the emerging mores of the peer group prevail. This challenges the parents to modulate their demand for compliance by their teenager with in-home mores.

As I said in chapter 3, where relationships with family have been good over the years, the peer group selection will most likely not impose a dramatic change in already acquired life mores. The demands of the selected peer group are not likely to be incompatible with those of the family. While there will be challenges for both adolescent and parents, they will most likely be modest.

Where parent-child relationships have been burdened with conflict, be it that parents are unduly demanding and controlling, or have used too constraining limit setting and discipline, or kids have been oppositional and too defiant, or any other strain factors have existed between parents and child, parental limits may now trigger more rigorous adolescent resistance if not rebellion.

Where parent-child relationships have been outright hostile and parents have been abusive, parental limits will just not work; the shift to the peer group will be welcome and drastically diminish compliance with parents' demands.

**What to do?  Limit Setting:** The 15- to 18-year-old will still occasionally need limit setting, certainly so in those whose self-discipline continues to need fostering and encouragement. This will also occasionally be required for getting the teenager to let parents know where he or she is after school and on weekends; who she or he is with. The 15- to 18-year-old will not always tell parents the truth; the need for privacy and autonomy will at times make this necessary. Parents need to sense when they have to accept their adolescent's behavior without further cross-examination—and hope for the best.

Supporting, complimenting, and encouraging the development of yet stronger self-discipline with regard to studying always facilitates the teens' efforts. Some 15- to 18-year-olds do very well and, like all of us, are gratified by acknowledgment and reasonable appreciation of it from those they value. Where the self-discipline is weak, this period of development is crucial for parents to make their best efforts possible to encourage it in their kids. If such has not be sufficiently secured before, parents might consider outside tutorial help if they cannot themselves tutor their teenager without getting into battles of wills.

Enormously challenging for parents and teenagers at this age are the issues of sex, smoking, alcohol, and street drugs. These especially are best addressed with the teenager in the spirit of helping her or him find ways to navigate her or his way through very real peer pressures. Parents' using shaming and humiliation strategies or insulting ones, all destroy more than they build. They cause resentment and they generate hostility and hate. In many teenagers these will trigger a negative backlash against the parents and what they stand for—including their mores and expectations. In some, they will trigger rebellion.

Where limits fail, punishment should be instituted. Giving up on the teen is likely to push him or her farther away from family values.

**Punishment:** Privilege withdrawal is the only option. But as always, exercise care to not withhold privileges that will benefit the adolescent's well-being. Grounding can be used effectively. Allowance withholding where allowance has become ritual can be effective. In older ones, disallowing the use of the car can weigh fairly heavily.

*Physical punishment now is outright destructive to all concerned; it can be deadly.*

See chapter 1 for details of research over the past century on the effects of abuse on kids, especially adolescents.


## NOTES

1. One mother said that she worried that insisting on compliance would "break her child's *spirit*." Note that in this, the parent's worry seemed to be that her child's *sense of self and autonomy* would be broken. This mother's anxiety is in crucial contrast to that experienced by the mother who believes the principle that recommends strict, harsh child rearing, that "the child's stubbornness must be broken" (see chapter 3). But by backing away from limit setting to avoid the child's anger, the overanxious parent risks making her child *insufficiently compliant*—with all the problems this brings (see chapter 3)!

2. For instance, (1) *The Challenging Child: Understanding, Raising, and Enjoying the Five "Difficult" Types of Children* by Stanley I. Greenspan and Jacqueline Salmon (1996), and (2) *The Difficult Child: Expanded and Revised Edition* by Stanley Turecki and Leslie Tonner (2000).

3. Parens, H., Scattergood, E., Hernit, R.C., & Duff, S. (1979). *Parenting: Love and Much More.* Thirty-nine one-half-hour programs produced by CBS for Broadcast on WCAU TV, Channel 10, Philadelphia, PA. First aired June–July, 1979. Program #9: "Am I Crazy If I Talk To My Baby?"

4. Some quite healthy kids with an obsessive-compulsive disposition, or the ones "with a mind of their own," will not be able to accommodate as easily to mother's or father's expectations of behavior; These kids will require greater patience and compromise on the part of the parents to eventually be able to abide by their expectations.

5. We must distinguish between "high-energy" and "hyperactivity" in children. "High-energy" or "high-activity" level is a *normal* variation in inborn disposition in kids. High-energy kids are well-regulated, energetic, but they are readily controllable. In contrast, "hyperactivity" is an energy level that is high but it is also impulsive, more or less hyper-reactive due to a modest, built-in, brain hyper-reactivity over which the child has weak or no control. Fortunately, such kids tend to respond well to specific medications that tend to decrease the brain hyper-reactivity and with that increase the child's ability to better control his reactivity, concentrate better, and altogether, slow down. The problem is that these medications, at the time of this writing, are not recommended for children under six years.

6. Communication stated in public by Dr. Brisch at my Munich Lecture on "Obedience versus Compliance" May 20, 2011.

7. H. Parens (2007). Malignant prejudice—Guidelines toward its prevention. In: *The Future of Prejudice,* ed. H. Parens, A. Mahfouz, S. W. Twemlow & D. E. Scharff, p. 278.

8. See especially, H. Parens, S. Scattergood, A. Duff & W. Singletary (1997 [2010]). *Parenting for Emotional Growth (PEG)—which includes PEG: The Textbook; PEG: A Curriculum for Students in Grades K thru 12;* as well as H. Parens & C. Rose-Itkoff (1997 [2010]). *PEG: The Workshops Series.* All these *PEG* works are contained in H. Parens (2010). *CD: Parenting for Emotional Growth* (see http://jeffline.jefferson.edu/peg/).

9. In the set of materials we just produced into a CD entitled *Parenting for Emotional Growth* (H. Parens, 2010). *Parenting for Emotional Growth (PEG)* consists of (1) *PEG: The Textbook* and *PEG,* (2) *A Curriculum for Students in Grades K thru 12* by H. Parens, E. Scattergood, A. Duff & W.S. Singletary (1997), as well as (3) *PEG: The Workshops Series* by H. Parens & C. Rose-Itkoff (1997).

10. Erik Erikson (1959). See note 21.

11. Psychoanalytic child development theory holds that each phase of psychological-emotional development brings with it challenges or "tasks" the child has to achieve. I have here listed those that adolescents have to achieve.

12. Cooney wrote this article for the *Globe* which via the Internet was distributed to its members by the Regional Council of Child and Adolescent Psychiatry of the Greater Philadelphia Region. Cooney can be reached at ecooney@globe.com.

**5**

# HELPING CHILDREN LEARN TO EXPRESS HOSTILITY IN ACCEPTABLE WAYS—AND REDUCE TEASING, TAUNTING, AND BULLYING

*If you want your child to talk to you when he or she is an adolescent, start talking to your child when he or she is a baby!*

"You're not allowed to hit me!" 2-year-old Jane's mother half shouted at her. "If you're mad at me, tell me. But it's not OK to hit me!" Jane smirked, but soon seemed subdued and looked like she felt scolded.

When 16-year-old Mike's mother told him he could not make a phone call just as the family was about to sit down for dinner, he stormed "What the fuck is this! You're not at the table yet!" Showing that she felt offended, his mother said, "Don't talk to me like that! I know you're mad, but you can find a better way to let me know that than by acting like some foulmouthed kid!"

It is unavoidable that children become angry, even hostile toward and at times even enraged with their parents, even in the best of child rearing. Because children's ability to control their anger, hostility, hate, and rage is not built-in, all children, whatever the age, have to be helped to find reasonable and acceptable ways to express these feelings. When hostility, hate, or rage is generated in us there is a built-in tendency to discharge it. Given its inherent pressure, we have to do something with it:

1. We discharge it outwardly, against others or the environment, or,
2. More commonly than parents think, kids discharge it toward themselves.

Hostility does not evaporate. That which is not discharged toward others or toward oneself is retained and accumulates within us, and is likely to seek a target for discharge. Where the level of accumulated hostility and hate is high, the child or adolescent will be a time bomb.

When hostile destructiveness (hostility, hate, and rage—see chapter 2) is not appropriately and constructively dealt with by the child, it accumulates and becomes part of the child's personality. And this aspect of personality continues into adolescence and beyond. As such, it then leads to behaviors that create all kinds of problems and can color painfully all aspects of the individual's life.

It falls to parents to help their children learn from early on in life how to cope with their own hostile feelings. It's built-in, that as the child's caregivers parents have to do so. Parents know only too well that, as their caregivers, our children unavoidably become very angry with us, feel hostility toward us. But, unpleasant as it is, this is an *opportunity* to help children learn to express these feelings in ways acceptable to us and to the community in which we live. The approach I have found that works well in my clinical work is to help the child or adolescent recognize when he acts and therefore most likely feels angry or hostile, and we then try to sort out what it is that is causing him/her emotional pain at this time—it may be something that is happening now or that he/she is remembering and thinking about just now. We then consider what he can do with and about it. Most helpful, I have found, is to find ways to talk about it. The younger the child when she/he learns that when she/he feels angry there is some psychic pain causing it, the easier it is for the child to find ways to deal with it constructively.

Often, the child under 2 will try not to hit, but control over this automatic reaction is then unreliable. I have found evidence for this from two observable facts:

- Commonly when a 1-year-old has hit someone, the infant reacts with anxiety, as if he expects something painful to happen to himself. In addition,
- From about 10 to 12 months of age on, infants begin to use defense mechanisms to try to govern the impulse to hit, such as by displacement, inhibition, and others—see below where I take this up with examples.

This comes from the fact that the child has already seen that when he hits another person (child or adult) he gets an unpleasant reaction from his parents, from those around, or from the one he hit. There is a universal fear of retaliation when one hits another, unless the other is seen as much weaker than the one who hits. This is easily seen in adolescents—even if the individual puts on a brave face—and continues into adulthood. To be sure, acting tough often hides being afraid.

From 2 to 6 years of age the child's efforts will be increasingly effective, and self-discipline will increase, based on conditioned learning, especially due to: "Mother always gets upset with me when I hit!" And in many families, though regrettably not in all, "Mother gets upset with me when I'm being mean." Later in this chapter, we'll talk about "being mean" when we talk about *Dealing with Teasing, Taunting, and Bullying* that begins to appear in some kids from about 12 months of age on.

We must make a distinction between "being angry" and "being mean."

## A CRITICAL DISTINCTION BETWEEN "BEING ANGRY" AND "BEING MEAN"

Let me detail here why I make the distinction between "being angry" and "being mean." I assume that like in English, in all languages, we have developed an array of words that in one way or another describe and define the various ways humans discharge aggression. In chapter 2, I detailed why I find it useful to consider the different major trends that make up this complex thing, human aggression, which in a variety of ways serves us in adaptation and survival. One trend, I say, is nondestructive aggression which, without destroying anything directly, serves adaptation and the achievement of our goals. Another trend is non-affective destructiveness, which is destructive but is not driven by hostility; that is, we destroy living things, animal and plant, to feed ourselves, not because we hate them, in fact we love some of the things we destroy; we destroy them but not out of ill-will. And the third trend, hostile aggression (with its sub-trend hostile destructiveness) gets generated in us physiologically, in the face of a threat to our well-being which is what feeling pain alerts us to. For instance, the pain that we feel when we accidently burn our finger on a flame on the stove leads us to reflexively pull our hand away. It protects us against getting a still more destructive burn! When we allow that which causes us pain to go to extreme it might destroy us.[1] This too then, hostile aggression, and even its sub-trend hostile destructiveness, serves self-preservation.

This last trend, hostile aggression, I said in chapter 2, is generated in us by the experience of psychic pain, and hostile destructiveness by excessive psychic pain. There also I said that hostile aggression has the distinctive feature that, the intensity to which it is generated correlates with the intensity of the psychic pain experienced. Given that the intensity of the psychic pain we experience mounts over a wide range, from very low-level to very high-level intensity psychic pain, so will the intensity of the hostile aggression generated vary accordingly.

When we consider the intensity of the hostile aggression generated, this is when we get into using different words to describe what is felt. I have written[2] about the spectrum of manifestations of hostile aggression which runs the gamut from irritability to rage. I consider annoyance, then, irritability, and then, anger to be generated by mild to moderate psychic pain.

- At the level of feelings of *annoyance* and *irritability,* one generally just wants the psychic pain to stop. One may walk away (if one can) or tell the person to stop it!
- When the pain-induced feelings mount to the level of *anger,* some degree of force may be put into wanting the psychic pain to stop; a warning may be given: "You better stop what you're doing!" Even if some physical force is used, like pushing the person causing the now moderately higher level of psychic pain he/she is causing, there is no wish, conscious or unconscious, to harm that person; we want the person to just stop it!!

I have put these lesser levels of feeling pain and the type of aggression they generate into the trend of hostile aggression because they are caused by the same experience: psychic pain; but they are felt less intensely; they are at the milder end of the spectrum of psychic pain experiencing. It is when the psychic pain crosses the line of the individual's psychic pain tolerance, such as feeling, "This is too much, I can't stand it!" that the hostile aggression generated brings with it a very significant dimension:

*It converts hostile aggression into hostile destructiveness (HD)—wanting to inflict pain on the one who is causing us psychic pain.*

Until this threshold is crossed there is no intention to inflict pain on the other; you just want the other to stop what he's doing to you. When this threshold is crossed is highly variable among individuals, and even within each of us, it varies depending on how we feel at a given time. In all of us, this threshold tends to be lower when we are hungry or tired or sick, etc.

Once this tolerance-of-pain threshold is crossed, as the level of psychic pain heightens, the reactive hostile destructive feelings we experience tend to be spoken of as hostility, hate, and rage. Here's what is useful for caregivers to be aware of.

- *Hostility* tends to reduce once the psychic pain caused us is stopped.
- *Rage* is an explosive reflex-type reaction to very intense, unbearable psychic pain; *rage* too will tend to stop once the psychic pain stops (see chapter 6 for a full discussion of it).
- *Hate*, on the other hand, which the child can begin to experience from about 18 months of age on, is a state of feeling HD that has persistence, and that continues *whether or not* the particular individual or condition to which one has attached hate is, in fact, actively then and there causing one psychic pain. When we hate someone, it's for the duration. And to undo hate, the relationship needs to be repaired—which requires much work. To undo a condition that causes us to hate, that condition needs to be neutralized.

Now we can talk about the difference between "being angry" and "being mean." In children, young ones especially, being angry often elicits "wanting to hit." It is part of our biological, self-protective reflexive tendency to want to push away someone or something that is causing one pain. It originates even before the infant is able to think. In chapter 3 I talked about the fact that while infants are able to have simple thoughts and ideas associated with what they experience prior to age 2 years, it is from about 2 years that cognitive processes begin to develop that will by 7 years or so achieve the youthful level of being able to judge, and to grasp the consequences of one's actions. But I want to emphasize that the reflexive "wanting to hit" when one feels angry is not driven by enjoying causing someone pain.

"Being mean," is enjoying causing someone psychic pain. Later in this chapter, we'll talk about teasing, taunting, and bullying where we see outright pleasure in causing someone psychic pain. Enjoying causing someone psychic pain is where many highly troublesome interrelational and social ills have their beginning. It is the essence of sadism, of enjoying hurting another physically, emotionally, or both, individually or as part of a group. It drives not only teasing, taunting, and eventually bullying, but also causing harm to others and destroying property, and pushed to extreme contributes centrally to malignant prejudice, which pushed to its utmost limits, leads to murder and genocide.

Now let's return to when and what we can expect from our children.

From 5 years of age on, especially from 6 to 7, the child will begin to understand the moral reasons why not to hit. He/she will be able to weigh, to evaluate and judge the meaning and the distinction between "wanting to hit" when angry and "being mean." This growing understanding will be facilitated by the child's learning that emotional pain is what is making him angry or hostile. By 7 or 8, he/she can and should be expected to make the link that: "When my feelings are hurt it makes me feel angry and then I want to hit." And so too, "When my feelings are hurt too much, I really want to hurt the other (person)!" It is understandable that a child would want to hit, even to hurt another, but that it is not a good way to let his/her feelings out. Once the child develops sufficient self-discipline in looking for what caused him/her pain and then, to find constructive ways to deal it, the less will he/she be prone to lash out at others. And as the child succeeds in finding constructive ways to express his/her hostile destructiveness, the less will it accumulate in his/her psyche—and the less burdened by it for life!

This ability to look for and understand the cause of feeling hostility and increasingly develop self-discipline over lashing out can begin to be expected by 6 to 8 years of age although acquiring this self-discipline will vary from child to child depending on his or her inborn dispositions. Of course, one cannot expect a child who is temperamentally impulsive to easily develop the ability to control the discharge of his hostile feelings; parents will have to be patient, do much more work, and will have to take longer to help this child achieve sufficient impulse control. Also the child's reactivity type, whether the child is a slow-reactor or a quick-reactor[3] as well as her/his threshold of irritability, will make for variation in the child's ability to learn to control her/his discharge of hostility. And in addition, the child's life experiences—which, for example, by 6 years of age means: 6 x 365 x however many times a day he is maltreated—are strongly determining of how much hostility he/she has already accumulated and how difficult the challenge will be for that child to develop reliable self-control. We have found that in traumatized children, the challenge will be so large that their efforts to cope with their accumulated hostility is likely to range from total (defensive) inhibition to explosiveness.[4]

Increasingly then, from 8 to 12 and from 12 to 18 the self-discipline to not hit and not be mean, to the extent that each child achieves these, will establish. So will the understanding that emotional pain makes one angry and hostile and that this leads to one wanting to hit, and if the hurt is caused by a mean-spirited person to also be mean in return.

In helping our kids not hit when angry and not be mean toward others, we will not only prevent the interrelational and social ills I mentioned before, but we will also open up ways that will lessen the likelihood of their feeling unduly guilty and make them less fearful of their own burdensome anger and hostility. And doing this will foster their assertiveness and healthy competitiveness. And that will make them freer to learn and strive toward their personal goals.

## RATIONALE

Many people believe that being angry or feeling hostile within the family is bad. Many parents ascribe anger and hostility to some "evil" tendency within the child. In both clinical work and behavioral research we have found that hostility is reactive to life experiences that range from painful events to traumatizing experiences. We have found no evidence that children are born with an "evil" tendency within them.

To recognize that hostile feelings are mobilized by experiences of excessive emotional pain gives us a very different picture of what makes our kids angry and hostile. And it means that any human being—child, adolescent, or adult—subjected to sufficient excessive emotional pain will become hostile.

When parents understand that their child is hostile because she/he is experiencing emotional pain rather than because she/he is "bad," parents tend to be less taken aback by their child or adolescent's hostility and more interested in helping the child, young or older, deal with the underlying cause of the psychic pain. And by focusing on the pain while helping their child cope with his/her reactive hostility, parents will tend to reduce the child's hostility more readily. They will help rather than make matters worse for the child and between the child and themselves.

When feelings of hostility are expressed, while unpleasant to witness and certainly to be subjected to, it gives parents an opportunity to progressively help their child understand what gave rise to his own feelings, and learn to mediate them more positively. Stepwise then, parents help their child learn to gain reasonable control over these troubling feelings. By doing so, parents protect their child against developing automatic trouble-producing reactions.

When such feelings are not allowed reasonable expression, the child internalizes them and fails to learn to deal with them in positively adaptive ways. It is therefore problematic when well-meaning parents disapprove of all signs of anger from their children, let alone hostility and hate, especially when they occur in the family. Like it or not, it is at home that these feelings are first experienced and expressed; and it is invaluable when it is at home that the child is helped to learn how to understand and deal with these in growth-promoting ways.

Unfortunately, in one way or another, many a child, young or older, is told that it is very bad to feel angry, let alone to feel hostile. In some cases the child is told she is evil, which of course is painfully injurious to the child's healthy narcissism and developing sense of self. It often, in fact, leads to the child's believing there is something bad about her; her sense of self will likely be "I am bad," or "There's something wrong with me."

One adult told me that when she was an adolescent her father told her that "smart Jewish girls don't get angry!" As an adolescent, what was she to do with that? Surely, she felt, there was something very unacceptable and wrong with her. Even as an adult, while she had by then long known that this statement was not based in good psychological, philosophical, religious, or simply everyday reasonable fact, she recognized that it had troubled her. The problem is that, even knowing that a given statement of disapproval expressed by a mother or father is unreasonable and even false, the sting of disapproval the statement carries makes it difficult for the individual to ever totally dismiss. Even though false, the statement hurt, and generated hostility toward her father. In addition, the father's declaration not only made the adolescent feel that having anger or feeling hostile is a very bad thing, but it at times made her doubt her own intelligence (which also meant her self-confidence, self-regard, self-appraisal)—which, however, her academic performance eventually helped her see her abilities more accurately. This type of handling of a child's, young or older, anger and hostility is furthermore troubling and baffling, given that on a number of occasions she saw her father, mother, and siblings also get angry. That, however, did not eradicate her feeling that there was something wrong with her. In time, this adolescent saw the falseness of her father's remark, which not only made her feel sad and angry with him, but it also lowered her esteem of him. The fact remains that while growing up, she felt that having angry and hostile feelings made her less of a person than she wanted to be.

Here's another problem I have encountered more than once in the way many parents deal with their child's anger and hostility that is directed toward them.

> Very upset with her mother, 3-year-old Susan shouted at her, "I hate you!" Her baffled mother immediately reacted with, "Oh! I know you don't mean that."

Well, even though the meaning of the words Susan used were not yet fully reliable, she said that this is what she felt. Interestingly, although a 3-year-old's words may not carry the meaning we all have in mind, some words and things young children say are not complicated; they are not rocket science.

When we tell a 2-year-old "I love you" or "I'm angry with you" or "you're a bad boy" or many other commonly used phrases, the child grasps the meaning of the words by virtue of the emotional color with which he hears them said to him. I'll talk later about how to deal with that.

The point I want to make here is that a number of problems follow from 3-year-old Susan's mother's intervention. Among other things, the child feels that she is not supposed to feel what she is feeling. The child is told to disavow, or that she cannot have, the feelings she knows she is experiencing. She overtly agrees with Mother, but feels she is a little monster since she knows that she feels "hate." Generally even by 3, a child will have a pretty good grasp of the progressive difference between saying "I'm angry" or "I'm mad" or "I hate you." The child knows that "I hate" is much stronger than "I'm angry." But Mother's saying "Oh! You don't mean that" leads to the child's doubting what she is experiencing. Her evaluation of what she feels is undermined, and this may lead to her feeling confusion about her own feelings. Because she may come to believe that what she is feeling is unacceptable, she may unconsciously set herself the task of denying the feelings she has, which is an undesirable way of coping with whatever feelings we have.

In clinical work, I have many times found that a person I am treating may not know what he or she is feeling. It doesn't feel good; but the person is uncertain what it is that feels bad about what he or she is feeling. This may apply to good feelings as well. It is a serious problem in that not knowing what one feels robs the individual of finding ways to lessen feelings that are unpleasant and even painful. Equally serious, it may make uncertain one's feelings of love, or how to accept another person's expressions of love— even when these are directed toward oneself.

There is a further consequence of the parent's disallowing that the child hates his mother. Children themselves label feelings of anger and hate as signs of being bad. They do so sometimes even in the face of parents' telling them that these feelings are normal. Children are the first to judge that they are bad when they experience hostility toward the parent they love. This is because, as I have emphasized throughout this book, feelings of hostility toward those we love create within us a conflict due to ambivalence, which brings with it a profound reaction of disapproval of oneself by oneself. This conflict often leads to self-accusations and self-hate, which we all know as guilt. A child needs the opportunity to resolve these feelings of ambivalence because they produce guilt, and they can lead to the development of too harsh a conscience—psychologically a very costly problem in that a harsh conscience robs the self of well-being. While we all need a conscience to guide our behavior, too harsh a conscience can be crippling emotionally in a number of ways—for instance, not being able to accept another's expression of love and respect because one feels one does not deserve these; sinners don't deserve love and respect! So when a parent cannot tolerate the thought of the child's hating her, a thought difficult to hear to be sure, she denies the child the opportunity to deal with these feelings of hate constructively—a process in which the parent can have the most meaningful input. This is an incomplete listing of the unfavorable consequences of not allowing a child to experience his feelings, whatever they are.

The principle is this:

*When your child is angry with you, you have an opportunity to help the child deal with such feelings constructively. You'll care more and put more loving-constructive effort into it than anyone else!*

It is important for parents to know that when feelings of hostility toward those we love are insufficiently "dealt with and metabolized," what in psychoanalysis we speak of as "working through," these feelings produce within us all kinds of emotional disturbance and misery. Feelings of hostility cannot be worked through unless

- they can be acknowledged,
- the factors that caused them examined,
- the feelings given reasonable ways of expression and discharge, and
- they are dealt with by the self and the parent (or therapist) in a growth-promoting way.

Over the past century, psychotherapists have found that the great interactive facilitator of working through troublesome feelings of hostility is to be given permission to verbalize them in the context of a meaningful, empathic[5] relationship. In the child, young, school-age, and even in adolescence, the best relationships available to him are the ones with Mother and Father. The well-cared for child naturally feels: they more than anyone will understand me, be sympathetic and loving toward me. Siblings can also become meaningful facilitators of the working through of loads of hostility, although they also often become the victim of that hostility. My aim is to help mothers and fathers (and other caregivers), and their children develop an emotional dialogue with one another in which anger, hostility, and hate can be talked about meaningfully in growth-promoting ways, which means in ways that reasonably, sympathetically, and responsibly reduce hostility.

## INTERVENTIONAL STEPS

When it makes sense to the parent that the hostile feelings her child is experiencing are the product of some excessive emotionally painful experience, she can frame her interventions in that context. As I said before, it is psychologically constructive to convey to the child that some hurt is causing the child's anger rather than that some inborn evil force is at work in him; it makes for an interaction of large beneficial consequence to the child's perceptions of himself, of his mother, and eventually of others, and to his well-being. It frames the child's experience in a positive quality of human relatedness.

Another thing this reaction will do is make it less threatening and noxious for the child to experience the hostile feelings he is having. Consider the atmosphere for a dialogue between yourself and your child, young and older, when you tell him he is being rotten again! Now compare that to telling your son caringly that you know something is hurting him, but you expect him to express his angry or hostile feelings in reasonable ways. Can he talk with you about what's going on; you would like to know. With your teenager add, ". . . if it's not too personal."

I have said many times that even the best of parenting cannot prevent numerous experiences of psychic pain, occasionally even excessive psychic pain. The generation and mobilization of hostility within family life is unavoidable. Let's take up again the example we talked about earlier: the unpleasant and at times difficult task of setting limits with one's beloved child.

In setting limits—even in the guiding model I developed—the caring parent is the instigator of the psychic (emotional) pain experienced by the child and, therefore, instigates the child's hostility. In our child development project[6] (chapter 1, this book), we became aware of the important but distressing fact that

> *the person(s) the infant first feels angry with, and even first hates is the one to whom the infant is forming his or her foremost attachment(s), the infant's most emotionally valued caregiver(s), the mother (and father).*

Because other (substitute) caregivers are not as emotionally important to the baby as are the parents, the frustrations or disappointments substitute caregivers cause the child do not produce as high a level of psychic pain. As a result kids tend to be less angry with them than with their own parents— babies somehow "know" that those who most invest emotionally in them, their parents, are supposed to love and take care of them.

In general, the mother, in most animal species the biologically primed best caregiver, unavoidably becomes the first to frustrate her child. When, as we have seen increasingly in the last several decades, the father is prominently engaged in caregiving to his infant, the same will apply to him. Therefore, because the parents are the first "frustrators" of the child they love, they become the first toward whom the child's feelings of anger, hostility, even rage, and later hate, become directed. Difficult as this is for parents, it is, in fact, a very good thing! After all, who would put up with that! Who would be as committed to care and help a child learn to cope with his rage or hate, as is a loving parent? Who else is going to be as willing to put up with such bratty behavior!

Thirteen-month-old Mary was absolutely adored by her mother and father, the only daughter and the youngest of several children they had. Mary was a quite alert but rather calm infant until about 6 months of age when we began to see in her a striking upsurge in her activity level which by ten months was high. From 6 months on, Mary became a vigorous explorer of her environment.

From about 6 months, the time of this upsurge of healthy *nondestructive aggression,* Mary's explorations and autonomy driven activities from time to time came into conflict with Mother's efforts to keep her safe and sound. Battles of wills would now occur and by the time she approached 12 months of age, these battles began to heat up rather sharply. Mother, who was not a high-activity-level person, occasionally had her hands full. A large battle of wills occurred when Mary was about 13 months of age.

As nearly 13-month-old Mary's autonomy strivings intensified and began to organize, she at times wanted to go into the hall, extending her explorations to a cleaning cart that would occasionally be there at a given time during our child-parent observational sessions. Because of her concern about her daughter's interest in that cleaning cart, Mother repeatedly told Mary she was not to touch it and when Mary did not comply, Mother enforced her limit by picking Mary up and carrying her back into the large observational sitting room. Mary's heretofore moderate objections gave way to loud vocal complaints, her body tensing, shaking, face reddening. Contorting her body to pull herself out of mother's hold, she cried angrily, waved her left arm in a striking movement against her mother several times, kicked her, both without making contact but twice she actually struck her mother with her arm. She once also struck herself.

We saw clear evidence of her distress. For the first time, Mother could not calm Mary as she had quite easily done so many times. Whether Mother held Mary or tried to put her down, Mary's crying and expressions of hostility continued. Whether she tried to explain, comfort, or distract, Mother could not calm Mary. Mary physically rejected any efforts Mother made to reduce her distress. Once her crying stopped, Mary looked angry and serious. She sat on Mother's lap, erect, as if frozen at the edge of her knees, resisting Mother's gentle efforts to bring her close and sharply complaining when Mother tried to help her. After about 15 minutes in this statue-like state, Mary's body tone gradually softened, she relaxed passively into her mother's body, thumb in mouth, and stayed there, awake, thoughtful, and downcast for twenty to thirty minutes more.[7]

One of the most salient points I make from this example is how troubling the conflict due to ambivalence, to be furious with someone one is attached to, is for all of us. Not yet knowing how to deal with it, Mary was immobilized; in fact she seemed paralyzed. We have to deal with our ambivalence. In order to not feel paralyzed by the anxiety ambivalence causes us the way it did to Mary, we use defense mechanisms. But, as I will show later in this chapter, while defense mechanisms do help us cope with anxiety and depression, they at times lead to no end of problems. This is why we have to foster in our children the ability to talk about and to express in acceptable words and feelings, the pain they experience as noxious—which might otherwise end up making them "trouble-makers."

But first, how does one deal with one's child experiencing what Mary did?

First of all, once Mother had determined that a limit was needed, she stuck to it. When Mary expressed her anger, then her mounting feelings of hostility at her mother, to the degree that she experienced them that day, Mother felt hurt and bewildered; this intense outburst of hostility to the point of rage was a first with Mary. Mother asked what she should do. She felt embarrassed, because we were observing them, all of us, surprised at so strong a troubled reaction by this child with her mother whose relationship we all knew was so good. Of course, all parents are embarrassed when their child has a fit in public. I recommend to mothers or fathers to ignore the public reaction and just tend to their child's distress; not by giving in, or by "giving the child something to cry about," but by listening, holding to the limit, and trying to comfort.

Mother was stung by the feelings expressed by her baby; but Mother did not stifle her child's expression of feelings. When a child cries and seems to curse at her mother (even before she has learned to curse with words), clearly expressing strong hostile feelings, the child is choosing the most normal pathway one can use: direct expression. This, given its clarity, actually facilitates the mother's dealing with her child's feelings of outrage and hostility. Therefore, it is best not to prohibit the child's crying, protestations, and nonverbal "cursing"; the child is truthfully telling you what she is feeling.

Although pained and distressed to see her daughter so upset, and embarrassed even though she knew the group of mothers, kids, and staff would not criticize her—interestingly, there was no criticizing in our naturalistic group project (see chapter 1); neither the mothers nor the staff criticized; we just talked about whatever went on, knowing full well that such things do go on probably in all families everywhere—Mother patiently waited. She thoughtfully tried ways of comforting Mary, but Mother recognized that Mary did not accept Mother's efforts to comfort; Mother painfully waited. She sensed that Mary was struggling with something large; she just felt she had to continue to hold Mary and wait. After a long period of observation, I proposed (quietly, as subdued as the rest) to the mothers that Mary's sitting upright on the edge of her mother's knees meant that she rejected Mother's wanting to comfort her. None of the mothers disagreed: Mary was not ready to be comforted. Yes, she was still very angry with her mother. However, I proposed to them, Mary was struggling and needed time to figure out what to do. Mary, I suggested, was furious; but it was with the mother she values beyond question. Furious with the mother who meant so much to her, she did not yet seem to know what to do—with this conflict of ambivalence: she was furious with her dear, dear mother.

Note that I am avoiding using the words "love" and "hate." This is because I am among those developmentalists who believe that the ability to "love" and "hate" requires sufficient brain development for the child to be able to link

- the deeply felt *feelings (emotion)* with
- the *idea* of attaching these positive or negative feelings to someone or something, and that
- both "love" and "hate" are states of feeling that are *enduring*. "Liking" someone is not as deeply felt nor does it necessarily last over time.

*"Love" and "hate" are more complex emotional states that last, that have duration; they generally develop from about 18 months of age on.*

So, 13-month-old Mary at the time of this conflict was furious with the mother to whom she was securely attached; whom she valued deeply and would soon develop the capability to love. Mary's secure attachment to her mother continued well into our 37-year follow-up study. But this day, 36 years before, Mary was very troubled by her conflicted feelings toward her soon-to-be-beloved mother. A mother could not have handled this crisis better than did Mary's mother.

When we think of helping our children verbalize their feelings of anger, hostility, and hate, we have to distinguish between words that hurt and words that insult. While we want to encourage our children to verbalize difficult feelings, we do not want them to go beyond certain reasonable bounds of what one can say to another person, particularly to one who is valued and loved.

I take note of this distinction and say that parents should not tolerate words that insult them, but should allow words that may hurt without insulting. We have found that some parents find certain words intolerable, whereas others do not. Perhaps "intolerable" is a dimension we should add to words that insult.

Not only are we sensitive to certain words, but we are also sensitive to the tone in which words are expressed. The tone often carries the emotional quality and coloring of the feelings expressed. In helping a child verbalize feelings of hostility and hate, a boundary must be drawn. *Words and intonations that are insulting or intolerable should not be allowed.*

For instance, a young child's outburst of "I hate you" at her mother, even in its most deeply felt hostile intonations cannot be viewed as an insult. A parent may find the words painful, yet they should not be disallowed. This example shows how difficult it is to say where to draw the line in allowing a child to verbalize feelings of hostility and hate. We each need to draw our own lines. But we have to bear in mind that it is necessary, in order to help our child, to find a range of expression that is permissible. Otherwise, there will be no verbal pathway to the resolution of hostility, and that will unavoidably create emotional and behavior problems that are preventable.

When 16-year-old Mike stormed at his mother "What the fuck is this, you're not at the table yet!" his mother was insulted. Yes, Mike just said words; he didn't throw anything, didn't break anything, he just said "°#&^%!" But the word he used was not acceptable. His mother told him without insulting him that she experienced him then as a "foul-mouthed kid"—which at that moment he was.

We all have our acceptable and unacceptable swear-words. This author would have distinguished between one of his exasperated teenage sons calling him "a jerk" versus "a bastard" or "a son of a bitch." To be called a "jerk" by one's own son is a distasteful event. To be called a "bastard" or a "son of a bitch"—which fortunately never happened—would not have been acceptable to this parent.

In fact, we are talking about a far-reaching aspect of how to get along with someone one values and loves. How to argue and even fight with those we love is a challenge to all of us. It certainly is a challenge to children. It is good when arguing or fighting (whether with loved ones or otherwise), to learn reasonable rules. For instance, even in boxing, there are rules: at all times, no blows below the belt. We might use that model in family fights, to draw the line between words that are hurtful and words that are out of bounds, inappropriate, insulting, and intolerable—below the belt!

Of course, parents get upset by their children's expressions of hostility toward them.

When 3-year-old Susan shouted at her mother "I hate you!" Mother was crushed: "Oh! I know you don't mean that!" Well, Susan said it. And it's more helpful to assume that she meant it rather than in essence saying to her daughter, "You can't be feeling that way—because I'm your mother!" This, as I said, creates problems.

But consider this. I have said this to many parents. I have asked them: And how often does your child say this to you? And when she says it, for how long do these enduring feelings of hate seem to be felt by your child? Commonly the young child's "I hate you!" soon gives way to much kinder, more caring enduring feelings. In most cases, once the feeling of hate is verbally expressed, it tends to lessen and then the feelings of love that were momentarily blanketed over by the hate feelings, these much longer enduring love feelings resurface. I ask the parent to consider "How much does she hate you, for how long does she hate you?" This much (I put my hands, palm to palm, and stretch them apart for about 6 inches)? And how much do you think she loves you (and I stretch my hands full arms length as wide as I can stretch)? The intensity and duration of the child's hate toward the parent is far less, by far, than how much the 3-year-old child thinks Mom (or Dad) is great! And I add that it's helpful for the parent to say this much to the child: "I know sometimes you get real mad at me; I get pretty angry with you sometimes too, you know! You're not an angel, and I'm not an angel. But I'm so glad that most of the time I know that you really love me—and I sure love you!" (Use your own words.)

It's actually good that we get upset when a young child explodes with, "I hate you!" If we did not get upset by it, it would mean that we are indifferent to our child's feelings of pain. However, some parents tell their child not to be angry, that it is bad to be angry, and—most unproductive of all—is the parent's, "I'll give you something to really be angry about!" In general, a young child's exclamations of hostility, even rage, as when 13-month-old Mary had "had it" with her highly emotionally invested mother, are desirable means of expressing what the child is feeling. It is helpful, of course, *for the mother to recognize that the child is reacting to something Mother is doing to her.* Then the anger being directed toward Mother cannot be surprising. It's not as though Mother had not repeatedly interfered with Mary's strivings for autonomy!

Thirteen-month-old Mary kicked her mother from a distance (without making contact) and twice with her arm actually struck her mother in the arm. Once she struck herself. Discharging hostile feelings by striking out physically is usually not a good way to express one's feelings. The 13-month-old cannot be expected to be able to control her impulse to hit out in reaction to being flooded with feelings of hostility as was Mary. Were such hitting of Mother and herself to continue, this would set in motion the task of helping her express hostile feelings in vocal tones and words, not in striking out. Yet, there are times when a child's physically striking out may be warranted. There is a debate going on as to whether or not in response to being continually bullied and/or attacked by someone else, the child or teenager might choose to strike out. Some parents tell their child that when bullied by someone he should just walk away. We'll talk more about this issue below (see Teasing, Taunting, and Bullying).

However, discharging feelings of anger, hostility, and hate by striking out physically at one's mother—I assume that a school-age child and certainly all but a few very troubled adolescents would no longer do that—produces a double jeopardy. It is usually more difficult to reverse a physical act than a verbal statement. The exception is a mother's swat on her young child's clothed bottom (see chapter 4). Also, often, an act tends to be more hurtful, more unacceptable than angry words. Given the type of circumstance we are discussing now—Mary's having a fit in response to her mother's limit setting or Mike's curse directed at his mother—the old saying "sticks and stones can break my bones, but words will never harm me" may have some merit; but it is not always, nor altogether true, given that words that insult can in fact hurt more than a physical blow—racial slurs are a good example.

My overall impression is that children tend to feel more guilt when they physically strike out at their parents, than when they say "I hate you." Given that there is a natural, almost reflexive, tendency in young children to hit when they feel angry, it is helpful for the parent to intervene and not let the child strike her or him, that he should say what he feels and thinks, but he is not allowed to hit you. By the way, one can say to a less-than-2-year-old who does not yet speak in phrases or use words to "*Say* what you feel and think, but don't hit!" The child will get the message.

For the young child who persists in hitting Mother, setting limits on that act becomes necessary. It is a worthwhile project; the limit-setting strategies proposed in chapter 4 should be brought into action. When the limits do not work, the parent should go on to privilege withdrawal.

Doing to the child what the child is doing to the parent "in order to teach him a lesson," is not as desirable as withdrawing a privilege or, if comfortable with it, with a young child, administering a swat on the child's clothed bottom. For example, with a young child who bites, biting the child back is not a constructive way of teaching him not to bite. It works; the child will stop biting; but it teaches the child that it's OK to do mean things to others. And the child will hate you for biting him or her. With a less-than-one-year-old, express hurt ("Ouch!"), set limits and verbally scold. With a 2- or 3-year-old, set limits and if he or she persists, go to a time out. Beyond 3 years, it's uncommon for kids to bite.

Equally important, just as the mother should prohibit the child's striking at her, so should the mother prohibit and protectively disapprove of the child's striking herself, as Mary did. Parents will commonly find that children (even less than 1 year of age), when excessively angry, will not only lash out against others but also against themselves. In very young children, this may occur as a result of both lack of control over reflexive reactions and insufficient differentiation between self and other—not knowing who is the self and who is the other instigating the experience leading to rage.[8]

Even in children just around 1 year of age, when there is an acute hostility overload, the child may restrict himself from directing his hostility toward Mother or Father. Even this young, as we saw in Mary, hostility toward those to whom the child is attached creates internal conflict. The alternative frequently used by young children is to direct the hostility away from the valued and needed parent and turn it toward himself or toward an innocent by-stander (by displacement which I'll talk about shortly).

We find that children often tend to use the same reactions over and over. Thus the parent can recognize the pattern the child uses to deal with hostility overload. Parents will recognize it if their child tends to direct his hostility against himself as a selected way of dealing with hostility overload. As patterns of hostility expression and discharge are tried by the child, parents should endorse constructive ways the child uses.

Three-year-old Phyllis seemed somehow to frequently get bruises, scratches, or cuts on her arms, legs, or face. We had noticed that she would fall or bump into chairs, even though she was not a clumsy child. We soon came to see that when she got upset with her younger sister and teased or hit her, and her mother would then scold her, Phyllis would scratch her own arm or bite her own hand. We inferred that she did this because she was unable to find reasonable ways to express her feelings of hostility and rage. When this was drawn to the mother's and Phyllis's attention, she began talking about her feelings in a matter of a few weeks. The physical attacks on herself began to decrease and eventually stopped.

Restrictions on lashing out against Mother, as well as against the self, should take essentially the same form.

- First, one states the prohibition against doing just that.
- Second, one comments as to the reason for that prohibition, which is invariably in the form of: "I love you, and I don't want you to hurt me or to hurt yourself—and I don't want you to do things that will make you feel bad about yourself!"
- Third, if this type of behavior has been going on for some time, point it out to the child, explain that you disapprove and expect the behavior to stop. Again, the child's lashing out against himself may require the setting of limits and where these fail, some benign form of punishment.
- And where the parents' efforts do not work, some professional help may be warranted—because self-hurting, self-defeating tendencies can have serious lifelong implications.

## WHY REDUCE OUR CHILDREN'S NEED TO ERECT DEFENSE MECHANISMS TO COPE WITH THEIR FEELINGS OF HOSTILITY?

Helping children find acceptable ways to verbally express their feelings of anger, hostility, and hate reduces their need to set up psychological defense mechanisms to protect themselves against the anxiety these negative feelings create in them. Most parents don't need this encouragement, but it is in our children's best interest that we consider this task seriously. When a child is not helped with the expression and discharge of his hostility overload against Mother or against himself, the child does not feel protected against his own hate reactions and accumulating inner pressure to destroy. The child may then become afraid of what his own rage may lead him to do and even become afraid of this rage himself—like he has this destructive force in him which may even destroy him.

One of the largest challenges to the young child comes from her/his unavoidable experience-produced feelings of hate and rage, which at moments stir up in her/him the wish to destroy the mother the child loves! Consider 13-month-old Mary's paralysis. What a remarkable illustration of the challenge to the child: What was she to do? How was she to deal with this eruptive force inside her? Yes, she'd been angry with her mother before; but this! She was mortified and paralyzed. To be sure, it was the mounting of anger to hostility, then intensified into rage. The indignation that her sense of self was being trashed by, of all people, her dear, dear mother! We were all awed by this lovely child's bewildering dilemma. Her mother was pale with pain and helplessness.

Because her mother, despite her own distress, handled this challenging situation so patiently, so empathically, so sympathetically, Mary was able to deal with it directly. And she was then eventually able to quiet her eruption and accept her mother's comforting. What would have been the consequences for Mary if her mother had just let Mary thrash around on the floor and maybe even called her a spoiled brat! The rage we saw would have stayed inside Mary—and who knows when and how it would eventually have been discharged.

Being afraid of one's own hostile or rage feelings commonly leads to having to self-protectively set up defenses to not feel them, to not act on them. Then a child may simply repress them, or deny them, or inhibit the discharge of these feelings, blocking their reasonable expression and discharge. Without such defenses the child's emotional life might be frozen—as we saw only briefly, fortunately, in Mary. These defenses, and there are others in addition to those I mentioned, may, however, lead to distortions of feelings, including those of hate which will then not be metabolized or resolved and will accumulate. These may then impede feelings of love and affection, which may then negatively affect love relationships, and eventually sexual gratification. Defenses erected to contain one's hostility, hate, and rage may also lead to *inhibitions* in learning, and may eventually create school and work problems.

Here is an example of what I have found many times.

A 6-year-old boy is surprisingly quiet when with grownups, even with his own father. He tends not to talk to them, even at times when it is expected (as with a teacher in class). He tends to talk most easily with his mother. He does well with peers. He also is subject to temper tantrums that distress his parents greatly, and he is most enraged with his younger brother, who he believes is the source of much difficulty for him. Because at 6 years he has not yet learned to control his rage well enough and is in constant dread of its bursting forth, he has to set a big clamp on his feelings. This leads to inhibitions, which among other inhibitions includes not talking with grown-ups other than his mother.

Here is another type of event I have seen that needs a comment.

Sixteen-month-old Michael bumped into a chair because he was not looking where he was going. In response to Michael's being upset, his mother tapped the chair and said, "Bad chair!"

This is neither a constructive nor socially adaptive type of problem solving. Clearly the chair did not walk up to Michael and hit him. The accident occurred because he did not pay attention to where he was going. It is better to help Michael's evolving sense of being someone who can reasonably prevent some accidents from happening to him, someone who initiates things and who is responsible for his own actions. "Look where you're going! Be careful" is far superior to "Bad chair!"

The fact is that blaming an innocent thing or person for having gotten hurt by one's own actions facilitates the use of the defense mechanisms of *displacement* and *projection* in dealing with hostility overload. It also encourages the child to avoid dealing with situations realistically, which can only complicate his/her own life. It is more to the child's advantage to learn to watch where he is going than to encourage him to believe that chairs magically move and hit you. Blaming chairs distorts facts, encourages frightening magical thinking—which all children experience, even into elementary-school years and later—and interferes with the child's developing healthy adaptive precaution and reasonable self-care.

Here's what makes this so important an issue: Blaming an innocent object facilitates a highly problematic mechanism for dealing with one's hostility and hate: it's somebody else's or something else's fault. "I didn't do it; he, or it, did it to me!" This is a form of the defense mechanism we call projection. This psychological mechanism of projection—of ascribing, by externalization, one's own hostile destructive feelings onto someone else—is a close cousin to the defense mechanism displacement. The earliest form of displacement seems to me to show its origins: it's a defense mechanism whereby, when the child (young and old) feels an overload of hostile feelings toward his mother or father, a person he loves, it stirs in the child an internal conflict which, as early as from the first year of life on the child may solve by displacing these hostile feelings onto something or someone else. Let us return to an event I already mentioned.

Twelve-month-old Jane was having a difficult time with her mother this morning. In the midst of one of their mild but then frequently occurring battles of wills, Jane picked up a small wooden block, raised her arm, and turned to her mother somewhat defiantly. Mother looked at Jane quite sternly, and although she said nothing, her expression was clearly a statement of prohibition. Jane's arm came forward, and as it did so, she rotated her body slightly and threw the block at Mrs. G., who was sitting next to her mother.

I inferred from this that Jane's target was her beloved mother, but the prohibition from her mother and from within herself led Jane to displace her attack onto an innocent bystander, Mrs. G. All psychoanalysts and many other thinking people see such events as a displacement, a self-protective coping mechanism implemented by all human beings to discharge hostility we feel toward someone we love, through discharging it against someone who is less important to us. This hostility discharge creates less conflict for us because that person is not as valued as the loved one.

I want to repeat here what I wrote in chapter 1: In our observational research, we saw a striking cluster of defenses young children erect when very angry with their mothers. (I should note that we saw the infants with their mothers; except on some occasions, their fathers were not able to join us in our Tuesday and Friday observational meetings. Occasionally also, we saw some of our subjects' older siblings, as when there was no school a given day.) For instance, already by 12 months of age we had seen much evidence of

- *Displacement:* when angry with mother, Jane picked up a block and threw it not at her mother but at the woman sitting next to her mother,
- By 18 months of age we saw clear evidence of *projection:* a strategy where the child projects her own hostility onto someone else: "I'm not angry at her, she's angry with me,"
- *Rationalization:* "I'm angry with her because she was mean when she told me to brush my teeth", and
- *Denial:* "I didn't do that; it was an accident."

Then, especially organizing of prejudice, starting from 5 to 6 years on, we saw behaviors from which we could infer "reality-distorting defenses," including

- *Reductionism:* "All Blacks wanna do is rob you!"
- *Caricaturing:* "All Jews have hooks for noses,"
- *Depreciation:* "All Spics are lazy and don't deserve to be paid like Whites," and
- *Vilification:* a recently minted "All Muslims are terrorists!"

These are all defenses that play a key role in the organization of what I call "malignant prejudice."

In the use of all these defenses, someone other than the person toward whom hostility, hate, and rage was initially experienced has become the recipient of that now externalized hostility, hate, and rage. And this can happen even many years after the noxious experiences took place and seem to be forgotten. But both psychoanalysis and neuroscience now inform us that experiences of intense psychic pain get registered in the brain from very early on in life and continue to reverberate in us indefinitely, unless they are metabolized or revised either by reparatory life experiences or intensive psychotherapies (see chapters 1 and 3).

This is one of the major reasons why reducing our children's need to set up defense mechanisms to cope with their feelings of hostility, hate, and rage is of great advantage to them and to society.

Like limit setting, learning how to control one's anger and hostility and to discharge it in socially acceptable ways requires time and repeated efforts on the part of the parent. Helping kids express their hostility in acceptable ways continues well into the elementary-school years and at times into adolescence. As I emphasized in chapter 4, in adolescence our efforts to get compliance, to set limits, and now to help our kids establish acceptable ways to discharge hostility takes special care. When an adolescent needs help in improving his way of discharging hostility, the effectiveness of the parents' efforts are highly determined by the adolescent's past history in interaction and relatedness with these parents. Perhaps more so than before, the history of secure, good relatedness will now make helping our adolescent gain further control over how to discharge hostility constructively both more feasible and less necessary. By contrast, where there has been much hurt and negativity in relationships at home, especially where there has been abuse and neglect, helping teenagers discharge high loads of hostility in socially acceptable ways will be most problematic, if not outright ineffective.

With kids, during both their school-age years and adolescence, whose relationships are quite loving and secure, but in whom personality traits make limit setting and compliance really challenging, helping them progressively develop skills in controlling the hostile feelings they experience cannot be achieved without more or less substantial struggle, negotiation, and compromise. Some kids with obsessive traits, or some burdened with self-disappointment due to some learning difficulty or some other inborn challenging trait, may have more difficulty dealing with their hostility and require more effort on the parents' part to help them continue to make efforts to discharge these problematic feelings in reasonable ways. It continues to be challenging to parents to help such kids when they go into adolescence; but the parents' efforts need to be continued. With some of these kids, a "tough love" approach may be very helpful. In this approach, limits are set with firmness (not hostility!), even in the face of much distress felt by both adolescent and parents, and punishment must be reasonably but clearly measured, and it must be limited to privilege withdrawal. Side by side with this then, helping the teenager continue to improve his ability to express his hostility in acceptable ways is paramount, because much hostility will get stirred up by the "tough love" approach. Physical punishment with adolescents is not part of "tough love"; it's abuse, and it's very risky.

What complicates the parents' efforts to further help their adolescents discharge their hostility in ways parents believe to be acceptable is that the parents' standards of what is acceptable increasingly carries less weight in adolescence due to the shift of the center of their universe from the parents (the family) to the peer group. The consolidation of self-identity has to include mores (philosophy and methods) of hostility discharge that are acceptable to, have to straddle the standards acceptable to, both the adolescent's family and his/her peer group. Again, where relationships are good, this may not be difficult to achieve; where relationships are painfully troubled, the likelihood is large that what's acceptable to the peer group may not be to the family, and what is acceptable to the family will likely not be acceptable to the peer group. By the way, with teenagers whose challenging behavior comes from having been traumatized or neglected, "tough love" strategies work only with a limited number of them.

> The essence of this book, which applies centrally to the task of parenting discussed in this chapter, is that the statement: *"an ounce of prevention is worth a pound of cure"* is a gross underestimation. Prevention may in fact be the difference between a fruitful, gratifying life and a life of trouble and misery.

It is well to bear in mind that there are ways of discharging one's hostility in graduated doses and in ways that are tolerable to both the self and the target of one's hostility. Verbalization of one's hostility in a positively meaningful relationship allows for the lessening of its accumulation in the psyche and prevents its coloring the personality. It also facilitates the development of internal controls over how one discharges hostility and hate, a process that develops gradually, with much help from parents. As with limit setting, teaching children to verbalize hostility often requires repetition to gradually achieve a working through and resolution of feelings of psychic pain and of the hostility and hate it has generated.

The parents' efforts to develop, maintain, and enhance a positive dialogue with their child—which can be put into play even when dealing with feelings of anger and hostility—not only provides a vehicle for the working through of painful experiences, hostility, and hate, but also secures the vehicle for healthy development in the child, including the formation of good relationships and heightened well-being.

We should also toss into this promise the idea that if parents want their child to talk to them when they become adolescents—something that is not guaranteed in all families—they must talk and listen to their child and encourage their child to talk about feelings and experiences from infancy on.

## TEASING AND TAUNTING, THE BUILDING BLOCKS FOR BULLYING

We have to help our children understand that teasing and taunting are not acceptable ways of expressing one's feelings of hostility or hate toward others, because teasing and taunting have the potential of becoming highly destructive ways of coping with these universally unavoidable painful feelings—in everyone's life, there are pleasures and there is pain! Parents should recognize that although teasing and taunting may initially look quite innocent, given any substantial stress or pressure, these behaviors can easily slide into bullying. While a child's teasing another child, or a parent teasing a child may have a playful intention, it "attacks," however mildly, the other's healthy narcissism and causes pain, even if only mild pain. It is well to bear in mind that while a teaser may intend to be playful, the victim may experience it as taunting or even bullying, and that how the victim experiences the teaser's playfulness is what should determine the parent's intervention. It is an occasion to help the child who teases learn to empathically look for how the victim experiences his "playfulness." If the other child does not experience it as playfulness, the teaser should be helped to apologize and make amends for his playfulness having been experienced by the other as hurtfulness.

This event becomes an unplanned opportunity for the parent to teach his/her child to learn to look for how people react to what he/she does. Even when the young child under 4 or 5 years cannot yet "judge" or "mentalize"[9] the effects of what he/she does, the young child is capable of empathy, of feeling what the other may be feeling and the parent's saying, "How would you feel is someone did to you something that makes you feel like [the other child manifests—facial expression and vocalization]?" In the parent's own words, "put yourself in his/her shoes."

To be sure, it is desirable to help our children tolerate some pain, learn to cope with it in self-protective ways, and we know that tolerable pain experiences activate the child's highly desirable resilience capabilities; but "everyday life" does a good enough job challenging the child and causing him/her pain, without "everyday life" needing the help of a "playful" but nonetheless sadistic other person—especially one's own father, the universal playful parent, who unfortunately, too commonly falls into being a child teaser!

The recent national and professional attention given to acts of bullying of drastic consequences, as the minority group "social outcasting" that triggered the deadly violence at Columbine High School, and the tragic individual teenager suicides such as those of Phoebe Prince, Jared Benjamin High, 11-year-old Carl Walker-Hoover, and those of Jessica Logan and Hope Wisel,[10] all triggered by shaming and humiliating bullying, as well as the more recent suicide of Rutgers University student Tyler Clementi; these were all direct by-products of escalating teasing and taunting. The wider social community of which each family is a member, as Twemlow and Sacco[11] point out, the social community in which children live must mobilize to prevent such tragedies. As Twemlow and Sacco observe, "Blaming the children misses the point."[12] Twemlow and Sacco hold that the adults in the community, parents and school staff (teachers, counselors, principals) must act to prevent such events from happening in our schools.

There is a most welcome recent push in many schools and universities nationally to prevent and intervene constructively where bullying is taking place. While these efforts are enormously important, given that teasing, taunting, and bullying commonly occur in and among peer groups (i.e., in schools and neighborhoods), foremost these behaviors have their origin and start at home. As parents we must be aware of the fact that this now highly amplified by "cyberbullying" social problem begins much earlier in life than most of us imagine. As primary caregivers, the issue demands our attention and constructive action. We must recognize that:

> *Bullying is intensified teasing, and taunting. It is perpetrated by the child individually or as a member of a group. Its consequences have long been demonstrated.*

Of course, the terms *teasing, taunting,* and *bullying* are commonly used. But I want to emphasize that there are meaningful distinctions between them. The *Oxford English Dictionary (OED)*—which many consider the most definitive for the English language—defines them like this:

> *Teasing:* Let me start with the word "tease": To tease is "to irritate another in a trifling or sportive way" (*OED* 3247). *Teasing* is to be "pettily irritating, annoying, or vexatious" to another (*OED* 3248).

**Taunting:** First, a "taunt" is "an insulting or provoking gibe or sarcasm; mocking or scornful reproach or challenge" (*OED* 3242). *Taunting* is "to reproach (a person) with something in a sarcastic, scornful, or insulting way" (*OED* 3242).

**Bullying:** First, a "bully" is "a tyrannical coward who makes himself a terror to the weak" (*OED* 293). *Bullying* is "overbearing insolence, personal intimidation, petty tyranny" (*OED* 293).

I should note that Twemlow and Sacco rightly point to the fact that "bullying is a process." It occurs over time and involves three sets of characters: bully, victim, and bystander. It can occur between a bully and a victim, or between a group and one victim (as in a lynching), and between groups of bullies and of victims (as in racism and other forms of malignant prejudice), each of which always have some involved bystanders, even if they are so totally passively, I would say, "just uninvolved but interested onlookers." In schools especially and widespread in society, it occurs between a bully and a victim in an environment of "bystanders." Too commonly, bystanders allow the bullying to go on and even when there is an appeal by the victim for help, the bystanders may not act to intervene; they are "passive bystanders." This in essence supports Twemlow and Sacco's position that the bullying process "is controlled by the bystanding audience" be it in schools or in the neighborhood. There is a large literature on the fact that Social History is full of illustrations of this phenomenon, in the context of very variable environmental conditions.

Here I will not address bullying as a process, given that my concern in this book is to help parents, caregivers, and educators deal with the individual child, and later the adolescent, as a teaser, a taunter, and a bully. Even though I do agree with Twemlow and Sacco that bullying occurs as a process, I hold that each member of that process, the bully, the victim, and the bystander, can be taught to understand that the "bullying process," that being either one or the other of its component parts, bully, victim, or bystander, is not acceptable! After this discussion we'll consider the child/adolescent who is the teased, the taunted, the bullied, i.e., *the victim.*

*I should also note that parents need to consider helping their child understand that just being a bystander, allowing a weaker child to be victimized by an intimidating or a terrorizing victimizer is not acceptable either! How the child then intervenes requires thoughtful strategy the center of which should be: "How would you feel if some kid bigger than you would do this scary or hurtful thing to you, and*

*people standing around you did nothing to help you? Be thoughtful;
be considerate; but be careful!"*

So back to the individual child/adolescent who by his teasing and taunting
behavior may veer toward becoming a bully.

Note that the hostile destructiveness that drives each, teasing, taunting,
and bullying, heightens and that it causes the person teased, taunted, or
bullied a progressively higher level of emotional pain:

- *To tease* is to irritate, to trifle with; it's petty ("no big deal"). It causes
  the least intense level of psychic pain along the range of emotionally
  painful feelings.
- *To taunt* is to be sarcastic, to scorn, to insult; it is not just *hostile,* it's
  *mean.* It's intending to and enjoying causing the other emotional pain.
- *To bully* is to push around, to intimidate in a rather persistent way. It
  may go to the level of petty terrorizing, that is, to make someone's life
  miserable without going to the point of seriously crippling or killing
  that person or persons.

Correlating teasing, taunting, and bullying with the level of hostile destructiveness experienced by the perpetrator which drives his/her actions, note
that

- *Anger* generally does not lead one to tease and taunt. Once the factor
  causing the psychic pain that triggers anger stops, in most kids and
  teenagers the anger is likely to wane; apology usually facilitates the
  lessening and stopping of anger. However, given that accumulated
  *hostile destructiveness* is commonly found in many maltreated kids and
  teenagers who tease, taunt, and bully, *anger* is likely to mobilize some
  of their accumulated internalized *hostility* and then what surfaces is
  no longer simply *anger.*
- *Hostility* and *hate,* which feed meanness, may and often do lead to
  teasing, taunting, and bullying. Hate may especially do so because it
  does not waver or change from day to day—remember that hate endures, whereas hostility tends to be episodic, though the hostility that
  has already accumulated can readily be activated. While these may
  lead to teasing, taunting, and bullying by one kid, group processes
  (whether a group of buddies or a gang) can easily activate teasing or
  taunting into bullying of an individual, or of a specified group—as
  occurs in malignant prejudice and racism.

- *Rage*, interestingly, does not commonly lead to teasing and taunting; rage is explosive, it tends not to allow for "playfulness" (in teasing) or scheming and planning (in taunting and bullying). Rage tends to be an individual response and is only uncommonly activated by group processes.

Having said this, in our project we saw behavior at about 12 months of age that took us by surprise. I am referring to what I catalogued as aggressive behavior that seems to suggest pleasure-related destructiveness (see chapter 2). As I said, we had not seen this type of aggression before about 12 months of age. Let me remind the reader of the three examples I recorded in chapter 2.

The first example is the one that took place between 11-month-olds, Jane and Tammy.

Jane was exploring her environment in her usual way. She came to Tammy, who was also just going about her explorations, pacifier in her mouth as was usual for her at this time. Jane paused a moment standing in front of Tammy, both looked at each other, when Jane just reached for and plucked Tammy's pacifier from her mouth! Jane's mother reacted immediately, getting up and returning the pacifier to Tammy while telling Jane not to do that. Jane didn't seem particularly troubled by her quite reasonable and loving mother's reaction. Jane walked away, looking around. Then she circled back to Tammy and looking at her, reached for Tammy's pacifier and again pulled it from her mouth. Jane now seemed intent on doing this. Tammy got upset. Jane's mother's tone was more urgent and firm this time. Jane walked away seemingly not too dismayed about all this. In fact, she had a bit of a smirk on her face. After a few moments, there she was again, in front of Tammy and again, pulled the pacifier from her mouth. This time Jane smiled as she did this; Tammy now started to cry!

I was very puzzled by this behavior. Here rather than experiencing psychic pain, 11-month-old Jane was causing another child psychic pain.

Here's another of the examples of this type of behavior:

Two-and-a-half-year-old Susan seemed rather restless one morning. As she went from one toy to another, she noted with interest a toy 1½ year-old Tommy was exploring. With a half smile on her face, she reached for that toy and pulled it from Tommy's hand. Her mother was looking elsewhere and did not see this. Within moments, Susan, again smiling, grabbed the next toy Tommy picked up. Again, she watched Tommy's reaction with pleasure and some satisfaction. Tommy fussed. He picked up yet another toy, and in a moment, Susan grabbed it. Her smile now left no doubt that she was getting pleasure out of being nasty to Tommy. Now Tommy was heard, and Susan's mother, now tuned in to what was going on, intervened.

No one would argue: this was intentional, it was taunting. The third example here was more complex but helped us see and understand what could have been at the base of both 11-month-old Jane's and 2 ½ years old Susan's behaviors.

When Candy was about 18 months old, she and her twin sister were exploring among the other children as we carried out our usual observations (during the project I described in chapter 1). For no reason visible to us, 2½ year old Donnie approached Candy, suddenly thrust his arm around her neck and grabbed her head—in the wrestling move called "a half-Nelson." We were all startled! The mothers, the observers, and certainly, Candy! Mothers intervened quickly. Candy did not retaliate against Donnie. She moped; and she disrupted her sister's play with some toys. Her mother calmed her sympathetically.

At our next group session three days later, Candy, her sister, and her mother came as usual. Candy seemed subdued. Some 20 minutes later, I saw Candy's face come to attention as she focused across the Unit's Day Room where we met. Donnie, his younger sister (one of our research subjects) and their mother had just walked in. Quite directly, Candy walked up to Donnie and without a sound, raised her fist and struck him in the arm! With this she smiled softly, a bit like Mona Lisa. Donnie was startled but interestingly did not strike back. Candy's mother readied to get up but saw that the event was over. It made clear sense to me; it might have to Candy's mother as well. In fact, I commented to the mothers that it seemed as though Candy had been planning how to let Donnie know that she was very angry with him for what he had done to her 3 days before. I wondered if Donnie's reaction of doing nothing might have suggested that Donnie too understood that this was retribution for what he had then done to her three days before.

Parents should intervene and help their child know that teasing and taunting creates problems. Most parents agree that this is not acceptable behavior, needs to be interrupted and, even with less-than-2-year-olds, a firm mini-lecture is called for. Teasing and taunting must be addressed as early as it occurs in a child's behavior, with a mini-lecture that conveys to the child: "this is not acceptable behavior," because such a mini-lecture helps the child internalize this as a principle of behavior that becomes part of his/her early conscience formation. As often as it occurs over the years, that often it is to be addressed with firmness. And each time, talking about it again later, when things have quieted down, fosters the internalization of this principle. By contrast, teasing and taunting during childhood and adolescence that is not confronted with loving firmness by parents can lead to an increasingly stabilizing pattern of abuse of others that can create painful problems for others, for society, and for the child herself/himself.

Given that teasing and taunting in time may become bullying, it is important that parents know that in bullying, both the victim and the bully are children/adolescents who are at risk for emotional-social problems. My clinical experience confirms Twemlow and Sacco's position that both bully and victim may develop emotional (psychiatric) symptoms that will cause them misery: for the victim, in depression or anxiety or shame and low self-esteem, for example; and in the bully, in being a behavior-disordered kid that people don't like, and in having adaptation, relationship, and social problems.

History has shown that a time comes when the taunters and bullies (individual and in groups) create for themselves problems of socialization that often have led peers (and society) to reject them as shameful members of society. Note that groups can act as one bully or as a pack of bullies—as is common in malignant prejudice, racism, in all ethnic groups that promote what I have called "malignant ethnocentrism." To illustrate my point, because from a societal perspective it is of enormous importance, let me develop a bit further this leap I have just made in talking of groups as bully/bullies, before I get back to speaking to parents and educators of the individual child/adolescent bully and point out that he/she will eventually pay for his/her bullying.

Some of my colleagues have worked at finding ways to reduce the suffering of both the children of victims as well as those of perpetrators of the Holocaust, one of most outrageous bullying-begotten crimes against humanity ever perpetrated. Yes, this is what I am talking about: The Holocaust and most of the other genocides that have brought shame to civilization—and there are many since the fifteenth century when they began to become massive[13]—have their start in a child's developing the easily come-by tendency to become a bully, carried out to its extreme: individually, in crime; and in groups, in genocide.

In their efforts to help the children of victims as well as those of perpetrators—because it has become known that they too suffer painful consequences following on what their parents did (see chapter 3)—these mental health researchers brought together volunteer grown children of both, children of Holocaust survivors and children of active perpetrators, i.e., Nazi officers and atrocities executers. Once they were able to express some of their feelings and talk to one another, a daughter of a Nazi officer, very distraught, blurted out: "You, children of the victims suffer, but you suffer in dignity! We suffer too, but we suffer in shame!" She meant of course, "I suffer shame at what my parents did to you!" This second generation as well as the third generation—according to studies by German mental health and other professionals—suffer shame at their parents having directly or indirectly tyrannized innocent others.

The reader may feel skeptical or bewildered by the leap I have just made, but historical facts bear out what I am saying, like other mental health professionals I say that atrocities against others have their roots in childhood, even early childhood.

Let's get back to helping the individual child and dealing with the individual adolescent to express his/her hostile destructive feelings in acceptable ways. Let's look at the 3 examples I mentioned a few pages ago.

Already at 11 months Jane needed fairly firm limits by her mother, given Jane's rather hefty disposition. Jane was not teased by her mother; but she may have been teased by her father or one or more of her older siblings. It did seem that her behavior just came up spontaneously, as part of her exploring her universe, including people in it, especially so, kids her own age.

It was not clear to me and my coresearchers what Jane experienced as pleasurable when she saw Tammy upset. I wondered if she derived pleasure from making something happen; she caused a change in her universe! Did she have a drive to be nasty? Some would believe this. I don't. She certainly already had had run-ins with her mother in which we saw Jane get angry with her! She may also have had such experiences with her father. No doubt she did as well with her siblings. Was she taking her anger toward her mother, father, or siblings out on Tammy? My inclination is to assume that all of these might have contributed to her first exploring, which then turned into teasing Tammy: her need to have an impact on her universe, opened to her the fact that *she* could cause another annoyance and psychic pain as she felt was done to her, this being pushed by her already accumulating anger. This event gave her the opportunity to discharge by *displacement* her accumulating hostility; she found she could do so by being nasty to another.

Susan's actions toward Tommy are easier to understand. He was her unwanted baby brother! No one consulted her about having another baby in the family to share her parents with! She liked being the only princess in the house. Now her privileged position was being challenged! By whom? Like every first born, Susan didn't blame her parents—who of course did all this planning to have another baby—instead, she displaced upon her brother her resentment about being displaced from cherished priority status to common plebian: all because of that brat!

The dynamics of Candy's behavior were clear: she had outright been attacked. Given the pain she experienced, it registered firmly in her young mind. Days later she acted to get back—quite mildly I should say. It gave her satisfaction to pay Donnie back for what Donnie had done to her! But here too we need to be careful: isn't too much satisfaction in getting back at someone the slippery slope to revenge! Candy did not look like she was about to push her success in getting back at him; had she, her mother would have been wise to intervene and help her learn when enough is enough.

It all begins when we experience too much psychic pain—which unavoidably begins at home. But it is fortunate that it is at home that it begins because no one is more qualified emotionally than the parent to help the child learn to discharge the *hostile destructive* feelings he/she experiences in acceptably constructive ways.

Parents should address teasing and taunting by their child because this may evolve into his/her becoming a sadistic individual, one who derives pleasure from being mean to others. Then, no doubt his/her relationships with loved ones, with peers and others will include his/her causing them psychic pain. In addition, and most troubling, the teaser may from here evolve during childhood into a bully or later in life into someone easily drawn to harmful behavior toward others as occurs in acts of malignant prejudice (see above and chapter 1).

From early childhood on, setting limits is the first order of things. But with that, talking to the child/adolescent about teasing and taunting behavior is essential. With preschool kids and school-age ones, parents need to take the time to get the child to try to explain why he teases or taunts, and to follow this up with telling the child, young or older, that complaints he has toward others are better dealt with by talking with the other where possible than by teasing and taunting. Where talking to the other does not work, talking to someone who can listen sympathetically and be supportive is a very wise way to go; early in childhood, to talk to Mother or Father; later, talking to them and to friends can help a lot.

Twelve-year-old Marty's mother told me that he had been irritable for several days. "It's not like him; he's a warm, friendly kid, a good student, gets along well with adults (including teachers) and his friends." Essentially his mother told me that after some questions to find out what's troubling him, Marty told her that Jay, that big kid from a block away, has been picking on him when he sees him, in school and in the neighborhood. Jay is a head taller than Marty, a year older and not doing so well in the same grade, in the same school. Jay's family is known in the neighborhood as always seeming to be in some turmoil; "his older brother isn't such a nice teenager either," she said. According to

Mother, Jay doesn't hit Marty but he seems to always be around and annoy, even insult Marty. Jay's bullying Marty's friend Aaron too, but not as much.

In talking with her further about this, what Marty's mother told me suggested amply that Jay was a young teenager who for some time was known to not do well in school and to not be treated well at home—his mother was known in the neighborhood as being a difficult and angry woman. There is consensus among Child Mental Health professionals that unfortunately parents whose kids turn out to behave like Jay tend not to seek psychotherapeutic help for the child, let alone for themselves. And some of these kids end up getting troublesome attention in reaction to their "behavior conduct disorder"—as we diagnose them. So Jay was in the process of becoming a bully. We have to bear in mind that there is a rather direct line between kids feeling maltreated—be it being abused and/or neglected at home, and/or when feeling ashamed by his/her own school failures, or when being rejected by peers and by teachers in school—and their later taunting and even bullying others. Displacement and projection of the hostile destructiveness they accumulate brings this about.

But while this is so, there are also many young people who tease and taunt and some among them may bully others, who, like Jane, are not "maltreated" but nonetheless experience the psychic pains of everyday life—and even in the best of circumstances kids experience a good deal of psychic pain, at home, at school, and in the neighborhood. Hurtful experiences, disappointments, frustrations are part of normal life; hostile destructive feelings get generated in each of us, all of us. There is, however, no doubt that "the psychic pains of everyday life" are not likely to produce bullies at the high rate we find in kids who are abused or neglected at home. Nonetheless, even with children who are not really maltreated at home, the challenge remains: how can we best help our children learn to discharge their hostile feelings in ways that minimize causing others undue pain? To pull together what I have said in this chapter:

## For the young child:

- Talk to your baby so that he/she will learn from early in life that talking together is a highly desirable thing to do: it facilitates relationships, it helps share pleasures and concerns, it helps solve problems, it relieves stress, and it's the easiest way to get comforted, and more.
- Talk to your baby so that he/she will talk to you when he/she is an adolescent; putting a high value on talking together gets started in

infancy and continues through the years. Adolescents who have not been talked with meaningfully as babies will not suddenly come to see the value of talking to you as an adolescent.

- When your child is irritable, or angry, or hostile, or says "I hate you!," talk to her or him! Try to find out what's hurting him/her like Marty's mother did. Encourage him/her to tell you about it—but respect her/his need for privacy, especially so with teenagers.

- When your young child is mean to his/her siblings, peers, anyone—is the child mean to an older person—or, when your child takes another's toy, teases or taunts one way or another, intervene! Stop the behavior and administer a time out. After the time out give the child a mini-lecture; be serious about the unacceptability of such behavior. And ask your child how he/she would feel if someone did to him/her what he/she did to the other child.

## For the school-age child:

- When your child is really angry with someone, insist: talking is a better way to deal with and solve whatever problem he/she is having than hitting the other.

- Help your child choose her/his words; let the child know that insults are as trouble-making as hitting.

- Set limits when the language your child uses makes things worse, as do insults, like Mike's mother did.

- When your children are angry with each other, the same principles of talking rather than threatening, hitting, or breaking the other's things applies.

- Intervene with firm disapproval—don't be mean—when your school-age child lies, cheats, or takes others' things or damages them.

- Bear in mind that the development of the ability to reflect on his own behavior and to reflect on what the other may be feelings emerges from about 4 to 5 years of age on, and that to evaluate or judge what others think of one begins from about 6 to 7 years. Reflecting to the child during the early elementary school years that his/her behavior will reflect on him/her begins to have weight for the child; this self-reflection becomes then highly determining of how the child will act. Encouraging the child in a positive way to reflect on the impact of his behavior can optimize his/her behavioral self governance.

- It is also unfortunately common that being angry with a peer may lead your child to suggest to his friends, "Let's not play with him" or to say directly to the peer, "You can't play with us." When rejections of that kind are not stopped by parents, this may become an easy way to bully peers, with the potential for ostracizing a vulnerable peer to possibly dire ends—leading some kids to suicide.

**For the adolescent:**

- All the above apply, but must be applied in a context appropriate for the adolescent's age.
- As I emphasized above, recent neuroscience work tells us that the adolescent's remarkable brain development does not progress at a similar pace in all cognitive (thinking) functions. While a teenager may show stunning leaps of growth in learning, memorizing, math, and physics problem solving, his/her judgment and prediction of consequences of his/her actions tends to lag behind. Some brilliant kids may in fact be virtually blind and irrational regarding the consequences her/his actions. Many an adolescent believes that taunting and bullying may be only annoying and pestering, and at best push a selected other or others outside their group. Blind to the potential consequences taunting and bullying can bring about, they are jarred by the tragic reaction that erupted at Columbine High School and dismayed and shocked by Tyler Clementi's tragic suicide—all brought about by their reckless lack of control over their conscious and unconscious *hostile destructive feelings*. And to think that all of this got started as it did with 11-month-old Jane.

Yes, bullying is universal, and over the centuries has led to tragic harm to others. And that's why parents need to take most seriously the fact that teasing and taunting are at the crest of the slippery slope to bullying.

## THE CHILD OR ADOLESCENT WHO GETS TEASED, TAUNTED, OR BULLIED NEEDS HELP TOO

Marty was getting bullied. For various reasons, like many a teenager, he did not tell his mother about it. But knowing her son, Mother knew something was troubling him; and she reacted by wanting to help him. The fact is that many a bullied kid needs help too.

Of course, being teased is common in many good families and among friends. However, it's not a good sport in families because, while the teaser enjoys the game, the teased child or adolescent commonly—even while trying to put up with it—does not, given that the teasing tends to be at her/his expense. But, because it will likely go on, it is desirable to help the child try to read if the teasing is playful or is really depreciating. There is a big difference between truly being playful and being nasty—as we talked about before. Nonetheless, for many kids, being teased even playfully does not feel good. In large measure this is because even many a well-developing child does not feel fully secure in his/her own skin.

A parent's assessment of the teasing can be very helpful. A mother saying that the teasing is playful—when she truly feels it is—can lessen the child's feeling that she/he is being laughed at. At the same time, if the teasing has a nasty edge to it and Mother perceives this, her helping her child develop the ability to judge such teasing can help the child affirm his/her own perception of the character of the teasing. The child can then be helped to learn to tell the teaser to stop it. This may not always work and the child will be left to decide what to do, whether to tease back or to stay away from the teaser. If the teaser is the father, Mother is likely to step in on the side of the child, who will then feel protected. It is wise for fathers to find more constructive games to play with their kids, young and adolescent; probably having been teased as a child or at work, many a father rationalizes that it builds character. Well, learning to deal with teasing is important, but it does not build character.

Many a teenager has been and is being teased. The challenges facing the adolescent are enormous, and for all adolescents, invariably these challenges lead to insecurity and anxiety (see chapters 3 and 4). In families where kids and parents talk together about all kinds of matters and have done so from early on in life as part of the way they are together, when the kid is being teased it will likely creep into conversation. This presents an opportunity to reassure and help the adolescent feel listened to by caring family members, and it also makes it an occasion for talking about how to deal with being teased.

Taunting and bullying are a different matter. The help needed by the child will depend on the child's sensitivities and age.

First of all, some children with certain inborn personality traits are more likely to get taunted and even bullied than others. These personality traits show themselves from very early on and are likely to continue to be part of that child's personality for years to come. Children who are shy, or timid, or easily embarrassed, are more likely to be taunted than children who tend to be assertive, go after what they want, and are likely to resist being "pushed around."

*Such personality traits are picked up at a glance; just in an interactive glance in fact, these traits can reveal to a taunter that this kid can or cannot be victimized.*

Children are not evil! But, as I explained in chapter 2, they all have a tendency to displace and project hostile destructive feelings that have accumulated in them over time—most commonly, these are residual feelings generated in important relationships where they were not given opportunity to talk about them, and in which such feelings cannot be discharged toward those responsible for generating them. We can say this about kids at virtually all ages, starting as early as we saw in Jane and Tammy: a timid 11-month-old or 4-year-old, just as much as a timid 9-year-old or 17-year-old, is likely to become a target for a maltreated kid's accumulated hostile destructiveness.

Among school-age children and adolescents, much less so among less-than-5- or 6-year-olds, an overly anxious child, a child who is overweight, a child who is quite a bit smaller than the average for an age group, a child who is unduly clumsy, sometimes a child who is "slow" (not as smart as the average) is more likely to draw hostile attention from peers than another child who does not exhibit such self-image factors. Ethnic and racial differences among kids, such as in skin color, "foreign" facial features, can also—more so among adolescents than among elementary school-age kids—become triggers for taunting by troubled kids who are looking to displace or project their restless inner hostile destructiveness.

Depending on his or her age, the taunted child may at first need to be protected and progressively helped to self-protectively find ways to handle such situations. This is a highly desirable project which will serve the child for many years to come. Some young children protect themselves automatically, with confidence; they act to stop the aggressor. Others, like Tammy, are stunned, may become frightened and end up feeling helpless; they turn for help to the caregiver. Whatever way the teased child reacts, when needed the parent should comfort, then the parent should help the child, whatever age, by discussing ways to deal with a taunter or a bully; most school-age children and adolescents will surely be confronted by one at one time or another.

Recently, more than ever, the topic has drawn the attention of mental health, education, and even law and order professionals. Here are some thoughts about how to help one's child handle a taunting or bullying situation. Among mental health professionals, a highly relevant study currently in progress was recently reported in *Psychiatric News*.[14] Because the study is in progress, and has its limitations—as do all such studies—what these authors report should not be taken, nor do they wish us to take it, as the last word on their findings. Nonetheless, they give us meaningful information. What comes of what we tell our kids to do when taunted or bullied by another kid or kids?

The study[15] tells us that in response to a survey of questions among a population of 13,000 students in 12 states—age range was not specified but I assume they were elementary school–age kids and teenagers—here is what they found. Important to note is that while any given strategy (solution) at times made things "better," this same solution at times was reported to make things "worse." No solution worked uniformly to make things "better" or "worse." The question is: which solution made things "better" more frequently while at the same time could also make things "worse" least frequently.

*Note that this problem is sufficiently noxious that no solution is a predictable prescription for improvement.*

The solutions kids and adolescents selected that most often made things "better," included:

- "[Telling] an adult at home"; this seemed to be the solution that got the best results for the victim—made things "better" a little over 30 percent of the time. Only a little over 30 percent of the time did kids feel there is a way of dealing with bullying predictably well! Then close after came,
- "[Telling] a friend" about being taunted and/or bullied.
- These two solutions not only made things "better" most often, but also made things "worse" the least: less than 20 percent of the time.

Note that these support one of the principle theses of this chapter (indeed of this book):

*(1) helping your child learn to tolerate a reasonable load of psychic pain, which is essential for all humans since we just can't prevent psychic and physical pain from happening, and (2) helping your child learn to talk to an emotionally interested and sympathetic other person who is meaningful to your child, will contribute enormously to your child's resilience—a point on which all researchers on resilience agree.[16]*

Following the 2 best solutions (a tentative conclusion since the study is not finalized) came the following:

- Telling "an adult at school" and
- "Making a joke about it [when being taunted or bullied]."
- While these two solutions made things "better" almost as much as the first two, they did not succeed as well in reducing the bullying situation, at times making things "worse" more often—just under 30 percent of the time.

According to Davis and Nixon, the kids responding to their questions reported that the next four rather well-known strategies worked less effectively:

- "[Hitting] the bully or [fighting] back" got favorable results less than about 30 of the time, but managed to make things "worse" nearly 50 percent of the time. More kids said it made things worse! I will comment on this below.
- "[Making] plans to get back at the bully" was less favorable but, on the other hand, it made things get worse less often than "hitting the bully back"; things did not get better, but they less often got worse than by actually hitting or fighting the bully.
- "[Telling] the person to stop," and
- "[Doing] nothing" were both the least effective and made things worse 3 to 4 times as often as it helped.

Here are two important things to note regarding these findings which in my clinical and research experience are credible. First, all efforts to deal with being taunted and/or bullied we parents commonly recommend to kids, while at times help somewhat, they make things somewhat worse a large percentage of the time: from 20 percent to 50 percent of the time, the taunting and bullying continue "unchanged." The 20 percent of the time the bullying "does not change" are the times when action by the victim makes things "worse"—such as hitting the bully back or making plans to do so. We are seeing more and more clearly the pernicious influence of taunting and bullying and the drastic consequences to which these can lead.

*It is high time that we parents, caregivers, and educators are coming to recognize that taunting and bullying must be dealt with as more than "that's just what kids do." We must teach out kids about human rights from early in on in life, along with realistic morality in behavior.*

Second, we have to consider not only how to deal with our own kids teasing, taunting, and bullying others, but we also have to help them learn to deal with *being* teased, taunted, and bullied. The development of skills for coping with all kinds of pain begins very early in life and the challenges children face, including teasing, taunting, and bullying, change over time. So, let's consider the age of the child being taunted or bullied, and what do we help the child learn to do to cope with it as constructively as the child can. Let's consider the commonly used strategies Davis and Nixon explored with their large population of school-age kids and adolescents.

## The Young Child

We know what 11-month-old Jane's mother did when her feisty little girl taunted Tammy: she scolded her increasingly more forcefully as Jane's taunting behavior continued. What did Tammy's mother do? She immediately comforted Tammy and tried to secure that Jane stop taunting Tammy. She might have added, "Tammy, don't let Jane take your pacifier; hold on to it when she tries to pull it out of your mouth, and I'll help you and tell Jane to stop doing this." Now, Davis and Nixon found that "telling the person to stop" works favorably only infrequently. But that is among elementary school–age kids and adolescents. And it might not have worked with Tammy at 11 months of age. But in the early years, I would suggest this as a first step to take. In using this strategy, the way each, the victim and the taunter/bully, presents himself/herself matters. The tone, the strength and directness of the message communicated, the sternness of the glance, the "you better stop it!" do matter. While these may lead to an escalation of challenge, the child's trying out self-protective strategies that tend to come naturally to her will help the child learn what works and what doesn't, when and with whom. In this, Mom or Dad can be very helpful. Helping our children self-defend in diplomatic and reasonable ways, avoiding hitting where possible, helps kids learn to cope constructively with such miserable but rather too common events. Fathers who have a tendency to act big and tough and bypass diplomacy would be very wise to temper this common macho male tendency.

We also know what 2½-year-old Susan did to her 1½-year-old brother Tommy. She was being nasty. Tommy fussed, but did not directly call out for help from their mother and did not counter Susan's actions. Tommy was not of an inborn disposition to counter such an act offensive to him, nor had he yet developed the ability to tell his sister to cut it out! Nor was he the kind of child who would simply hit reactively. Once mother saw the scene which she quickly grasped, she intervened on behalf of the younger of the two. In addition to setting limits with Susan, which she did, Mother could have instructed Tommy to not let his sister take his things. He doesn't have to be mean about it; he can just pull his toy back and tell her to stop it! Depending on Tommy's effectiveness and Susan's reaction, Mother would have been wise to follow through with the necessary instructions to both. No need to be mean, just insistent that they heed her suggestions for dealing with such a challenge, both with being a taunter and with being a victim.

And we know what Candy did when Donnie mortified her with his half-nelson! The mothers quickly got Donnie to stop his attack on Candy. That we saw. It worked. But we did not see Candy's mother suggest to Candy how to deal with it; she did immediately rise to her rescue and comforted her daughter caringly and effectively. Nor did Mother intervene when Candy annoyed her twin sister, perhaps because Cindy handled it pretty well herself; she scolded Candy and held on to the things she was playing with. My impression is that three days later, mother was as surprised as the rest of us by Candy's retaliatory action against Donnie, which suggests that she and Candy probably had not talked about how to handle Donnie at the next visit.

Candy hit Donnie back! All indications are that it worked well; very well. She was relieved and Donnie gave evidence of understanding that Candy meant business—and he did not continue at any time (that we saw) any pattern of bullying her. Parenthetically, about 2 years later, after seeing no sign of bullying on Donnie's part, to all the adults' distress we witnessed Donnie declare to one of the African American kids visiting that he could not play with them because he was "Black"! Donnie's mother was mortified, verbally apologetic and quickly intervened with Donnie with a pained mini-lecture—which, we learned later, she continued after they left the group session.

While according to Davis and Nixon "hitting a bully back" works about 30 percent of the time and makes things worse about 50 percent of the time, this time it worked very well. But Candy was only 18 months old. Also, we can't be sure that she and Donnie were among the 30 percent for whom it worked well or whether during the early years, what applies to adolescents may not apply similarly to younger kids. I am not inclined to advocate what Candy did; although I have in the past suggested that sometimes, the only thing that stops a bully is for the victim to hit the bully back. Thirty percent of the time it may work, but I think that it may work better at an early age than in adolescence, given that with the passage of time into adolescence, years of pain experiences may have led to the accumulation of much hostile destructiveness and led to evolving strategies, however maladaptive, that include bullying. In addition, I assume that the little child who hits has not yet learned about the disadvantages of negotiating an argument with a peer by hitting, whereas an adolescent has learned the problem bullying often creates having, witnessed that perpetrators are often ostracized for being bullies (see chapter 3; also note that Twemlow and Sacco to whom I refer in this chapter, rightly see the bully as a youngster who needs help as much as—if not more than—does the victim). In addition, many a young child may launch an attack as did Donnie who himself was not maltreated by his/her parents—though he did have older brothers who may at times have pushed him around. More on why hitting back may not work well in adolescence when we talk about being bullied in adolescence, below.

## The Elementary School–Age Child

Parents need to be aware, and most are, that a child who is shy, or over-weight, or of a different ethnic background than the majority of kids in a school or neighborhood, may become unwittingly selected by a bully for victimization. Even very nice kids like 5-year-old Donnie may be guilty of such hurtfulness. Without overdoing it, inquiries as to how things went in school today from the vantage point of both school learning and socializa-tion are a valuable entry point into facilitating a child's dealing with being taunted or bullied in its early stages. Such attention, when not overdone, can prevent any taunting or bullying from taking hold.

For the elementary school–age child, Davis and Nixon's findings, even if not firmly substantiated, provide good suggestions for parents to follow. As a first strategy, the child should be encouraged to (1) talk with an adult at home; (2) talk to a good friend; (3) talk to a teacher or other school author-ity; and (4) if the child can, have him try to laugh it off; but laughing it off has to be done with care, given that the taunter or bully may feel laughed at which might only fire up his feelings of injury—which, I have no doubt, lie at the bottom of his/her being a bully in the first place.

If the child's various efforts at this first line strategy do not work, the issue may have to be taken up directly by the bullied child's parents with adults of influence in the life of the taunter or bully. First the bullied child's parents, one or the other or both, may need to go to the school to discuss this matter with their child's teacher or principal. It is often problematic to try to talk with the bully's parents, unless both sets of parents are on good neighborly terms. This is because the bully's parents may not respond favorably to complaints about their child. That is, (1) they may react violently against their own child—which they most likely have done in the past, given that the most common cause of bullying others comes from having been treated harshly at home—and, (2) they may not be able to accept, to tolerate the idea (a) of their child's doing this (we saw the humiliation of Donnie's mother at his rejecting a young visitor's wanting to join him and a peer in play, "because you're Black!"), or (b) of his being accused of being a bully, which these parents would experience as an accusation of them. Given the weight we now give to school bullying, school adults and administrators are more inclined to discuss strategy for intervening in taunting and bullying. Elementary school administrators, faculty, and staff are more engaged in dealing with this problem than they have been in the past due in large measure to some of the problems that have recently mushroomed and gotten so much well-deserved press.

Distressing to many parents is that some school-age children will not tell their parents they are being teased. This is often due to the shame they feel about having allowed themselves to be intimidated and humiliated by a bully. Such a child is then likely to be upset and this will, fortunately, most likely express itself at home. Trying to get the youngster to say what is upsetting him might well bring this out—and parents are well advised to try to get their upset child to talk about what's upsetting her/him. Once a parent learns that the child is being taunted or bullied, the door is opened to helping the child deal constructively with this problem.

A parent ridiculing his or her taunted kid, of whatever age, is extremely hurtful and generates hostility toward the ridiculing parent. Helping the taunted child should be a priority and it presents an opportunity, unpleasant as it is, to talk about and offer suggestions to the child as to how to deal with a taunter or a bully, knowing that often, this may be more difficult than anyone wishes.

## For the Adolescent

Again, parents of kids with vulnerability traits for being taunted and bullied are well-advised to ask, casually and habitually, how things went in school today, both in terms of school learning and with the peer group. While many of these parents have been aware of these risk-factors in their kids from even in elementary school years on, these kids continue to be vulnerable as adolescents and may require active parent participation in protecting them in schools even as teenagers. But to the traits of shyness, overweight, ethnic variance, and others, we now need to add the taunting and bullying-vulnerable variance in gender-related tendencies, especially of effeminacy in boys—which becomes a red flag for many a teenage boy and girl, given that their gender-specificity may not yet be sufficiently solidly established. This last vulnerability-for-bullying trait will require parental reflection and acceptance, because in many such instances, biological factors heavily determine this character trait, not conscious choice-making or preference. The old ideas that such tendencies can be easily changed by force or by clinical treatment have not proven to hold up after years of efforts. And over-insistence on the part of parents and others that such changes in character can and must be achieved creates no end of pain and problems for adaptation in the adolescent so disposed.

Many an adolescent who is taunted or bullied will now, even more than before, feel emotionally injured by the experience. This in large measure is because the adolescent years are the time when psychological development imposes on youth the imperative to shift the center of his/her interest in relationships from the nuclear family to the peer group. As a result his/her being taunted or bullied by someone in the peer group tends to be experienced especially painfully because the adolescent feels rejected by someone in this increasingly valued group during a time of uncertainty as the adolescent transitions the center of his/her relatedness from his/her nuclear family to this much less secure universe.

Still, being taunted or bullied by someone in the peer group will be much softened when the adolescent's nuclear family relationships are favorable. Intermittent retreat from the peer group to nuclear relationships will provide a break from feeling badly treated and opportunities for getting emotionally refueled and self-esteem repaired, and to talk about difficulties in school or the neighborhood and help plan strategies for coping with this unpleasant life challenge.

Of course, being taunted and bullied in the adolescent peer group will be experienced as more troubling by the adolescent whose nuclear family life has been and continues to be laden with abuse and neglect. For the home-abused and neglected adolescent, the peer group taunting and bullying will further generate rage in him/her toward others, which is likely to lead to an escalation of antisocial behavior of all kinds in such victimized adolescents. It is likely that what happened at Columbine High School may have been the coming together of a small group of teenagers who, whether by strict (harsh) upbringing or outright abuse or neglect at home, when marginalized and ridiculed by their peers in school for their different dress and behavior codes, felt pushed by intolerable psychic pain to explode as they did, with disastrous consequences.

While we can assume that many an adolescent who is taunted and bullied by a peer, is so by one who has most likely been abused or neglected at home, this are not the only pathway to being taunted and bullied by others. Sometimes, a relatively innocent adolescent wanting much to please another, may put himself or herself in a place of inviting victimization. Given the new instantaneous communications vogues of texting and "video-camming," and its inflammatory vehicle, cyberbullying, one such adolescent can become a victim of bullying of yet unprecedented dimensions. While some cyberbullying has reached dimensions that have led to disasters such as the cases of Jessica Logan, Hope Wisel, and Tyler Clementi as well as a recorded number of other suicides following cyberbullying, many more cases of cyberbullying occur daily in which naïve teenagers manage to get themselves targeted. While cyberbullying, especially texting, often takes the form of ridiculing, denigrations, and efforts at marginalizing one or another of the kids with taunting-vulnerability traits, the ones of a given minority ethnic group, or who are shy, or overweight, or gay or lesbian, etc., some "video-camming" has led to a new variant in cyberbullying.

This specific mode of cyberbullying comes under the category of "sexting" in which a naïve teenager may either on her/his own or under the influence of a pressured request for such self-exposure, decide to send a phone or computer image of himself/herself in some state of nudity. While such self-exposure may occur just once, such single self-exposure can end up weighing heavily for the naïvely self-exposed adolescent. Such a one-time event falling into the hands of one or several self-absorbed irresponsible adolescents can have serious reverberations. These events demonstrate with clarity the finding that the adolescent brain does not develop the ability to predict and judge the consequences of her/his actions at the same pace as her/his ability to memorize a piece of literature or solve an algebra problem. While such self-exposure may have been intended for a single individual, the receiving adolescent may not have the sense of responsibility of holding to his/her promise of maintaining privacy. In the adolescent, bragging rights can far outweigh responsible judgment and concern for the other who naïvely gave occasion for such perpetrator bragging rights.

One mother told me with much concern and dismay that her 14-year-old-daughter had after some pressure by her boyfriend sent him a computer video of herself naked. How Mother came to find out is not pertinent—it was not by outrageous measures to invade her teen daughter's privacy. While this mother was understandably troubled by her daughter doing this, her trouble was pretty well outweighed by her daughter's humiliating discovery that her boyfriend had in fact forwarded copies of the video message to several of his friends! The girl was incredulous that her boyfriend might have so betrayed her. She too has an adolescent brain! What initially seemed like an occasion for a teen's mother to talk to her daughter in scolding tones, turned into an occasion for the mother to help her daughter see some of the unfortunate consequences naïve behavior on her part can produce for her and to strategize how to try to get some closure to the incident with the erasure of the "sexted" video with due apologies from the boy, then quickly no longer "boyfriend," enforced by his family who got informed of the event. I have heard no more of the reverberations of this event. Things seemed to have ended with no tragic outcome but it did yield a humiliating lesson in self-protective rules of behavior.

This is surely not the easiest way for a teen girl to learn the limits of what to do and what not to do. It did give her mother occasion to underscore how to not subject herself to the abuse of others, how to avoid becoming the victim of someone's teasing, taunting, and even bullying. While every parent wants to prevent behavior that may lead to their teenager becoming a victim of abuse, we see, as in the instance with this 14-year-old, that it is not possible to cover all possibilities. It is well though for parents to impress upon their kids, from the time they get a cell or iPhone or access to a computer, that what gets written into or shown on a computer will not be controllable by them; once out on the internet, it belongs to others—including their thoughts and images of their bodies.

## NOTES

1. To simplify what we know in medicine, excessive, unbearable pain (physical and/or psychological) can not only cause one to lose consciousness; it can, by virtue of causing extreme stress on our physiology, lead to the breakdown of the functioning of the systems in our body and cause death.

2. Parens, H. (1993). Rage toward self and other in early childhood. In: *Rage, Power and Aggression*, S. P. Roose & R. Glick, eds., pp. 123–47. New Haven: Yale University Press.

3. Reactivity type is to be distinguished from impulsivity, the latter being due to a weakness in the organization and regulation of discharging feelings which makes it much more difficult to learn to control them.

4. See (in chapter 11) the case of Richie who was well nurtured until 6 months of age, when a painful change in his teen mother's life soon led to his being sadly neglected and painfully abused, which severely arrested his up to then normal development. Richie's history demonstrated painfully how he turned from a loving, beautiful little boy to a shriveled, failure to thrive, raging child (Parens, H. [1987]. Cruelty Begins at Home. *Child Abuse and Neglect*, 11:331–338.)

5. In psychotherapeutic work, it is critical that the therapist be "empathic" or be capable of "empathy." By this we mean that the therapist must be able to not only listen, but to emotionally perceive, grasp, and understand what the patient is feeling and trying to convey. It is being able to feel what the other is feeling; not

to feel the same way, but to grasp that the other has these feelings. The therapist must *resonate* with the patient's feelings not just his or her words. Such *empathic relatedness* is not just reserved for therapists; it is a highly desirable capability in any relationship, intimate or not, but it is especially so in the parent-child relationship; indeed, it is an essential requirement *for growth-promoting parenting* (Parens, H. [2010]. CD: *Parenting for Emotional Growth: A Textbook, Two Series of Workshops, & A Curriculum for Students in Grades K Thru 12©.* ISBN 0-9726910-0-6. Thomas Jefferson University, Media Division, Philadelphia, PA).

6. Findings presented in H. Parens (1979 [2008]). *The Development of Aggression in Early Childhood.* Lanham, MD: Jason Aronson/Rowman & Littlefield Publishers, Inc.

7. Parens, H. (1979). *The Development of Aggression in Early Childhood.* Lanham, MD: Jason Aronson, pp. 204–205 [Revised Edition, 2008].

8. Margaret Mahler's development theory of "separation-individuation" proposes that infants experience themselves as if they are one with mother (the caregiver; which may also be the caregiving father) and that the full psychological recognition that the self and mother/father are separate individuals becomes established during the period from about 18 to 36 months of age.

9. Peter Fonagy and Mary Target have coined the concept "mentalization," which essentially means that the child can perceive that the other person has feelings and ideas (thoughts) that are different from what the child experiences and has. This capability is crucial to understanding others and essential for living constructively in a relationship and in society. For the interested reader who wishes to understand this concept further, see Fonagy, P. and Target, M. (1997). Attachment and reflective function: their role in self-organization. *Development and Psychopathology* 9:679-700; and, Fonagy, P., Gergely, G., Jurist, E., & Target, M. (2003). *Affect Regulation, Mentalization, and the Development of the Self.* New York: Other Press.

10. All these examples are referred to by Stuart W. Twemlow and Frank Sacco in chapter 7 of their book, *Preventing Bullying and School Violence—A Modern Psychiatric Perspective*, which is soon to be published by American Psychiatric Publishing, Inc.

11. See prior footnote.

12. (p. 310, pre-publication manuscript)

13. For a substantial accounting of the history of genocide see Ben Kiernan's 2007 *Blood and Soil—A World History of Genocide and Extermination from Sparta to Darfur*, published by Yale University Press.

14. Article by Aaron Levin in January 7, 2011 issue, pp. 22 & 24.

15. The authors of the study reported in Aaron Levin's article are Stan Davis, L.C.S.W., a child and family therapist and a school counselor in Wayne, Maine, and Charisse Nixon, Ph.D., an associate professor of psychology at Penn State Erie; see www.youthvoiceproject.com/.

16. Boris Cyrulnik, a French psychiatrist and resilience researcher of strong reputation, makes this the center piece of resilience.

# 6

# HOW TO HANDLE TEMPER TANTRUMS AND RAGE REACTIONS IN GROWTH-PROMOTING WAYS

**O**utbursts of *high-level hostile destructiveness* (HLHD) create enormous difficulties for both parent and child. It is a large mistake to assume that these reflect only the child's "willfulness." Remember that hostile destructiveness is generated by an experience of excessive psychic pain. When the psychic pain experienced is intense to the point of being unbearable, in some individual kids it tends to activate an outburst of HLHD.

Not all outbursts of HLHD are the same. There are temper tantrums and there are rage reactions. There are differences between the two types of HLHD outbursts which, when recognized and understood, can facilitate one's dealing with them constructively. Temper tantrums have structure. Knowing their structure can guide the parent to more effectively handling them and increase the likelyhood of achieving their reduction. Rage reactions are not structured and call for different handling than tantrums. Interestingly, while simpler in structure, rage reactions are more variable than tantrums. There are three types of rage reactions:

- Category 1: caused by intense pain-causing physical dysfunctions of early childhood;
- Category 2: caused by challenges to the child's healthy narcissism;
- Category 3: caused by a very painful event in a child with a history of substantial abuse and neglect.

# DIFFERENTIATING BETWEEN TEMPER TANTRUMS AND RAGE REACTIONS

In order to help demonstrate the differences between temper tantrums and rage reactions I describe here two young children: David who had temper tantrums, and Richie who had rage reactions.

## Thirty-Eight-month-old David's Temper Tantrum

David was born with a low threshold of irritability, a tendency to quick reactivity, difficulty in organizing intense feeling states and in calming himself. He is an intelligent lovable kid, who, however by virtue of his inborn dispositions, quickly gets upset and very angry. This of course, causes both his parents much distress. From about one year of age on, his outbursts of hostile destructiveness (HD) began to organize into temper tantrums.

By the 38th month, David's outbursts gave the impression that, at moments of disappointment or frustration, his efforts to contain the distress and the HD mounting within him became overpowered—these days we might say like by a tsunami. This particular morning David seemed on edge when his mother rolled him and his eleven-month-old sister in a stroller into our Children's Unit Dayroom. Mother, who was overtaxed by his outbursts, did not immediately respond to his pressured need to get out of the stroller. He squirmed vigorously, made efforts to get out himself, much distressed that he could not get on his feet and do what he just seemed driven to do! Once she was able to, Mother helped him out of the stroller, while trying to calm him as she facilitated his strained efforts to get out.

Phew! He could now move where he wished. He darted to the fruit on the table; smiling, he signaled to his mother that he had noticed it there. He went to the toys, briefly interacted with two peers there, and busily examined some toys. Meanwhile, Mother had gotten to his sister, a much easier child, and helped her out of the stroller. Ten minutes had passed when David brought an apple to his mother; it was not clear if he wanted her permission to eat it or simply to inform her that he was about to do so. Mother did not want him to have it because he had complained of stomach pain, and she told him, she feared it might upset his stomach more.

He erupted! Virtually at once his face showed intense pain and hostility, crying, blustering nonverbal vocalizations, he dropped to the floor, kicking and flailing at his mother who had just taken the apple from him. Mother looked pale, embarrassed, and moderately bewildered—she [and we] had been through this with him before—as she tried sympathetically to calm him, telling him why she had taken the apple from him. His kicking and flailing made her pull away slightly, but as he calmed a bit, she came closer and continued her effort to explain that she didn't want him to get sick and to calm him down. Within thirty seconds he let her hold him, and now seated in a soft chair, she continued her efforts. Both child and mother looked pale, drained, and tensely in pain still—both, it seemed, trying to contain David's still palpable potential for eruption.

About one minute into the calming phase, as another child picked up the car with which David had been playing before the tantrum he erupted again, though not as harshly. David, blustering and demanding the return of the toy, picked up a block and threw it toward and nearly hit, not the child who was playing with the car, but another group mother, a person totally uninvolved in the event. Further frustrated by the second child's not returning the car, David in quick sequence picked up his sister's bottle, threw it at her, picked up another block, and threw it at me [the parenting group instructor], nearly falling off the chair in doing so. He looked at me anxiously, more surprised than enraged as I told him I was sorry he was feeling so bad but that I did not want him to throw things at me or to fall off the chair. I wished he could talk to his mommy or me about the things that were making him so upset. Simultaneously, his mother, scolding softly, was telling him not to hit his sister, that Dr. Parens had not done anything to him, and made good efforts again to calm him, telling him he could not throw things at people. With his mother's help, the second child returned the car to David, and David became calm as his mother continued to talk to him. Both David and his mother looked exhausted and pained.

As he recovered gradually, David began to annoy his sister by taking the toy with which she was playing, looking at his mother as he did so, smiling provocatively. The teasing continued and intensified into taunting. Mother now became angry with him. At the moment when he was on the verge of going too far, David abruptly changed his activity, asking his mother to take out his letter cards and play with him at identifying the letters of the alphabet. David and his mother continued to look emotionally drained.

## Fourteen-Month-Old Richie's Rage Reaction

The second child, Richie, is a child who was severely traumatized. I select him to describe rage reactions because his reactions were clear and give us a sad opportunity to compare a rage reaction with a temper tantrum. Richie's rage reactions were quite harsh and explosive, corresponding to the degree to which he was traumatized. Like with tantrums, rage reactions have a wide range of intensity, frequency, and degree of difficulty. Fortunately, not all kids who have rage reactions have them because they have been traumatized to the degree that Richie was. Generally, the less the child feels miserable as a result of excessively painful experiences due to environmental (foremost, caregivers') actions, the more moderate the rage reactions. Of course, kids who have rage reactions, as well as tantrums, need thoughtful parental help—difficult as it is for parents to deal with them. To make clear why Richie's rage reactions were so harsh, I will give more details as to how I postulate Richie got to be the way he was when we saw him.

When we first saw Richie he was 14 months old. He was depressed, hyper-vigilant, with a painfully distrustful look and very sad eyes. He was subdued, his movements were sluggish. He looked no more than 8 months of age. Richie was brought to our group by Mrs. V because she was deeply shocked by what had happened to Richie (she knew him since his birth) by what had become of him, and by how difficult he was now to care for.

Given the child we saw at 14 months of age, it is important to note that Richie was well developed and physically healthy at birth and was in good physical health and good mental health (ascertained both by history and by a series of photographs of him) until 6.5 months of age. At this time, Richie's teenage father gave his 17 year-old mother the alternative of moving away with him from where she lived with her "grandmother" or that he would leave her. Bewildered, she moved with him into a rented room. Within two weeks, the young father abandoned them.

Acutely depressed and hoping her boyfriend would return, rather than returning home, Richie's mother stayed in that room with her baby. Becoming more and more depressed, Richie's teenage mother could not tolerate his complaining, whining, and not eating. Bear in mind that Richie had been very well cared for by his young mother and those around her while she was in the protected setting of her home.

Increasingly bewildered and finding her baby's crying and refusal to eat unbearable, Mother began to put him in the hall when she could not get him to stop crying. According to Mrs. V, at 9 months of age Richie had changed dramatically and became withdrawn. Her description suggests that he became "anaclitically depressed."[1] At 9 ½ months of age, Richie was brought to the emergency room at our hospital due to a clothing-iron burn on his back. Mother said that during a fight with Richie's father, the iron fell and burnt Richie. Seeing mother and child's emotional states, emergency room staff assumed child abuse and Richie was placed in city custody. He remained there until he was 14 months, at which time Grandmother took him into custody. Now very difficult to care for, through the intervention of Mrs. V, Richie's "grandmother" brought him to get some help in our observation-educational setting. Here are a few excerpts from our data recordings.[2]

At 1(year) -2(months) -25(days), depressed Richie continued to be emotionally and motorically sluggish. His exploratory activity was minimal; but he was hypervigilent. He occasionally smiles, bounces on his knees; several times seemingly spontaneously, he throws toys harshly in just any direction, the pressure of his hostile destructiveness eliciting immediate limit setting (p. 332). Interestingly, even though his "grandmother" was there, he turned to Mrs. V for comforting.

At 1-3-1 of age, mood was unstable, depression dominated. But he smiled broadly for the first time, when 2.5 year old Doris engaged him to play ball with her. She rolled a 3 inch rubber ball to him, and he brusquely rolled it back to her. She rolled it to him again, and again he returned it her. In the spirit of play, Doris hid the ball between her legs. He appeared confused, suddenly unbearably frustrated, he cried, contorting his body harshly and fell back banging his head on the floor in the process, all to Doris' pained dismay. Mrs. V intervened. Soon thereafter he went into a rage reaction when he could not have a toy he wanted (p. 332).

At 1-3-8 of age his depression was softer, he seemed less morose, smiled more at people. Exploratory activity expanded and he reached out to several project children. He used toys more appropriately. Nonetheless, in exploring the toy cart he continued to throw toys out harshly one by one, which elicited the need to contain him. We felt that the load of HD he was experiencing "invaded" his physical activity, that his activity became too harsh and destructive (p. 332). Relatedness with others was improving. He now began to waken during the night screaming. "Grandmother" could comfort him within minutes. We assumed he was now having nightmares.

Twelve weeks later, at 1-6-7 of age, he was walking without support, wobbly but upright. He had bursts of explosiveness, suddenly throwing toys sometimes in a wide trajectory that would alarm the mothers and bring immediate intervention.

At 1-7-23 of age, his feelings seemed much improved. Aggressive outbursts with toys continue. But he did not attack kids or babies, whom he now approaches with interest. He then seems low-keyed. Relatedness with others is enriching.

At 1-8-23, we saw large strides in development; improved mood stability, control of hostility, coping behavior at a more advanced level, relating to others more positively (p. 333). Now when he searches the toy cart there is no explosive toy-throwing. Rather, he now folds his hands on his chest as if to control himself and at such moments shakes his head "No." He then continued to have about 3 nightmares per night. He is now saying things that make people laugh. "Grandmother" and Mrs. V said that it brought back memories of how he was entertaining at 5 months of age.

## Prevention and Damage Repair

As we consider what temper tantrums and rage reactions are and how to intervene constructively, two terms stand out as we aim to optimize the development and well-being of children (1) *prevention* and (2) *damage repair.* Prevention requires knowing what causes these reactions and what can be done to lessen the likelihood that they occur; lessening the frequency of their occurrence is a start. Some cannot be prevented; but, some can—this especially applies to those category 3 rage reactions that result from child abuse and neglect. Damage repair requires knowing what can be done to reduce the pain and repair the damage these can cause the child, the caregiver, and the relationship between them.

Close observation of children like David and Richie revealed that it is helpful to understand what drives them, why they are happening, and when and how to intervene. Observation of what seems to provoke them and of their characteristics has led me to propose the following working model.

## Complexity

The structure of temper tantrums is complex; the structure of rage reactions is not.

A full temper tantrum has two dimensions or, we could say, two curves or waves. As illustrated in figure 6.1, the first dimension is "the entire tantrum period." This I represent as an overall curve (wave-like) event that has a beginning, mounts rapidly, reaches a crest (or peak), then gradually more or less slowly wanes and dies down. The second dimension consists of tantrum outbursts, which I represent as smaller, "episodic waves" that ride on the full tantrum curve. Each of these episodic waves has a climbing limb, followed by a crest and then, a down limb (see figure 6.2).

A rage reaction has a simpler structure; it generally is an outburst. It tends to start suddenly and to stop when the child (or adult) runs out of steam or someone puts an end to it—either by giving the child (or adult) what he wants (which he feels like a "need") or often with a threat! It does not tend to give a warning, since it may not have a discernible "beginning" which can alert the parent that it's coming. We were all startled by Richie's sudden explosions. To be sure, if one is determined to get a rage reaction from a child like Richie, one can predict that at some moment, the explosion will occur.[3]

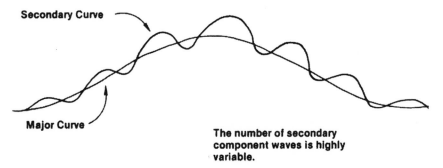

Figure 6.1    A Full Temper Tantrun

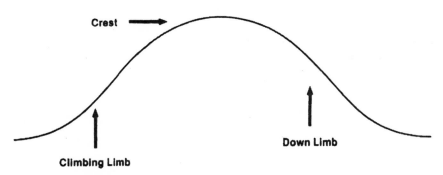

Figure 6.2    Component Wave of Secondary Curve

## Time of Emergence in Development

Another difference between temper tantrums and rage reactions is their time of emergence in development. A rage reaction is a reflex-like reaction that is built into the infant's biological tendency to react to experiences of intense pain with a correspondingly intense emotional-physical reaction. In essence, a rage reaction is a life-preservative reaction to a perceived life-threatening event. I would guess that 7-month-old Richie may have experienced his mother not tending to him as she had up to then as a threat to his life. Suddenly the "good-enough" nurturing mother was lost and he was helpless to get what he needed to survive. This life preservative reflexive rage reaction can occur from the first days out of the birth canal.

By contrast, a temper tantrum does not occur until there is a sufficient degree of development of the child's conscious emerging sense of self. The experiencing of one's "sense of self" does not occur until about the middle of the second year of life. Some research findings help us identify this development. Margaret Mahler[4] described how the infant begins to experience himself as separate from the mother, as beginning to conceptualize himself as a separate entity, from about 18 to 24 months of age on. Of course, common to all scientific endeavors, not all researchers agree on this. In my research experience, Mahler's theory holds up well. Also, Rene Spitz[5] reported the observation that a child will begin to assert his emerging sense of self by saying "No!" when he does not want to comply with his mother's or father's expectation. In this he is asserting his sense of self and sense of autonomy: "I" don't want to do that!

As I discussed in chapter 3, when supported, the emerging sense of self grows out of and becomes invested with healthy narcissism, which gives the child a sense of being a valued individual. The well cared-for 18- to 24-month-old, beginning to consciously experience this self-valuation will joyfully ride this wave of self-valuation, but this will then bring with it some distress when he does not get what he wants—which he feels like a "need"! The more he wants what he wants, the more challenging he finds accepting not being able to get what he wants. Many not so joyful children will find this so psychically pain-inducing that some may have a tantrum. Not getting what he/she wants is not experienced as life-threatening; but it sure feels lousy, even very lousy.

## The Role of the Child's Early-Life Temperament and Experiences

When children don't get what they want, why do some children from about 18 to 24 months on have tantrums and some do not? In large measure, it depends on the child's developing early-life temperament that especially depends on the child's

- Threshold of irritability (low, moderate, or high);
- Threshold for pain tolerance (low, moderate, or high);
- Reactivity type (whether quick, moderate, or slow); and
- History of tantrums, which by "kindling"[6] make it that the more a child has tantrums the more easily they occur.

A child like David who has a low threshold of irritability, is a quick reactor, and has a history of tantrums is likely to have full tantrums. Some children known to have full tantrums may at times have only partial tantrums; these may start explosively or end abruptly after one outburst. Partial tantrums may be difficult to distinguish from rage reactions.

In contrast to what drives temper tantrums, rage reactions tend to arise from three quite different intense-pain inducing experiences/conditions. This includes from physical system immaturities or defects present at birth that, for example cause colic, painful gastrointestinal reflux, terribly itchy skin conditions like eczema, or from irritability of their central nervous system that comes from having been exposed in the mother's uterus to some infection or other toxic agent like alcohol or drugs. In addition, there are those that occur in normal toddlers who have a high energy endowment—which shows itself in their "determination" and push to do what they feel driven to do—when they encounter their parent's limit setting. And, finally, some rage reactions come from intense conditions of neglect and/or abuse at the hands of primary caregivers (parents).

While birth defects influence young children's temperament, in kids who have *category 1 rage reactions* these are induced directly by intense physical pain that arises from within the child's own compromised physical condition; once the pain stops, the rage subsides and stops. The parents' efforts to comfort him/her are registered by the baby. Even from the first days of life, parents' efforts to soothe and calm the troubled baby become part of the baby's experience that gets inscribed in the mid-brain where early experiences are recorded.

*Category 2 rage reactions,* the easiest to deal with, are those that occur when a vigorous toddler, well endowed with a high level of healthy non-destructive aggression (see chapter 2) encounters the parent's need to set limits (see chapter 4). The child's high-energy driven thrust to autonomy makes the child determined to explore her/his environment. But it is when this determined 1- to 4-year-old explorer is prevented from her/his goal by a duly attentive and equally determined parent who is now setting limits on the toddler's reaching that goal, that the toddler may erupt into a rage reaction—much as 13-month-old Mary did (see below). How the child experiences these crises, which depends on the history, intensity, frequency, and type of child-parent interaction that then occur, will get recorded in the midbrain. Over time, these too will contribute to the child's ways of coping and character formation.

By contrast, a *category 3 rage reaction,* like that of Richie's, comes primarily from what the child perceives as extremely hurtful actions inflicted on him by his own caregiver(s), his own home environment. How the child experiences such events becomes recorded in the mid-brain, which then too influences the child's moods and character traits. Such rage reactions come more from experiential events than from inborn defects or temperamental dispositions. In fact, Richie was healthy at birth and had a very good inborn temperament. Even as an infant of 5 months he was calm, interacted warmly, smiled delightfully, and could put on really cute faces. But then, when, as was Richie, children are harshly emotionally and/or physically neglected, or suffer caregiver abuses, the psychic pain these kids experience causes in them the generation and accumulation of increasingly large loads of hostile destructiveness (HD) (see chapter 2). Many children so maltreated, burdened with large loads of HD, will develop tendencies to act destructively toward others, themselves, and anything and everything in their environment (see chapter 1). When they experience an intensely painful event, they may explode in a rage reaction. Children who have tantrums or category 1 or 2 rage reactions do not tend to destroy. Children who experience category 3 rage reactions, do tend to destroy.

## RATIONALE

To be sure, children's temper tantrums and rage reactions are enormously worrisome and painful for parents. But they are also enormously troubling and painful for children and furthermore, they tend to be traumatic[7] for children. Here are several reasons.

Because they are unleashed by intense psychic pain, tantrums and rage reactions are driven by high-level hostility. While high-level hostile destructiveness (HLHD) is experienced in both, the dynamics that drive the discharge of their HD differ significantly. The dynamics that caused the experience of intense psychic pain in David, that in a child who has colic, that in a child like Mary, and that experienced by Richie are dramatically different. Very different strategies will be put into action by each child as he/she develops. In each of these, the way the parents react to and deal with the child's challenging behavior critically determines the strategies for coping the child or teenager will use.

Also important is that only part of the hostility in both tantrums and rage reactions is discharged in the child's crying, thrashing, and hostile behaviors. But given the child's recognition that the caregiver who is at the receiving end of and shares in the child's experience is very troubled by the child's behavior, in addition to the intense psychic pain that gave rise to the tantrum or rage reaction in the first place, the child, especially the young child, now experiences yet additional psychic pain due to his fear that his parents will stop loving him and may abandon him. David did give the impression of worrying that his mother might pull away from him and while testing how far he could go in discharging his hostility, he came to wisely protect against the danger of mother turning away from him by deciding to invite her to engage in a constructive activity he knew she prized, learning the letters of the alphabet. Depending on the caregiver's response, the young child with an inborn bodily dysfunction will experience fear of abandonment according to the negativity with which the caregiver cares for him/her. On the other hand, due to his traumatized psyche, Richie seemed oblivious to this danger while he was raging. But once the rage subsided, one has to wonder if he then did fear she would turn away from him and who knows what more—remember that he was brought to the Emergency Room with a burn on his back. Fortunately, most kids' rage reactions do not occur under conditions as drastic as were Richie's.

In general, even with good parental care-giving, the high-level hostile destructiveness generated by these experiences will be such that more HLHD will be retained in the child's psyche than will be discharged. Therefore, parents' efforts to help their children deal constructively with temper tantrums and rages can bring enormous dividends.

Also of concern, a temper tantrum is a massive emotional reaction that leads to an inner sense of disorganization and helplessness. This in turn activates anxiety which by its nature causes further psychic pain (see chapter 7). Such experiencing occurs even in 2- to 3-year-old children. Indeed, it is more likely to occur the younger the child, because cognition and psychic organization are less developed.

In addition, the traumatic effect of a tantrum or a rage reaction does not just stay with the child during its actual occurrence, but is re-experienced repeatedly as the child relives the event in his/her mind and attempts to master the bewildering state he/she had then experienced. In fact, clinical evidence reveals that such experiences are retained in the psyche for years after, where they maintain an undermining influence on well-being. The strength of this influence depends on the intensity, frequency, and duration of these tantrums over time. In working clinically with adults, I have learned about the unfavorable and long-lasting consequences—including a difficult to shake feeling of shame and of "something's wrong with me"—of having experienced temper tantrums during childhood, especially when they continued from the first years of life through early elementary-school years.

It is not my intention to alarm parents. Rather, it is to encourage parents to not take tantrums or rage reactions as evidence of "badness" or "evil" in their children but rather, as evidence that they are experiencing serious distress and psychic pain. And at the same time, while these reactions are difficult to experience and to deal with, I recommend that parents not let tantrums or rage reactions intimidate them; they need to be, and they can be dealt with constructively. In addition, I recommend that parents try to not let their child's behavior embarrass them—at times a difficult challenge. While sometimes parents are responsible for their child's tantrum—such as when a limit set is not really necessary—most of the time parents are not. Nor is the child—he cannot be held responsible for being burdened by his temperamental inborn givens which make it difficult for him to tolerate the demands of everyday life. Only infrequently, does a child have a tantrum just to get his/her way.

And let's face it, a child's tantrums can be a singular factor in making a parent dislike, resent, and distance herself or himself from her/his own child. Consequences to the parent are also very painful. But if a parent understands what goes into, what causes her/his child's temper tantrum, it is likely that the parent will empathize with the child's feeling intense psychic pain and sympathetically stay with the child physically and emotionally through the crisis.

To what degree the rage reactions impact the parent-child relationship depends on their causative factor. In the category 1 rage reactor the intense pain comes to be recognized by the child as coming from some inner physical torment and not from a caregiver. For instance, the child with colic will register the source of the pain as coming from inside; but as I said before, the child will then also register and record in his/her midbrain for years to come, the caregivers' efforts to soothe and comfort him or her.

This is quite different from what we saw in Richie, whose rage reactions occurred because of the trauma he experienced as a result of his teen mother's failure to meet his vital basic needs, physical and emotional. Beyond the earliest years, most rage reactions are caused by the child's having been or being maltreated by his/her own caregivers. And it is most likely, given what we have learned over the last century, that these caregivers were themselves maltreated, whether by neglect and/or abuse by their own families during their own childhood and adolescence. Category 3 rage reactions go even further than tantrums in rupturing parent-child relationships.

I want to repeat here that harsh, overly strict child rearing is often experienced, and often in fact is, abusive and traumatizing and generates high levels of hostile destructiveness in children (see chapter 3).

For these reasons, temper tantrums and rage reactions ought to be dealt with as soon as they emerge and, better still, these reactions ought to be avoided where possible, without making oneself hostage to a child's lesser fits of temper.

We must bear in mind that dealing with tantrums and rage reactions early in the child's life may not only reduce the cumulative pain and the HLHD these generate within the child, but that this will also reduce the "kindling" effect that comes with frequent tantrums and rage reactions; that is, the more frequent the tantrums and rage reactions, the more progressively they are facilitated and activated by lesser experiences of frustration and disappointment. We therefore want to pay special attention to them from the time they begin.

Most parents have a pretty good idea which type of the reactions I described their child tends to have—temper tantrums or category 1, 2, or 3 rage reactions. Some kids may have more than 1 type of HLHD discharge. Let's first consider intervening with temper tantrums; then we'll address intervening with rage reactions.

## INTERVENING WITH TEMPER TANTRUMS

Knowing the structure of temper tantrums can guide us as to when and how to intervene to help the child. Children like David are frequent temper-tantrum reactors. Others may have temper tantrums infrequently, and when they occur, these are easy enough to deal with.

In some children, the temper tantrum may seem to occur explosively, with little warning. Although the warning may be short, there are always signs of an imminent tantrum. We were not surprised when David's tantrum erupted, because, his mother told us, he had been cranky all morning, and on entry into our Dayroom was struggling to get out of the stroller—and we knew of his tendency to tantrum. His mood warned of a storm brewing. Most parents have a good sense of when their child may be on the threshold of having a tantrum. One of the problems is that the signs that point to the child's being vulnerable to a tantrum elicit a range of reactions in parents from worry and distress to challenge and even provocation: "Go ahead, have a tantrum and see what you'll get!" Just hoping that the child won't, or challenging the child to have a tantrum, does not help the child cope with it in a constructive way.

For the most part, even in children whose tantrums seem to emerge suddenly, one can see the following structure in them. A full temper tantrum has a beginning, mounts, reaches a peak or crest, then gradually wanes and dies down. This major curve (see figure 6.1) is typical of most tantrums.

Considering 38-month-old David, we could see by the way he struggled irritably to get out of this stroller that this morning he would have greater difficulty than usual in coping reasonably and age-appropriately with frustration and disappointment. Feeling uncomfortable or irritable, in kids who tantrum or rage, is like the angry-gray clouds that forewarn a storm coming. This is a *pre-tantrum (or pre-rage) state*. This is a very good time to talk to one's child in order to try to reduce the feelings of discomfort or strain he is experiencing: "Heh, David, what's the matter? Calm down, Sweetie; slow down a bit." If David is able and willing to say what's going on, this may reduce his tension and discomfort, lowering the likelihood that a storm may in fact break out. Talking to the child ought to be in order to calm him down, to reduce the tension, which is best done with a tone sympathetic to his distress. Threats, "Listen, you better calm down before something bad happens!" only increase the child's tension by further burdening him with fear. Unfortunately some parents (and educators) do turn to threats to control their child's behavior. While David's mother was sympathetic with David, she did not intervene preventively. She admitted painfully that she didn't really know how to help David.

Looking at the overall event, David had two distinct tantrum episodes—when mother took the apple away and when he found another boy was playing with the car he had just let go—and he seemed on the point of having a third one, when he very wisely shifted his behavior in a positive direction. At a moment when he might have created more problems for himself, his mother, and sister, he changed the course of his behavior and asked his mother to play the learning letters game to which, much relieved, she agreed. This was a wonderful sign of David's efforts to control himself, to stop the potentially oncoming tantrum episode, and to comply with his mother's expectation—indeed, making it part of his own self-expectation.

Thinking of David's behavior diagrammatically, one can see that superimposed on the major curve of his overall temper tantrum there was a secondary set of waves consisting of tantrum episodes. Each of these in itself may become more or less intense as they ride the major tantrum curve (see figure 6.1).

Let's look at the structure of one of these secondary tantrum episodes that ride the major tantrum curve. Each of the episodes consisted of a *climbing (up) limb, a crest,* and a *down limb* (see figure 6.2).

Analyzing the first episode closely, I got the impression that during the climbing (up) limb—which, on this day, in David was steep so that his first episode "erupted"—the *HD* discharge mounted in intensity and David then seemed to be unreachable by his mother's efforts to help him calm down. There may be 2 reasons for this critical climbing limb fact:

1. The child seems to be in an altered state of consciousness (as if "in a fog") so that he can't attend to (hear or understand) what is being said to him; and

2. Once the climbing limb is set in motion, the child's adaptive/coping functions which serve the ability to pay attention to external stimuli seem to be overwhelmed by the mounting discharge of hostile destructive feelings rushing out of him.

What I assume happens in reason #2 happens as well in some rage reactions. For example, Mary, who I describe below, in her category 2 rage reaction, experienced such an overwhelming of her adaptive/coping functions too. Mary did not seem to be in an altered state of consciousness as occurs in tantrums; she did not seem to have lost awareness of the reality situation she was in, that she and her mother were in a struggle with one another! This overwhelming of coping functions without losing awareness of reality happens as well in rampaging category 3 rage reactions, even though we may say, "He went into a blind rage!" It may be that in some extreme category 3 rage reactions losing touch with reality may happen as well along with the loss of control of coping functions. But generally the "raging bull" knows what he is doing. Fortunately, the discharging of hostile destructiveness in a tantrum is better characterized by "flailing" than by "destruction." As I said earlier, a child who tantrums does not tend to destroy, given that the tantruming child does not experience the despair or the mistrust of those in his environment as do category 3 rage reactors.

During *the crest*, there was some leveling off of David's HD discharge which may be what allowed him to be better aware of his mother's efforts and to be responsive to what she was saying to him. It was, however, during *the down limb* that David was best able to hear and perceive his mother's efforts to calm and comfort him, because the flooding of adaptive/coping functions caused by the HLHD discharge he was experiencing significantly lessened. While once the climbing limb is set in motion it's too late to intervene helpfully, it is best for the parent to prevent the flailing child from hurting herself, hurting another (usually the mother), or accidentally breaking things by thrashing about. Generally, during this interval of time, it is best to allow the child to thrash on the floor and protect him from harm. It is usually not necessary to take hold of a child who is thrashing about during a tantrum because it is uncommon that the thrashing becomes violent and ends up destroying things.

During tantrums, *it is important that the parent be near and to be available to the child*, especially for children younger than 4. This is because feeling abandoned—of which the child will become aware as the tantrum begins its down climb—while in the throes of feeling disorganized, helpless, and bewildered by the intense HLHD discharge, is of itself further traumatizing and threatens to damage the parent-child relationship.

In the course of treating a young woman psychotherapeutically, she recalled a number of times one traumatic event that has never left her: that when she was about 7 years old, her mother walked out of a store when she was having a tantrum, leaving her momentarily behind. When she came out of her state of disorganization to find that her mother was gone, she was petrified. Much despair and hostility was attached to the fact that her mother had "abandoned" her in that state of helplessness.

For this reason, I believe that putting the less-than-6-year-old child, and some even later, in a room alone when she is having a tantrum may be harmful. The threat of being abandoned—based on "I deserve it, because I was very, very, bad"—is then superimposed on experiencing the trauma of the tantrum itself. To be abandoned at that time is to be abandoned when the child feels terrible about who she is, what she does, and feeling helpless—the HD it will then even further generate in the child will create a still larger psychological burden.

However, there is a time when such a separation may be warranted: it is when *the parent fears losing control of herself/himself and physically abusing the child.* We recommend that the parent then truthfully tell the child *why* she/he is leaving. When the child is sent to his room, the child is most likely to feel it is because he is unbearable. It is important that the parent be brave and honest with the child and tell him that the reason Mother/Father is putting him in his room is because she herself fears losing control. "You're driving me up a wall, and I can't help you right now. I am afraid I am going to hurt you. For that reason you're going to your room, and I'm going to go to my room for a while too." You should let a child know when she is driving you up a wall, even if it upsets him—which it will—or even if he may not be able to hear what you are saying.

Under these conditions, it is imperative that the parent talk to the child after the tantrum has subsided. Mother should say she regrets having had to put the child in his room, and the reason she did so is that she was so upset by what was going on that she feared she might lose control and do something she would later feel very, very bad about. I would add that a parent could then make it a task for the child and for herself to make every effort to try to deal with feeling so angry before it explodes. All parents get angry when we suffer experiences that cause us excessive psychic pain. In parenting, we need to develop sufficient controls over our hostility when it is mobilized.

The parent can try to calm the child during the crest of the tantrum episode. But she will be most helpful during its *down limb*. During the down limb time, the child is more responsive, can better perceive what is happening outside of himself, and will be more receptive to the parent's efforts to reduce his distress. When Mother feels the child's tantrum is in its *down climb*, offering to comfort the child, talking to the child about the pain he is experiencing, repeating again that the child can't have his way and encouraging the child to get a hold of himself, often succeeds in making the child regain control over his behavior. The parent's sympathetic tone helps the child feel that in spite of his troublesome behavior, he is still valued and loved. Also, although the child may not accept Mother's efforts to help right then, such efforts are advantageous because they reassure the child that Mother values him and this facilitates the child's accepting mother's expectations. Such efforts lessen traumatization and help the child develop a positive self-image even when he feels bad about his behavior.

Recall our discussion of limit setting regarding the fact that many a distressed child will turn to Mother and plead for comforting through signs of wanting or asking to be held, or by leaning into the mother's body. This is a highly favorable signal for the resolution of the tantrum; by this the child signals that he is ready to resolve the crisis. And it is constructive for the parent to respond by holding the child and, while doing so, continue her/his verbal and emotionally positive intervention. I say this with a sense of urgency because to not respond to the child's plea for comfort is a missed opportunity to resolve the parent-child conflict and simultaneously to enhance the child's compliance with parents' expectations.

As all mothers know, children will not always appeal for comforting during the *down limb* of their tantrum episode. Even when the infant does not appeal for comforting, the mother/father would be well advised to offer it then. Sure, when angry with the parent a child may reject the parent's offer of comforting. I encourage parents not to take this rejection too painfully. The child's rejection then simply means that at this moment, the anger felt is more intense than the need for comfort.

David's tantrum (the first episode) was triggered by Mother's setting limits on his eating the apple he showed her. Mother felt she had a good reason for setting this limit—she was protecting her son who had this morning complained of abdominal pain. She tried to explain this to him; but her explanation did not quiet his wish to eat it and his tantrum was unleashed. Mother was upset, embarrassed, and herself bewildered by her son's behavior; she'd been through this with him many times. It was no doubt helpful that, once the tantrum episode was beginning to lessen in intensity (its *down limb*) David was able to let Mother pick him up and let her repeat her limit and its reason. While calming him, sympathetically she said something like, "I know, it's hard to not be able to have what we want. But you can't have the apple because it could hurt your stomach more." He listened quietly. If he argued with her that his stomach wouldn't hurt, she might have simply gently held the line and told him she didn't want to take the chance. The child's arguing quietly is welcome; Mother ought to just (1) keep the tone sympathetic and (2) hold the line.

During the second tantrum episode, had mother not been still so upset, when David wanted to reclaim the car now held by the other child, and had the other mother not returned the car to him, David's mother could then have tried to calm him by reasoning with him that he had stopped playing with it and it was the other child's turn. She then could also have added something like, "I wouldn't let him take what you're playing with, and I can't let you take what he's playing with. It's hard, but you have to wait your turn again."

Now, if the child rejects Mother's efforts to calm him, this should not make Mother give up on her effort to comfort her child. The fact that the child is rejecting the mother's comforting or the mother's now-benevolent admonition should not be taken as a sign that the mother's effort is not working. We all know the positive impact such a gesture has on us when we are angry with someone. Before we are ready to respond in a conciliatory way, we may well be aware of the other person's efforts to be conciliatory. Most of us appreciate such efforts, even if we are not yet ready to reciprocate in kind. So, too, the child feels the mother's efforts, and even if he is not ready to reciprocate in kind, he is reassured by them. Few children vulnerable to tantrums derive gratification from rejecting their parent's efforts at comforting!

Let me add a note. It's helpful when a parent does not get too angry with the child who has a tantrum. Knowing that the child is experiencing acute and excessive psychic pain, feels terribly helpless, ineffectual, disorganized, and threatened, can help a parent not become too angry with the child. There are times when being faced with their child's difficult to handle reaction, parents believe the child is trying to manipulate them and is a spoiled brat. The fact is that if children want to manipulate their parents, they may have a fit that is much closer to a mini-rage reaction.

Turning to rage reactions, let me say that much of what I have said and recommended for dealing with temper tantrums also can apply to rage reactions.

## INTERVENING WITH RAGE REACTIONS

To facilitate the handling of rage reactions let's look at the 3 categories I propose.

### Category 1 Rage Reactions: Early Childhood Pain-Causing Physical Dysfunctions

An infant who has colic suffers from abdominal spasms that cause intense pain. Holding an infant who has colic, the parent will easily register the baby's torturing experience. Many an infant like this will have infantile rage episodes. Each episode will be directly related to the physical pain as it is felt. Once the pain alleviates, the rage reaction will subside depending significantly on the way the caregiver interacts with the child.

If the mother of the colicky infant has already had a baby who was well-developed and healthy, she will know that something is wrong with the colicky newborn. This mother (father too) will know that she was able to handle her first (or more) child(ren) well-enough and that she is a mother capable of caring well-enough for a baby.

It is another matter when a mother's first baby is one who has colic. A colicky baby presents a challenge for any parent. But when a first-time mother's infant is colicky, it presents an even larger challenge to her. Because a first-time mother has never taken care of an infant 24/7, even if she "baby-sat" a good deal when she was younger, will struggle with the dilemma, "Is it me, or is it the baby?" Initially the first-time mother will recognize that there is something troubling the baby and she will try her best to calm, comfort, and feed her baby. Unless she knows that colic is a biological problem that challenges even the best childcare, she will soon feel incompetent, empathically experience a great deal of pain herself, and get angry—with the baby and with herself!

And then, when Mother's mother comes over and much to her mixed pleasure and distress, she sees that her mother is able to make the baby calm down and feed better, she will be convinced that she is a failure as a mother! Due to her own distress at feeling inadequate as a mother, disappointed in herself and humiliated, she fails to recognize that her mother is not necessarily a genius-Mom who can fix everything. All the young mother needs to do is to remember what her Mom was like when she was a child! There are no "genius-Moms," or "genius-Dads" for that matter. But her Mom does have more experience at feeding and caring for a baby. And, perhaps more important, her Mom has not been struggling with this colicky baby 5 times a day for weeks now, or even months—most colic stops when the baby is about 6 months old. So, grandmother is not tense when she picks up the baby to try to calm and feed him, she doesn't expect that she will fail at it; often in fact, having seen such infants, Grandmother tries her best, does not despair the moment the baby fusses. Even when the baby fusses Grandmother continues to calmly, soothingly comfort the baby, manages to get enough food into his stomach to reduce the intensity of the hunger and maybe even the stomach spasms. Commonly, this is how the event unfolds, variations of it depending on the cast of characters, especially first-time-Mother and her Mother.

Colicky infants, or infants with other pain-inducing dysfunctions, will challenge any first-time mother and father. Not surprisingly, such infants who are difficult to calm are the ones who most need to be calmed and comforted. And this is the large challenge to the young first-time parent who has such a baby: "How do I calm my baby who is making me a wreck?" Mom has two people to calm: first herself, and then to do her best to calm her highly distressed baby.

It's like they tell us on airplanes, "If the level of oxygen drops in the cabin, a mask will drop from above your head. Put the mask on yourself first, so that you can take care of your child(ren)." To calm the baby—in fact to do anything for and with the child—Mom (and Dad) has to first tame her own frustration-induced angry reaction toward the child, and try to calm herself. This principle, by the way, applies to many caregiving situations where the child is doing something that upsets the parent. Easier said than done! Yes, but aiming for this often brings much benefit to both child and parent.

Then, doing two functions at the same time: calming-soothing and, gently-patiently feeding, the parent ought to just do the best she or he can. In addition, it is well for the parent to bear in mind that the infant is not really on a path to aggravate the parent whose help the baby needs badly. Nor is it that the baby is a bad, rotten baby; the baby is hurting!

Once the baby has gotten enough food, continuing to hold the calmed baby rather than immediately putting the baby in the crib will prolong the calming and health-promoting experience. This will inscribe itself in the baby's midbrain: that the holding parent will try and try, and eventually will be able to help, comfort, and calm the baby. This midbrain inscription will be reinforced when the same holding and comforting experience occurs again, and again. And eventually, the infant will "remember" that the parent is a comforting, soothing, helpful parent and that most of the time, this can be gotten from the parent when needed. This then becomes internalized and helps the child eventually do for himself, and later for others, what the calming and comforting parent has done for him many times. This continuing to hold the baby for a while after the feeding experience is over, is equivalent to later, when the child can talk, talking with the child about any given event that did not go well, which then, by talking about it together later and reviewing whatever the child and parent did that made the event turn out well, this can make a painful event lead to growth, enhance resilience, and consolidate positively the parent-child relationship.

With this type of child, parents' taking turns when the baby gets challenging can be enormously helpful to all—and tends to foster good relatedness between parents as well as between child and parents.

## Category 2 Rage Reactions: Healthy Narcissism Runs up against the Caregiving Environment

The two most common causes of category 2 rage reactions are

1. When the young child finds the pain unbearable that is caused him by his Mom or Dad's failing to meet his needs within the limit of his tolerance for delaying gratification. The pain he feels is experienced by the child as an injury to his healthy narcissism.
2. When the child's thrust to autonomy—driven by his healthy narcissism—runs up against the responsibly protective/socializing parent's limit setting. In both instances, the child's temperamental givens play a part. Let's look at each in turn.

A child with a low tolerance for delaying gratification will experience pain more quickly than one with a higher tolerance for pain. The first child will be much less patient than the latter.

Let's take the example of a 6-week-old infant having signaled (by fussing and crying) that he needs to be fed. Delays are unavoidable whether the baby is breast-fed or bottle-fed. However, today, Mother just could not get there quickly. By the time she got to her infant, his crying had escalated rapidly into an infantile rage.

Commonly, a mother finds that when she attempts to put the nipple in the mouth of her infant screaming from hunger-pain, her attempts will not immediately succeed if the infant is reacting in rage. Mothers of such babies know that the emotional storm will delay the child's ability to feel and respond to the presentation of the nipple. Often a mother will gently rub the nipple on the 6-week-old's lips, sensing that the child's attention has to be brought to the nipple—that is, the nipple has to be brought to the baby's mouth, and even rubbed against it in order to override the baby's rage feelings and when the baby can feel the nipple through the storm of rage feelings, the feeding process can start. It's that feelings of rage are stronger than and will override the baby's feeling the nipple. The rage reaction makes the infant blind and insensitive to the possibility of gratifying the need that started the rage in the first place.

Whatever the physical dysfunction:

- First, recognize that the child is in distress and the rage is not just the behavior of a "spoiled child" intending to protest not getting what he wants.
- Try to soothe and calm even when the child is not able to calm or to show appreciation for the caregiver's efforts.
- Whenever possible, when a child feels much psychic pain, Mom or Dad (or other caregiver) ought to stay with the child through the episode of pain, distress, and rage. As I have said, leaving the child alone in such a state is likely to lead the child to feel abandoned and disrupt the child's attachment to the caregiver. Beyond 12 months or so, leaving the distress-raging child alone is likely to make the child feel he is bad and unlovable.
- After such an episode—even in the infant who can't yet speak—it is helpful to talk to the child about the distress he was experiencing, how sorry the parent is that the child feels such pain and how good it is that the pain is over. It's useful to point out that pain does stop; it doesn't last forever. With a child who does speak, listening to what he/she wants to say about it and talking about this is invaluable; this is because talking about such experience with a sympathetic listener helps the child master the painful experience better.
- If the caregiver can engage the child in some activity from which he/she knows the child derives pleasure, it is wise to do so. This does not mean giving the child sweets or a new toy. Reading a book, or briefly playing a learning or fun game are far superior.

The second child, a child with a high-energy thrust to autonomy (the push to do what he seems driven from within to do [see chapter 3]) will experience limit setting much more painfully and much more quickly than one with a low-energy thrust to autonomy. Let's go back to 13-month-old Mary, that wonderful little girl who had been progressively running into more and more difficulty with her up to that moment very-dear-mother due to Mother's limit setting (chapter 4). As I said Mother had told Mary a number of times that she was not allowed into the hall when the cleaning cart was there because there were things on it that could hurt her. But driven by her high-energy internal engine, Mary persisted and this time, when Mother got to Mary and picked her up, Mary exploded. I described how while Mother carried her into our Dayroom, Mary cried angrily, waved her left arm in a striking movement against her mother several times, and kicked at her. Twice she actually struck her mother with her arm, and once she also struck herself.

After this explosion 13-month-old Mary was terribly distressed. For the first time that we knew of, Mother could not comfort her. She cried angrily, would not let mother try to make things easier for her; she would not accept whatever Mother tried to do. It was highly growth-promoting that Mother was so accepting of Mary's distress and did not get angry with her.

Mary was somber and serious; she sat upright at the edge of her mother's knees. Only gradually her body tone softened and she relaxed passively into her mother's body, thumb in mouth, where she remained, awake, for 20–30 minutes.

With regard to Mary's rage reaction, I read several things into what we saw.

- Mother did not react by rejecting her child when Mary rejected Mother's efforts to comfort her. Mother was dismayed by Mary's rejections, which was most unusual for her; but she recognized that Mary was struggling with something and seemed sympathetic to her daughter's distress. Mother waited and let Mary settle in her lap, where she gradually collapsed against her body, and let her child stay there, passively holding her in her lap.
- Mother's passively holding her infant was a superbly active intervention. Mother acted: she afforded Mary the opportunity to make good efforts to get hold of herself, and to quiet her rage and calm herself down. When at home, if a child were to have that kind of reaction, a mother might not find it reasonable to just sit there and hold her enraged and distressed child for a period of 20 to 30 minutes. Nonetheless, we saw the beneficial effect of Mary's being held by her mother and by her mother's emotional and physical availability to Mary while Mary was doing the internal work of getting over her rage reaction.

*It is sometimes difficult for a mother, who always has too much to do, to recognize the enormous benefit to her child and to their relationship of sitting for 20 to 30 minutes with an infant who is overcoming a rage reaction or a temper tantrum. But in fact, it is timesaving, emotionally*

*protective, well-being securing, and more, for a mother to spend that
kind of time in that kind of effort under such painful conditions of a
rage reaction or a tantrum experience.*

This, by the way, was the only time in the years that followed that Mary had
a rage reaction toward her mother. From then on, while Mary's hefty thrust
to autonomy did not take easily to limits and she would get angry with her
mother, she became more and more able to negotiate the problem of running up against her parents' limit setting increasingly reasonably.

With a child who is beginning to talk well-enough, talking sympathetically about such events when things have calmed down, and even at times
when things are going fine between child and parent, can be enormously
valuable in helping the child understand the reasons for her parents' expectations. To talk about such an event in a scolding or threatening way
makes things more difficult—for both child and mother. (See the ideas put
forward in chapter 4 on limit setting.)

## Category 3 Rage Reactions: A By-Product of Child Neglect and Abuse

Fourteen-month-old Richie was a severely neglected and abused infant.
Sadly, he is not the worst example of what some children, of all ages, are
subjected to (see chapter 1).

Several critical factors distinguish category 3 rage reactions from the
other two categories of rage reactions and from temper tantrums. Category
3 rage reactions

- Tend to be more explosive and violent.
- Aim to cause harm or destroy!
- Occur in the context of not trusting the environment and the people
  in it; and
- Tend to continue from earliest childhood through adolescence and
  adulthood.

The consequences of the conditions that lead to category 3 rage reactions
are enormous. Here are a few.

First, given that the development of "basic trust" or of "basic mistrust"[8] in
relationships occurs in the child's first year of life in the context of the child's
relationships to his parents, neglect and abuse at home tend to determine
the individual's trust not only in them but in other human beings.

*The die is cast in the abused or neglected child that humans can't be trusted.*

This means that parents will be ineffective as persons who can convince the child that it is in his best interest to control his rage reactions. Furthermore, later, efforts made by well-meaning persons to comfort the traumatized child and adolescent will not be trusted and therefore, difficult if not ineffective. This contributes to the difficulty encountered by helping professionals of all kinds, doctors and therapists, foster families, school teachers, police officers, and programs when they try to help individuals who were painfully traumatized by their parents.

The earlier in life the traumatization at home occurs, the deeper it is imprinted in the individual's brain, and the longer will it remain part of the traumatized individual's life. Thus unlike the other rage and tantrum producing vulnerabilities which have a more limited lifetime duration, category 3 rage reactions may continue from early childhood well into adulthood.

A serious problem that arises in some children who have felt harshly neglected or abused by their parents is that having frequently felt painfully hurt by those the child counts on for love and protection, these kids come to dread being hurt when they experience needs for comforting and love. They may then even hide such needs from themselves; they "don't need love." In fact, feeling the need for expressions of love and comforting makes them feel weak and vulnerable. But the high-level energy of feeling very angry and enraged gives them a sense of feeling strong. As a result, they will avoid expressions of the need for love or for help from their own parents, which will render their parents' efforts to deal with their rage reactions ineffective.

Also, these distinctions of category 3 rage reactions contribute significantly to the fact that in trying to prevent individuals convicted of crimes from repeating crimes by means of punishments as jailing—which while painful may be seen as preventing starvation and homelessness—tends to not prevent recidivism. Some studies suggest that rehabilitation and treatment programs tend to achieve a better result. But to help a child like Richie, as a child or a grownup, a number of strategies would have to be implemented.

Sadly, we did not have the opportunity to continue working with Richie who was not brought back to us after the summer break of our program. We would have strongly recommended a combination of strategies, including parenting education for his foster caregiver and counseling or psychotherapy of both child and caregiver. And in addition, as time passed, we would probably have added intensive psychotherapy for Richie. No child highlights more clearly than Richie, how prevention of his neglect and abuse could have spared him the suffering we witnessed in him.

The interventions open to us with kids who have category 3 rage reactions vary with the age of the child. With children under 3 years of age, counseling or therapeutic intervention with the caregivers is essential. Help should be set in motion as early in the child's life as possible. The strategies to help should be developed by people sympathetic to parents who have been hurtful to their children, given that these parents were no doubt maltreated as children themselves. Efforts should come from all angles possible: professionals working with the parents, with substitute caregivers, and with the child, individually and in sets. Abuse and neglect have to stop! Parenting education (through sympathetic counseling) in order to inform parents (and others) as to what is so hurtful in what they do, and how to better their handling of the child are enormously helpful. It is important to help the parents recognize the child's pain and distress; and to undo the notion that their child is "evil" by helping parents understand the causes of the child's behaviors. Much work will need to be done by sympathetic professionals.

With children 3 to 7 or so years of age, the parents' efforts to stop their hurtful child handling, and all that is considered above for the under-3-year-olds, must be put into action. The problem now is to labor to undo what is already imprinted in the child's brain with regard to his expectation that he will be hurt by the caregiver, and to painstakingly try to develop or regain the lost trust in the parents. Equally essential is first to help the parents change their view of and their approach to their child, as well as to not lose patience, and persist in these efforts to change and to make efforts to reassure the child of their new understanding of both the child and their own past hurtful handling—with due attention by professional interveners to support parents who try to bring about such changes in themselves and in their relationships with their child(ren).

With children older than 8 years to early teens, professional help is a must. Services for the child, for the parents, for the family are likely to be needed.

*Arduous and long efforts will be needed to turn things around; there just are no quick fixes for problems that have gone on for the first decade of a child's life.*

For mid-teens and older adolescents who have category 3 rage reactions, where professional help is not modifying the adolescent's behavior favorably enough, intensive individual treatment where it is workable, and treatment center placement with therapeutic school settings and group therapies are options that need to be considered. The road for such teens from here is very difficult and unpromising.

*The weightiest factor in all this is that many such outcomes can be prevented!*

## NOTES

1. In 1946, Dr. Rene Spitz, a highly regarded Swiss psychoanalytic infant researcher, described the reactions of infants who, when separated from their mothers at about 6 or so months of age for more than 3 months, suffered from this type of infantile depression, a very serious condition.

2. Parens, H. (1987). Cruelty Begins at Home. *Child Abuse and Neglect,* 11:331–338.

3. In a recent (2010) Spanish film, *The Secret in their Eyes,* an attractive female lawyer, acting like a detective, in an attempt to prove a given male suspect capable of the brutal rape and murder of a young woman, prods the suspect with denigrating, emasculating remarks about his body and sexual prowess—in essence saying "there is no way in the world this little runt could have committed such a sexual crime"—which, while he tolerates her mounting insults, ends up in the suspect's flying into a rage and attacking her. By assaulting her he documents his capability of having committed the crime in question.

4. Mahler, M. S., Pine, F., and Bergman, A. (1975). *The Psychological Birth of the Human Infant.* New York: Basic Books.

5. Spitz, R. (1965). *The First Year of Life.* New York: International Universities Press.

6. "The kindling phenomenon" was found in experimental studies of seizure disorders. Researchers found that seizures in research animals could be triggered by progressively lower voltages of electric brain stimulation; this occurred without producing pathological changes in the animal's brain.

7. Any event that overwhelms the child's adaptive capabilities has the potential for being traumatic.

8. See footnote 21 for reference to Erik Erikson (1959, p. 120).

# 7

## OPTIMIZING THE PARENT-CHILD RELATIONSHIP

In this chapter, I want to talk about what mental health professionals believe is among the most important goals parents ought to aim for in their efforts to help their children grow emotionally healthy: it is *to optimize their relationships with their children.*

Optimizing your relationship with your child does not mean that you should always be loving, pleasant, and praising. There are times to let your child fend for himself, and there are times to be annoyed and angry, to be troubled and to register disapproval and scold. Similarly, optimizing this relationship does not mean that your child should always listen and be sweet to you, nor should he never be angry, or hostile, or even occasionally feel hate toward you. It's the *ambivalence*—the balance of love and hostility—each experiences toward the other that is critical. Whatever the child's inborn dispositions, strengths, and vulnerabilities, the parent-child relationship is the most powerful vehicle parents have for mediating and influencing their child's emotional development and life.

In forming a positive relationship between parent and child, the parent is loading the love side of the inevitable ambivalence that occurs in every parent-child relationship. Loading the positive side of the child's ambivalence

- enhances love-based compliance rather than fear-based compliance;
- better motivates the child to develop controls over his hostile-destructive feelings;

- helps secure healthier conscience formation which will protect against the development of troublesome patterns of adaptation; and
- helps children work through and reduce the inevitable hate and hostility they experience.

In the first section of this chapter, focusing on the child younger than 6 years, I first spell out what I know best about attachment and touch on its role in the development of the child's sense of self and of autonomy (beyond what I have said about these in chapters 3 and 4). I then look at some influences of the young child's developing sexuality on his/her evolving family relationships. Then we briefly consider major trends in relationships during the elementary-school years and adolescence.

In the next section, I add a few additional key thoughts I have found important over the years toward optimizing the parent-child relationship.

And in the final section, I briefly state the central issue of this book, namely, how the quality of the parent-child relatedness correlates positively with the development of the child's aggression profile.

## WHAT I KNOW ABOUT HUMAN ATTACHMENT

Infants are born with instinctive mechanisms to form an emotional relationship with those who invest emotionally in them.[1] Within moments of birth human infants react responsively to a caregiver, and within weeks they begin the process of emotionally attaching to those who consistently care for them.

Much research has documented that infants are born with ready-to-go systems that compel emotional attachment. These inborn systems make learning by conditioning possible, pattern the newborn's responsiveness and the accumulation of memory. Once born, many a newborn will look at the human face more attentively than other features of his environment. For instance, 12-day-old Bernie, in the course of being fed by his mother, interrupts the feeding and looks at his mother's eyes and forehead. His looking is not indifferent; it seems as though he is trying to "take in" the image at which he is staring. He seemed to "take in" the experience he was having, linking the feeding and the gratification it brings with the features of his mother who was feeding him.

Rene Spitz proposed[2] that the caregiver's eyes, forehead, and hairline constitute a powerful configuration which triggers the infant's attachment. Spitz, following the work of Konrad Lorenz on *imprinting*,[3] identified this configuration in the caregiver as a "releasing mechanism" for attachment. At about 5 to 6 weeks, most infants will begin to respond to that facial configuration with a distinctive *social smiling response.*

In conjunction with a number of physiological and psychological maturations, the appearance of the social smiling response heralds the beginning of an emotional attachment that is critical for both infant and parent. Most parents react to the infant's social smile by a response of love and reciprocity. This, of course, is only the beginning of an infant's emotional reaction that will within the first 18 months evolve into love.

Some mothers are enormously disappointed and distressed when their 3-day-old infants are not smiling in response to their demonstration of affection. Knowing that the social smiling response does not occur until the second month or so of life will facilitate in parents the response that will complement their infant's earliest social smiles. The parent's response is enormously important in enhancing not only the social smile, but also the feeling of being responded to emotionally. This opens the pathway of mutual responsiveness, of "the emotional dialogue" between parent and infant.

Fascinating and critical, while the mother's response of smiling adoringly is specific to her infant, Spitz demonstrated that the social smiling response of the 6-week-old infant is, in fact, indiscriminate. But, parents are not to worry! The infant is prewired to respond to a configuration of the human face with a social smile. Therefore, the smiling response will initially be elicited by any face, even by a diagram of a face drawn on paper! But this indiscriminateness changes rather quickly. It is common that an infant will smile more readily and broadly at his own mother, because by 6 weeks, he already responds selectively to Mother's voice and odor, which the infant recognizes even before he recognizes her face.

When all goes well-enough, the process of discriminating specifically who Mother is, who Father is, and even who Brother and Sister are, occurs from about the second month of life through the sixth month. By about 6 months the infant's smiling becomes a specific social smiling response. Now the infant has a somewhat stable feeling of who his prime caregivers are and who he can rely on for gratifying caregiving. The infant seems to sense who emotionally values him.

Hand in hand with this increase in "specific" reactivity, the infant will no longer smile at people she does not know. In fact, the 5- or 6-month-old may even react to people she does not know with a reaction of distress. This *stranger response* can have a wide range, from sober curiosity in looking at a stranger to acute reactions of distress: *stranger anxiety,* which makes the

6-month-old turn away from the stranger and cling to Mother. This stranger responsiveness will reach a first peak at about 5 to 8 months of age, tend to subside from 10 to 14 months of age, and peak again due to developmental processes at about 16 through 24 months of age.

The stranger to the infant is not necessarily a stranger to the family. It could be visiting grandparents whom the infant has not seen for some time. Usually, if the grandparents take their time about descending on their grandchild, the infant will soon get used to them, sensing emotionally that these persons are important to her parents, a factor that will facilitate the infant's attachment to the grandparents.

Along with the specific social smiling response and the stranger responses, both of which are indicators of the infant's selective attachment to specific persons, comes the reaction of experiencing anxiety and distress on *separation* from the parents. A *separation reaction* is well known to all parents of children from the ages of 5 months to 3 and more years. *Separation reactions* and *separation anxiety*—which is simply a more intense response to separation—are significant indicators that the child is emotionally attaching to his mother and father.

While parents would prefer that their infants not experience anxiety, both *separation anxiety* and *stranger anxiety* serve a beneficial purpose for the child's forming emotional relationships. Given the problem stranger anxiety may create later in life, when it becomes a contributor to prejudice, addressing the problem of prejudice, I wrote[4] that "complementary anxieties are activated in the infant that orient the infant *toward* the . . . primary-[caregiver]. *Separation anxiety* means that the infant is attaching to a specific [person]; the threat of losing that [person] elicits this anxiety. *Stranger anxiety* . . . informs us that the infant is beginning to [know] that not every [person] is his/her mother or father. We might furthermore say that *stranger anxiety* serves to contain and direct the infant's inborn . . . attachment tendency *away from any non-caregiving [person], toward the [primary caregivers]"* (p 26).

Forming an attachment is critical to the preservation of the species, social adaptation, and personality formation. But not all attachments achieve the same result. Spearheaded by Mary Ainsworth,[5] *Attachment Theory* has catalogued attachment types: there are good ("secure") attachments; troubled (anxiety-laden) attachments that do not foster in the child a sense of security in the relationship or the world around; and there are unreliable, unpredictable, insufficient ("disorganized") attachments that do just that, they disorganize the child's experience of the world around and the people in it. Of course, each type will lead to varying separation and stranger reactions; each will also strongly influence the child's ability to or difficulty in relating to others and adapting to his/her social universe. A highly non-secure attachment will create serious problems in every aspect of the individual's life.

## Facilitating Attachment

Indicators of attachment to specific persons, the specific social smiling response, stranger responses, and separation reactions provide opportunities for parents to facilitate their child's attachment. Here are a few thoughts on such facilitation.

*To the infant's social smiling response:* When an infant smiles on seeing the parent and the parent reacts to that *smiling response* with a reciprocal show of warmth, tenderness, excitement, and pleasure, this enhances the infant's smiling response and his feeling of being responded to, of being cared for, and optimizes the child's attachment to the parent. It would be difficult to overemphasize the importance of the parent's and infant's experience of mutual joy and pleasure at this stage—or at any time.

Beatrice Beebe[6] detailed the troubling consequences to the infant-mother attachment process, in mothers who experienced post-partum depression. She demonstrated the distressing effect their infant's social smiling response had on them. As the infant's smile broke out, the depressed mother reflexively looked away. The infant's smiling response interrupted; the infant looked dismayed and in turn, gaze avoided. The mother tried quickly to return her gaze at her infant who had turned away; when the infant returned the gaze, mother again reflexively looked away! The depressed mother seemed not able to tolerate the emotional state expressed in her infant's powerfully warm smile. Just this miscarried reactivity disrupted the priceless process of attachment.

*To the child's stranger anxiety response:* when the infant experiences a stranger response, how the parent deals with that can enhance attachment to the parent. For example, when Grandfather comes in—convinced that he will be received by the infant with open arms—and receives a reaction of distress, and turning away, it is not uncommon for him to react with distress and either push himself onto the infant or, offended, pull away. If the grandfather forces himself on the baby, this will not help bring the infant closer to the grandfather.

When the parent of the infant can intervene and convey to Grandfather that he needs to take more time in approaching the infant, and then Mother attempts to calm and comfort her distressed infant, she will be helping both the child cope with his stranger response and the grandfather with his hurt narcissism. In this way, the parent will be decreasing the duration and intensity of excessive psychic pain, and lessening the generation of hostility in the infant.

*To the young child's separation anxiety reaction:* The mother who responds to her infant's separation reactions with a feeling of understanding and moderate personal distress, who tries to comfort her infant, who explains why she has to go, where she has to go, and when she will be back, is making efforts to decrease the intensity of distress the infant is experiencing. Although this will likely not stop the separation reaction, the mother's efforts will register with the infant. They will contribute to ameliorating the infant's pain and ill-feeling and will heighten the positive quality of their mutual attachment while decreasing the hostility generated in her child. I want to say again that by showing concern and making efforts to comfort—even where she cannot stop the pain—the mother's efforts will not be lost on the child.

While holding in mind this outline of the earliest manifestations of the development of attachment, let's look at another aspect of attachment from another vantage point. However immature the infant's experiencing, we assume that the infant has both: (1) *self* feelings, perhaps even the beginnings of a sense of self and, (2) has a primitive awareness of the caregiver, and is reactive to the interactions between this elemental self and the caregiver. The development of oneself as an individual person goes hand in hand with the development of one's feelings toward and awareness of the caregiver as an individual. It is an internally experienced reciprocity between oneself and one's caregiver. The degree to which we love others goes hand in hand with our love for oneself. Equally, the degree to which we hate others parallels our hating ourselves. In addition, the way others love and respect us makes a large contribution to our loving and respecting ourselves, as the experience of being hated by those we depend on and need contributes to hating and despising ourselves.

The development of a sense of self, the developing awareness of the caregiver, and the development of interactive processes between self and other begin from the first days of life. Dr. Margaret Mahler conceptualized this process which she called *separation-individuation* theory.

## SEPARATION-INDIVIDUATION: BECOMING A SELF RELATED TO OTHERS

Separation-individuation theory holds that in the earliest weeks of life, the infant's experiences predominantly consist of (1) the perception of his needs, (2) his expressions of these perceived needs, and (3) his experiences of his needs being gratified. He does not discern all that goes on in his environment outside of this "self-experience."[7]

Gradually, by about 6 weeks, Mother (the prime caregiver) becomes part of this "self-experience." The infant begins to have increased awareness of that which is him and that which is the caregiver—by virtue of what she does for him. At this time, the infant seems to experience self and Mother as if surrounded by an enveloping membrane enclosing the caregiver within the infant's self-experience—an emotional sense of oneness prevails.

Mahler called it the *normal symbiotic phase*. She used this phrase to describe what she inferred: that the infant seems to experience the mother as a part of the self, especially evident, she thought, during experiences of need and being cared for. This normal symbiotic phase peaks at about 5 to 6 months of age, and then without a definite termination point, wanes as this state of being evolves into the phases of the development of relatedness that follow.

I want to note that while I speak of the caregiver as the mother, we can say the same of the caregiving father, occasionally of a caregiving sibling. I mean those caregivers who invest emotionally in the infant in that very unique, "family" way.

At about 5 to 6 months of age, the child begins to experience a significant heightening of her awareness of herself and to gradually clarify the distinction between self and the caregiver.

At the midpoint of the first year of life we see increasing locomotion, an ability and interest in exploring, an increased capability in sensory modalities, and an increased capacity in cognitive functioning. At this point, the infant thrusts into the process of separation-individuation out of the oneness with mother. This occurs in two major subphases. The *first subphase* runs from about 5 to 6 months on through about 16 months of age. The *second subphase* runs from 16 months of age to 3 years.

In the beginning, the *first subphase* is characterized by the infant's pulling away from the mother. Next the infant begins to exercise her increasing motor skills and one sees an increasing pressure to explore the environment. I got the impression that the infant wants to learn and understand what the environment is all about and is attempting to gain mastery over it. At the same time, the infant is attempting to gain mastery over her own newly emerging capabilities and skills. A marked thrust toward autonomy, separateness, and individuation becomes evident. Often, at this time, a 12-month-old infant may be so active, so busy, so pressed to explore everything that many a mother experiences the infant as "getting into everything and causing all kinds of trouble and aggravation." It is regrettable when a mother feels this because she may be failing to see that the child is driven to learn about the world into which she was born, a world she had never seen before. The child is an explorer, a learner about her new world.

At the height of the thrust toward autonomy, the *second subphase of separation–individuation* is initiated by the infant's increasing recognition that the mother and she are truly separate individuals. Increasing cognitive (thinking) skills begin to make clear to the 16- to 18-month-old that her relationship to the caregiver is not secured by an enveloping membrane or an emotional oneness. Rather, it consists of being emotionally attached to the caregiver, each a separate individual.

This heightened recognition of the self as separate from the mother initially brings with it an emotional crisis. We also see behaviors that signal an internal struggle. Mahler emphasized that this internal struggle is produced by the fact that on the one hand, he wants to remain one with Mother, but on the other hand, he experiences a powerful inner thrust to be an individual self separate from her. We can assume that a parallel, although somewhat different, process occurs within the relationship of the infant to the father, and perhaps even with siblings.

During the second part of the separation–individuation phase, there tends to be a reemergence or heightening of separation anxiety and stranger responsiveness. We often find the resurgence of these reactions and the clinging they bring are sometimes alarming to mothers. Some mothers feel that the toddler, who two weeks ago freely moved away from her and was an explorer of her universe, has suddenly become an infant again, regressing, needing to cling, experiencing a heightened degree of separation and stranger anxieties. Many mothers construe this to be a loss of gains made earlier. In fact, this is an advance, signaling the infant's move from the first major subphase of separation–individuation into the second.

It is important for the parent to be aware of the fact that this second peak of separation anxiety and stranger anxiety is tied up with the potential stabilizing of a new sense of self, one able to tolerate separateness from the caregiver. I want to underscore that development will be enhanced by the caregiver making herself available for holding, comforting, and reassuring as the child works through this process. It is important for parents to allow the child's clinging, to give comfort when the infant experiences anxiety. The challenge is significant: the toddler is now attempting to separate, individuate, and consolidate the experience of being a self separate from Mother, while, in place of the symbiotic relatedness, the child develops an emotional attachment to her mother of a more mature order.

And in fact, the working through of this challenge progresses gradually during the third year of life. Gradually, the child defines the boundaries of his self and those of others.

What we have talked about so far pertains to the development of the relationship between child and parent during the first three or so years of life. The major thrust of that development occurs in twosome (dyadic) relatedness of infant and parent.

But parents know that during these first years of life, many infants at times experience anger, even hostility toward primary caregivers, when, wanting the parent's attention, Mother or Father pays attention to another person, most commonly a sibling. This kind of interaction is more complex than dyadic; it is now a threesome, a triadic interaction.

These early forms of triadic relatedness, as self-sibling-mother bring with them conflicts of rivalry. These too, like so much in the early years—and later—need to be dealt with emphatically, with reassurance, especially with a clear recognition that all siblings have equal rights to a relationship with the parent, with assurance that any one sibling is *not* more important to the parent than the others. Ultimately, each child will experience this as reassuring and protective.

Psychoanalytic clinicians and child developmentalists have long established that at about two and a half years of age, a development of substantial consequence to the child emerges; it adds a new dimension to the relationship between child and parents. It is the emergence of *infantile sexuality.*

## THE EMERGENCE OF INFANTILE SEXUALITY AND ITS IMPACT ON CHILD-PARENT RELATEDNESS

Many parents, worried about behaviors they see in their young children, claim that these behaviors surely can't mean what they think it might. But, parents who can accept their children's behaviors for what it looks like will see behaviors that pertain to their children's emerging sexuality. Infants younger than 2 years of age seem aware of and touch their own genitals, from about 2½ years with increased frequency and persistence. They will also notice a new or increased interest in, and tender attention to, babies, especially so in little girls. Many a little girl will then begin to ask questions about babies. Children will begin to ask all kinds of questions about genitals—their own and those of others, especially of siblings and parents.

Parents find that quite often, a 3- to 4-year-old girl's relationship with her mother becomes more troublesome. A mother of several children, who had a very warm relationship with her nearly 4-year-old daughter, found things were becoming quite difficult between them. Mother often got exasperated with her these days. Several times now her daughter dumped Mother's perfumes and powders in the toilet. One time she did so after she had put some of each on herself. Her father told us that she "fluttered her eyelashes and asked me to take her dancing and to the movies." A similarly parallel phenomenon occurs in the little boy with relation to his mother and father. One 3-year-old boy complained to his mother that he did not want his father to come home for dinner that night.

What causes these behaviors? At this age, a biological maturation of the child's sexuality begins to unfold. This is the first outright expression of the child's species-specific "sexual drive." Psychoanalytic theory holds[8] that this "sexual drive," also known as "libido," has 2 currents: (1) *an affectional current* and (2) a *sensual (or specifically "sexual") current*. I hold that the affectional current is the first to emerge in the early weeks of life and that it fuels attachment. It is experienced by the child as a need and is most gratified in good (secure) attachments. In troubled attachments it is insufficiently gratified. I think it is Mother Nature's work: this current is what binds people together; it is what makes what we experience as love toward those persons we most value, and binds us together in families.

The second current of the libido is the sensual current. Its function is the preservation of the species. This current of the drive makes its first behavioral appearance about the third year of life and leads to what we have specifically identified as *infantile sexuality*. The dramatic development these examples illustrate in a child's relationship to his or her parents have been variably conceptualized as the "Oedipus complex" for boys and the "Electra complex"[9] and other identifiers for girls.

*It is important to note that the attachment they have attained prior to the emergence of their sexual complexes in both boys and girls remains the same. But this attachment now becomes more complex with the additional molding that comes with the child's specific sexual development.*

These sexual development complexes unfold like this. At about 2½ years of age, a parent first notes her child's increased interest in his/her own genitals. This includes their manipulation through the child's using his/her hand or by some indirect means. And the child begins to ask questions about genitals: "Does so and so have a penis?"

At about 3 years of age, the child's behavior shows us that he/she has sexual feelings that become attached very selectively: in little boys, they tend to be preferentially directed toward their mothers. In little girls, dominantly but not exclusively, they tend to be directed toward their fathers.

One might ask: Why does the child turn his/her sexual feelings toward his/her own mother or father? Why not to just to any other male or female? Would it not be better if these feelings became attached to someone other than one's parents, to protect against incest? Yet, the child seems quite determinedly selective. For the boy, it tends to be his mother; for the girl, her father. It is because the sensual feelings the child is newly experiencing follow the path forged by the affectionate current. By this age, affectional feelings are already more or less stabilized in the child's relationships to her parents. This, along with the seemingly dominant inherent tendency of sexual feelings to be heterosexual, is why a little girl flutters her eyelashes and asks her father to take her dancing and the little boy would like Father not to come home for dinner so that he would not have to share his mother with his father. Of course, such wishes must and usually are reasonably frustrated. In fact, it is helpful that they be frustrated. And it does not take long for the child to recognize that someone else gets the gratification she/he yearns for, her mother, his father, respectively.

As a result, given the intensity of the sexual feelings young children experience, intense feelings of jealousy erupt. This creates a significant conflict within the child: The little girl wants to shoot the mother she loves; the little boy wishes that the father he loves would not come home. We all know how feelings of jealousy bring enormous pain. This then generates hostility and hate toward the loved parent of the same sex. It creates a difficult and threatening conflict within the child. Since the rival is a person the child loves and needs most, and the feelings of hostility and hate tend to be quite intense, the child feels a great deal of anxiety. This creates an internal state, a conflict due to ambivalence—as well as an external situation—that demands the child's attention and large coping efforts because the child begins to feel acute guilt. This guilt, reactive to the little boy's hating and wanting to destroy his beloved father, further organizes in the child his developing conscience; in fact, this inner conflict is a powerful motivator of conscience formation. And similarly this occurs in the little girl for hating and wanting to destroy her beloved mother. This seems to happen to a child even when the parent he or she rivals is not reliably in-home. Some early life notion of right and wrong seems to play a part in the child's reaction to his or her transgressive wishes.

Problematic as all this is, some very important positive developments are set in motion. Among the major developments that occur,

- The little boy and girl come to terms with their feelings and try as best as they can to give them up. What they cannot fully give up, they repress into their unconscious mind. When whatever is repressed of these fantasies resurge in adolescence (see below), teenagers will have to do more work to bring closure to these wishes and fantasies.
- The child takes on the task of learning to tame and control hostile feelings that have been generated within her/him toward the loved parent. The intensity of these feelings pushes the child to increase her/his capability to cope with and master feelings of hostility generated, not only by this conflict, but also by other life events for years to come.
- In addition, the child intensifies her/his identifications with—wants to be like—the parent of the same sex.
- Also highly salutary, the child develops the ability to *sublimate*, to do something creative—educational, artistic, or in any skills development—rather than act on some of these troublesome feelings and wishes.

One more highly important phenomenon follows from this conflict: The transgressive wishes that were pushed into the child's unconscious part of the mind remain active. In early adolescence, influenced by the large upsurge of sexual feelings and fantasies that come with the transformative maturation of the young teen's body, these repressed wishes and fantasies, in disguised form, are likely to re-emerge. This may apply to just the sexual feelings, or to both the sexual feelings and the feelings of rivalry. Obviously, these would bring about some further changes in the parent-child relationship.

Further documenting the biologically driven nature of this sexual maturation, clinical evidence shows that this conflict commonly also occurs in boys and girls of one-parent families. Just how a child reared in a one-parent family goes through this process is individual-dependent, but clinical evidence informs us that a number of factors play a part—foremost the child's fantasies, parents' divorce, a parent's new love affair, etc.

All in all, the child's emerging sexuality further modifies the child's relationships to his/her mother and father. As I said before however, the central conflict it creates brings with it highly salutary developments within the child including a higher level organization of his/her conscience, further identification with the rivaled parent, controls over transgressive wishes and hostile feelings, and remarkable abilities as sublimation, creativity and altruism.

## LATER TRENDS IN THE EVOLVING OF RELATIONSHIPS IN CHILDHOOD

Let us say a few words about trends in the evolving of relationships that occur during the child's elementary-school years and adolescence.

Current social trends bring with them large modifications in psychic life, such as sending children to school earlier and placing them in day-care centers even from the first months of life on. Such trends unavoidably influence the character and the quality of relationships, sometimes for the better and sometimes not.

Whatever parents do, relationships change significantly during the elementary-school years. There are gradations of relatedness, where those children's experience with their parents and siblings have led to the formation of *primary relationships*; and now adding to these—although these days many younger children already have done so—elementary-school-age children also form relationships with other adults and peers that we consider to be *secondary relationships*. This grading of relationships is dependent on the degree and quality of emotional attachment between a child and the other person. During the elementary-school years, persons outside the home, both adults (particularly teachers) and especially peers, become progressively more important to the child. During this period, siblings with whom children have primary relationships are the great bridging relationships between the family and the outside world. A child who has a sibling one or two years older commonly finds it easier to enter the world of school and the neighborhood. This occurs, both, when the older sibling is an active facilitator for the younger one, and, when the younger one sees his/her brother or sister manage and even do well, the younger one is eager to follow their older sibling's footsteps.

Relationships with peers and with teachers bring both gratifications and frustrations. Playing with one's friends is not always fun. Parents often make the mistake of thinking that the child who was outside playing with her friends was having a great time. When the child comes home, it is now time to set the table or do homework. The idea is: "You were out having fun; it is now time to get down to work!" The problem is that being out playing with friends may be painfully frustrating, disappointing, indeed, at times humiliating and infuriating following on the peers' own injuries to which they have been subjected at home, in school, or elsewhere.

During the elementary-school years, however, the shift to persons outside the home is limited. Indeed, parents continue to be vitally central in the elementary-school-age child's life and are turned to for continuing support in mastery of life's increasingly larger demands.

The next phase of development brings with it the many challenges I detailed in chapter 4 that lead to a dramatic shift in relationships. Highly challenging for both parents and their adolescents is the major shift in relationships that occurs during this developmental period: from the parents being the central persons of attachment in the younger child's life, and while remaining strongly emotionally tied to them, the adolescent gradually places peers at the center of her/his life. All parents know that the child's traversing this passage into adulthood is achieved with a good deal of difficulty, which indeed at times, leads to highly conflicted relatedness between the adolescent and her/his parents. This difficulty is particularly evidenced in the adolescent's behavioral and mood swings: in the need to be very close to the parents at one time and then at another time, fending for and coping with the realistic need for separateness and individuality and wanting nothing to do with parents. This leads the adolescent to at times be proud of her/his parents and at another time be highly embarrassed by them. Sometimes, teenagers go so far as to need to diminish the stature of, and at times even depreciate the parents, as well as at times needing to reject some of the parents' beliefs and attitudes, and more. Thus the quality of relatedness between parents and adolescents during this decade may vary widely over time.

## FURTHER THOUGHTS ON OPTIMIZING THE PARENT-CHILD RELATIONSHIP

*From Birth On, Children Feel Pain, Good and Bad,*
*and They Remember What They Have Experienced*

Years of research and clinical work in neuroscience, psychology, and psychoanalysis have proven that infants are sensitive to and feel their experiences, are affected by them and remember them—even for life.

In intensive psychotherapies, we find that even many years later, severe trauma in infancy can be reconstructed from pain-laden experiences these now, some much older patients report in fantasies and in what they tell us while in treatment. These affect-laden fantasies and verbalizations experienced within the relationship to the analyst—what we call transference—compel us to infer that these fantasies, feelings and verbalizations represent a re-living of what they experienced in early childhood.[10] The pain that is actually re-experienced in the treatment setting, un-repressed by the process of the psychoanalytic treatment method, is strikingly convincing that what is re-experienced in treatment, happened; fantasies of that order do not come from thin air!

*Infants can feel intense, even torturing pain, and they do remember—all their life!*

But, I also want to underline that traumatic events will not unavoidably cause the child pain forever—

*IF,* in the course of growing up, opportunities and experiences occur that can lead to the mitigation of the trauma, and allow for the repair of the harm the given trauma has caused. Parents should never despair about trying to undo, repair, and make up for mistakes they feel they have made that may have led to traumatic experiencing in their child. This applies even for parents whose children are already grown up.[11]

## Helping the Child Cope with Anxiety and Depression

In and of themselves, anxiety and depression, both of which cause psychic pain, need attention:

- It is established that by 5 or 6 months on, children do experience *anxiety.*
- Many people do not know that from about 5 months on, infants can experience depression—some, severe depression.

*Anxiety* is "the feeling triggered by a sense of helplessness in the face of anticipating some undefined danger"; the person is dreading something that is about to happen to him, but often does not know what the danger might be.

*Depression* is the reaction experienced after such a dreaded event has occurred; the threat of danger (which we felt as anxiety) has materialized. Now we feel depression; we feel helpless, hopeless, and we give up.

Not only is it impossible to prevent the occurrence of anxiety or depression, it may in fact not be desirable to do so. Any troubling feeling, anxiety and depression included, challenges the child to cope with it. While the challenge is unpleasant, by its making a demand on the child to cope, it leads to the further development of adaptive functions in him/her, including that of resilience—that marvelous ability to get oneself out of a fix, and some fixes can get serious. The challenge for the parent is to feel one's way to knowing when to let the kid fend for himself and when the anxiety or depression experienced is on the verge of causing too much psychic pain and may lead to a meltdown. Letting kids melt down when they know you are there and that you can help and you don't, causes more pain, mistrust of your intentions, and all the negatives that follow from this.

A number of factors contribute to one's becoming anxious or depressed. Some among us are endowed with genetic factors that predispose us to react with anxiety or depression more readily than others. In addition to one's being born with a genetic predisposition to these reactions, daily life brings challenges and traumas into our lives that produce these reactions in us. Mental health professionals believe it essential that we humans learn to cope with feelings of anxiety and depression because they are unavoidable.

## Recognizing Anxiety and Depression in Children and Adolescents

The child who experiences anxiety is likely to express "fear," cling, cry, look pale and seem troubled; older kids will express it by being irritable, short-tempered, etc. Depression seems more difficult to discern. What does depression look like in children? *The principal features of depressive feelings are the same in children (even very young children) as they are in adults.* Consider that a painfully sad thing has happened to you. Imagine that you have just lost someone you value greatly, or that you are severely disappointed and there is no hope that your wished-for expectation will ever be fulfilled. What will you feel? How will you look?

The infant will look sad: his facial expression will be flat. Children traumatized as was Richie, even infants as young as 5 or 6 months of age will tend to withdraw, be inactive, move slowly, and respond to another person's approach with little if any experience of pleasure. Some infants will even withdraw into sleep. Depressed children, even infants who crawl or walk will tend to move sluggishly. The child may refuse to eat and perhaps not even feel hungry, and will respond to efforts to feed him with sluggishness. A 3-year-old or a 7-year-old experiencing these feelings is not at all difficult to identify; just apply the same features to them. Some children will be able to say they feel sad, may get irritated if you push them to cheer up.

A teenager may mask these feelings, may avoid interaction, be overly quiet, stay in her/his room much of the time, not want to go outside even on a beautiful day. If she can talk about how she feels she may say things that a parent will probably find worrisome to hear—unless the parent makes the mistake of dismissing what the teenager says.

It may be that depression is more difficult to discern for reasons other than its not being recognizable. I learned a number of years ago, that adults have much difficulty on seeing a child experience and express feelings of depression. This is especially so with younger ones. How can a child be depressed? Well, they can—and too many are! That it is just too difficult for many of us to acknowledge that children can suffer so makes it difficult for us to help depressed children.

It is not only parents who have difficulty recognizing when a young child is depressed. So do teachers and other professionals including some doctors. My intention is not to criticize. It is, rather, to point out that to help a depressed child deal with his feelings, thoughts, and fantasies is extremely difficult for adults, even for teachers and possibly for some psychotherapists. But,

*Without opening oneself to empathically experience a young child's pain, anxiety, or depression, one cannot hope to help the child cope with it constructively.*

The best way to help a child who is anxious or depressed is to talk with the child about what the child is feeling and to try to get the child to express in words—when the child can talk—what is causing these feelings. A child may not know; but trying to talk about it, trying to comfort, can go a long way.

### When to Turn to Professional Guidance?

When a parent is troubled or getting exasperated by the feeling, "I just don't know what to do to help this kid!"—it's time to think of consulting someone who is trained to find ways to help parents do so. The earlier in life problems that impede healthy development and adaptation are handled in growth-promoting ways, the easier it is to undo these problems and get healthy development back on track. Good health, physical and mental, begins at the beginning of life. The old beliefs that future heart disease begins in adulthood; that obese children will thin out as they grow on—sure it happens with some—or that children do not develop gastric ulcers; and equally, that childhood is the easy time of life—these beliefs are totally wrong.

In short, consultation with mental health professionals when a young child is reacting to the difficulties of life with painful symptoms such as excessive anxiety and depression can save the child and the parents much further pain, reduce time spent worrying, as well as money spent for both mental and physical health care over the years. While we all agree that "an ounce of prevention is worth a pound of cure"—it often is worth much more—too few among us act according to this wisdom.

So, when to consult a mental health professional for excessive anxiety, when for clinical depression?

*Anxiety:* When the child or adolescent's anxiety interferes with his/her well-being at home, persists for too long about going to school or while in school, or going anywhere to do anything that we might reasonably expect from a child or adolescent of his/her age.

When symptoms known to be outright manifestations of anxiety occur frequently, such as

- Frequent nightmares,
- Inability to fall sleep or stay asleep nights before challenges,
- Developing gastrointestinal aches on Sunday evening or Monday mornings, or any weekday mornings—due to school-linked anxiety, etc. Also,
- When children with pre-existing biological conditions as asthma, diabetes, allergies for instance, seem to be developing illness "episodes" more frequently than usual—parents should know that stress lowers the threshold for such episodes.

*Panic Attacks:* Panic attacks make the child or adolescent not only miserable, but can in addition interfere with a child or adolescent's psychological and social development, learning in school, and more. If a child or adolescent has panic attacks more than once a week, professional attention is needed both for evaluating precipitants and to determine best treatment strategies. The intensity and duration of panic attacks are critical dimensions of when to seek consultation.

*Depression:* We all experience sadness, and even mild depression in the face of painful disappointments or minor losses. In the face of a serious loss, as a family member, we all tend to mourn. These are normal reactions. They generally do not require professional consultation. Reasonable attention, talking about the loss, the memories attached to the person, mutual emotional support and comforting can go a long way to recovery of reasonable well-being.

Other than following a serious loss, as of a mother, father, or sibling, when evidence of feelings of depression persist for more than 1 or 2 weeks, professional consultation can be highly advantageous.

Surely, children and adolescents who are subjected to traumatic stress experiences—whatever these may be, whether at home, in school, in the neighborhood—will be helped by due attention being given to these experiences. Children and adolescents who develop a post-traumatic stress disorder will benefit enormously from therapeutic strategies devised specifically for a given child or adolescent. While milder forms of such disorders can be handled reasonably well by the child or teenager and their caring families, when such conditions persist or are harsh, consultation is really required.

## Trust your Feelings—But Have the Courage to Wonder, Am I Right?

This only sounds contradictory; it's not. Trust yourself, but keep an open mind about what you feel. Hand in hand with understanding one's child, it is critical that parents trust their own perceptions and feelings as a guide to effectively dealing with their child's feelings, including their aggression, nondestructive and hostile destructive. But it is wise to check back on oneself to see if one was right, if one duly took the child's feelings and rights into consideration. Yes, I said, "the child's rights" because by giving the child rights you empower him and make him responsible for his actions.

## A Crisis Is an Opportunity

I learned somewhere that the Chinese symbol for *crisis* is the same as that for *opportunity*. In the ups and downs of normal development, growing up at times occurs in a pattern of 3 steps forward, 1 step back. Despite the burden it places on us as parents, when our kids feel anxious, depressed, or experience pain of any kind, maintaining a positive attitude in our efforts to help them is growth-promoting. Complaining about the child's yet again experiencing such an episode, humiliating the child, shaming him into "Be a big boy!" undermines the child's self-esteem and his potential for growth. And, if the child, feeling shame, tries to comply with the parent's admonition, he may play-act that he is a "big boy" with at times costly consequences—learning to deny what he feels, becoming intolerant of experiencing pain, in himself and in others, and more. In addition, feeling hurt by the parent's insult, his hostility toward the parent, which he will struggle to suppress, will mount. And he'll learn, "Don't expect your Mom or Dad to help you!"

As a clinician, I think that, burdensome as it may be in our very busy lives, when one's child experiences trouble of any kind,

*It is another opportunity for us parents to help the child continue to learn to cope with everyday's unavoidable pains, to solve problems, and adapt as best as the child can to the demands of life.*

## It's OK to Be Angry, Even Very Angry with One's Child or Adolescent

A parent may find herself/himself having very troubling feelings toward her/his child or adolescent, and yet the parent may not be able to rein in these feelings and respond helpfully. Parents are at times shocked at the feelings their children elicit in them. This is especially so when parents experience intense feelings of anger, rage, and even momentary hate. In unfortunate circumstances, some parents will lash out irrationally at their child; this is risky with young kids and adolescents. Or, intensely conflicted due to having these feelings, a parent may feel overwhelmed, immobilized, and "give up"—and will then simmer in hostility and guilt.

Whether or not the parent has exploded, a time out is required for both parent and child/adolescent. And then the event has to be revisited—without too much delay. How long either child/adolescent or parent stays so angry that he or she is inaccessible to communication—except by yelling and continuing in the rage mode—will determine when one can get back to what happened and talk about it. It is best for parents to mobilize themselves and to encourage the child or adolescent to go over the painful interaction between them. If such events are infrequent, the parent's starting with a sincere "I'm really sorry this happened" can have remarkable reconciliatory power. If they occur frequently, apologies will hardly undo the hurt experienced and the rage generated in the child/adolescent. Note that in "I'm really sorry this happened between us" or something of this kind, does not say it's the child/adolescent's fault or the parent's; "it happened between us."

Given that the parent is the adult and more mature, the parent should take the initiative to repair, not the child! If the child takes the initiative, the parent needs to wonder if it's out of fear of loss of the parent's love, or if it's out of generosity and "goodness" on the part of the child—which should be enormously appreciated and somehow be conveyed to the child. Regrettably, some parents think that it's weak, or not right, for the parent to initiate the reconciliation and repair. Big mistake! In fact,

*It takes maturity and strength of character to initiate reconciliation with a sincere apology.*

In addition, it provides the child/adolescent with a model for how to deal with conflicts in love relationships.

What started the painful interaction needs to be brought out. The child or adolescent needs to feel that he is allowed to say what he believes happened, and parents need to be in a state of wanting to know and understand what led to this kind of event. Passing judgment and criticism do not win in these talks; taking responsibility for one's actions that are detrimental to oneself or another, do much better. Clearly, one wants to prevent such blow-outs from repeating themselves too frequently.

It is also well to bear in mind that an important lesson may be learned during these unpleasant events. Again, this is usually occurs outside of awareness. The child will learn:

Can my father and my mother feel angry, even very angry, without being overwhelmed, without having a tantrum, without becoming destructive, without having to ignore how they are feeling?

What might the kid learn if Mother or Father just goes haywire? Life with someone you love is full of risks, full of hurts, and then, may go haywire on you. Who needs that? Hopefully, the kid may think: I'll never do this to my kids.

But what will the child learn when the parent is able to deal with such difficult feelings by controlling them and not causing damage? In this case, the child gains useful experience in managing anger and is likely to internalize this event, to identify with her/his parent, and learn to manage her/his own anger and hostility better.

## Does the Parent Always Have to Have It Right, Always Be There?

There are going to be times when parents will not be able to be physically or emotionally available to their children. When one cannot at a given time be emotionally available to one's child, one ought to make oneself emotionally available as soon as one can. If a parent is busy at work and can't be disturbed by a telephone call from an anxious child, it should be made clear that the parent will call as soon as possible.

A father who was grieving the loss of his own father was too turned inward to react with concern when his 4-year-old son, Tommy, fell and hurt his knee.

Tommy, seeing his father withdrawn, sulked, but said nothing. One half-hour later, as if coming out of a cloud, Father awakened to what had happened. He then took occasion, turning to Tommy to say, "You know, I saw that you fell. You seem OK; let me look at it. I'm sorry. I was thinking about Grandpa. Are you okay?" Tommy seems to resist for an instant, but he comes to his father, pats him on the shoulder, and says, "It's okay, Daddy." Indeed, he comforted his father.

In instances such as these, acknowledging a lapse of emotional availability can be reparative in and of itself.

Similarly, one does not have to always be responsive to a child at the moment of need. Of course, "as soon as possible" has its limits: if possible it should not go longer than a few hours. But there are conditions when a young child will be able to wait for longer than that. For instance, if Mother is sick and unavailable for several days, the young child will be able to integrate the fact that the mother is sick and cannot be responsive to the child's needs until she feels better. But if the young child can see that the parent is really OK, and the parent does not make herself/himself available to the child, the child is likely to feel hurt, feeling that the parent is not sufficiently accessible.

## The Golden Rule in Parenting

Another cardinal guideline every parent would be wise to use is the golden rule: "Do unto others as you would have others do unto you." One has to be honest with this exercise: Is the way you're thinking "This is what I would want," really what you would want were you in fact a child or adolescent, or are you rationalizing as a mother or father, that this is what you really wish the child would want? Sure you're right that there are times when what you know is best for the child is not what the child will want. Then, tell the child what you want the child or adolescent to do. You will not always be wrong!

It is well to bear in mind what neurologist Frances Jensen teaches us about the adolescent brain—that its development is complex, and it is not yet fully achieved in adolescence. While teens do deserve our admiration for their vast cognitive growth, their frontal lobes, that part of the brain that, as best as we know to date, governs "insight, judgment, inhibition, self-awareness, cause and effect, acknowledgment of cause and effect"[12] is not yet sufficiently developed. Despite their protests, adolescents at times absolutely need to be told to abide by our guidelines, mores and wishes! And then, no bargaining!

## THE QUALITY OF PARENT-CHILD RELATEDNESS LARGELY DETERMINES THE QUALITY OF THE CHILD'S AGGRESSION PROFILE

In considering how to help our children cope with their aggression in constructive ways, I have emphasized the importance of forming a positive and secure emotional attachment between child and parents. As my chapter 1 study documents, parenting in growth-promoting ways enhances the development of healthy nondestructive aggressiveness (such as, assertiveness) and prevents/reduces the development of excessive hostile and destructive aggression in children.

As I close this book, I look back to 1970 when my colleagues and I started the project I report on in chapter 1, a project for which, as the principal investigator and director, I take all responsibility. Having developed what we (the project designers) felt were quite good protocols to measure our observations, my colleagues and I set out to study whatever we might discern to be or to not be correlations between qualitative aspects of the mother-child relationship (we did not have regular access to the fathers) and the development of specified adaptive functions in their children. But forces operative in me of which I was not then conscious,[13] derailed my plans and compelled my attention to the development of aggression in childhood.[14]

In our 19-year follow-up study the data revealed a positive correlation between, on one hand, the positive, secure quality of the relationships between the project mothers and their children, and on the other, the children's aggression profiles. I ascribed the positive, secure attachment of the children with their mothers to the mothers' remarkably improved parenting skills into what I have come to call "growth-promoting parenting."

I now recognize that my original hypothesis was tested—but not with regard to specific adaptive functions.

Rather, I say again, the positive correlation I found was between the quality of parenting the children got, which secured good relationships between them[15] and their mothers, and the children's favorable aggression profiles.

## NOTES

1. I speak of "what I know . . ." because attachment is a domain of human experience that has been studied by different disciplines that concern themselves with mental health development. My orientation to understanding attachment is based primarily on what we know in *Ego Psychology* (a theoretical orientation in

psychoanalysis), that derives especially from the work of Sigmund Freud, Rene Spitz, Erik H. Erikson, Margaret S. Mahler, Louis Sander, Daniel Stern, and others, as well as on my own research and clinical work. I have some grasp of but am not as well informed as are others on the attachment theory of John Bowlby, Mary Ainsworth, and many others. Bowlby, himself a psychoanalyst, developed his own "school" in the late 1950s—which has come to be known as "Attachment Theory" in reaction to interpersonal conflicts that arose between him and (oppressive) psychoanalytic authorities of the day. As I see it, the work done by "ego psychologists" and "attachment theorists" is highly compatible despite disagreements on certain non-critical points of theory that do not invalidate the models developed in each school of thought. The crossover of students from each discipline into the other has increased progressively since the storms of the 1960s have passed with the passing of their instigators.

2. While Spitz's research findings on attachment date back to the early 1940s (published from 1945 on) he recapitulates his later aggregated theory of the infant's progressive emotional attachment in his *The First Year of Life* published in 1965 by International Universities Press, New York.

3. Lorenz, K. (1953). Comparative behaviorology. In: *Discussions on Child Development*, Vol. 1, J. M. Tanner and B. Inhelder, eds., pp. 108–17. New York: International Universities Press.

4. In "Toward understanding prejudice—benign and malignant," chapter 2, in: *The Future of Prejudice—Psychoanalysis and the Prevention of Prejudice*, ed. H. Parens, A. Mahfouz, S.W. Twemlow, & D.E. Scharff [2007], published by Rowman & Littlefield Publishers, Inc., p 26.

5. A close colleague of John Bowlby, Mary Ainsworth, operationalized Bowlby's theory of attachment into discernible categories, which led to highly productive research that has contributed enormously to both treatment and prevention in mental health. (Ainsworth, M.D.S., Blehar, M.C., Waters, E., and Wall, S. [1978]. *Patterns of Attachment: A Psychological Study of the Strange Situation*. Hillsdale, NJ: Lawrence Erlbaum).

6. Beatrice Beebe presented her study "Maternal Depression at 6 Weeks Postpartum and Mother-Infant 4-month Self- and Interactive Regulation" to the Vulnerable Child Discussion Group, Chair, T. Cohen, at the meetings of the American Psychoanalytic Association, January 22, 2004.

7. Separation-Individuation theory was detailed in Mahler, M. S., Pine, F. and Bergman, A. (1975). *The Psychological Birth of the Human Infant*. New York: Basic Books.

8. In Parens, H., & Saul, L. J. (1971). *Dependence in Man—A Psychoanalytic Study*. New York: International Universities Press. See pages 54–69 where I report on Freud's writings on this component hypothesis of the sexual drive.

9. A number of analytic scholars/researchers have pressed for a model of development specific for the girl, asserting, rightly I think, that the model for the boy, the Oedipus complex, is not competent to define the girl's development. Rachel

Parens has offered such a model, the Electra complex; other models have also been put forward.

10. In the course of years of clinical psychoanalytic work, with a handful of severely traumatized patients' agonizing cooperation, I have reconstructed—i.e., retrieved from repressed pre-verbal memory—extremely painful very early life experiences that have had lifelong, emotionally very costly, consequences. Two factors seem to account for the patients' difficulty in remembering what is inscribed in their midbrain: (1) that neural connections between the midbrain and the frontal cortex (the cognitive center of the brain) are not yet laid down at birth; they develop only from 2 years of age on through 7 (see this book, chapter 3); and (2) that primary psychic defensive mechanisms mask the remembrance of the pain experienced—as I have learned from my patients, by what might be a primary form of dissociation ["It's not happening to me!"], and by "spore formation" [walling oneself off to not experience the environment of pain].

11. See Daryl Sifford's *Father and Son* (1982) published by Bridgebooks, Philadelphia, for an example of a father working with his grown son who succeeded in diminishing and moving toward resolving his son's traumatic experiencing of his parents' divorce, which had created a major disturbance in the son's relationship to his father.

12. Cooney wrote this article for the *Globe* which via the Internet was distributed to its members by the Regional Council of Child and Adolescent Psychiatry of the Greater Philadelphia Region. Cooney can be reached at ecooney@globe.com.

13. In fact, I became aware of what had then driven my unexpected and unyielding interest in the development of aggression in the children as I was writing my Holocaust memoirs, *Renewal of Life—Healing from the Holocaust* (Parens, H. [2004]. Rockville, MD: Schreiber Publishing) which took place 30 years later. The reader may be skeptical about the veracity of my remark, but the fact is that I discovered in writing my memoirs that much of my life's work has been driven by what happened to me and my family as I began my teen years during the Holocaust.

14. I first reported on this study in 1973 (see H. Parens [1973]. Aggression: A Reconsideration. *J. Amer. Psychoanalytic Assn.*, 21:34–60.

15. Reported in our 19 year-follow-up study in 1993 (see Parens, H. [1993]. Toward preventing experience-derived emotional disorders: Education for Parenting. In: *Prevention in Mental Health*, H. Parens & S. Kramer, eds., pp. 121–148. Northvale, NJ: Jason Aronson, Inc.).

# INDEX

abandonment: fear of, 171; during rage reactions, 182; during temper tantrums, 175–76

abuse. *See* emotional abuse; physical abuse; trauma

adolescence: aggression profile in, 29; autonomy in, 109; bullying in, 148, 156–57; cognitive functions in, 105, 148, 158, 210; communication in, 136–37, 146–47; compliance in, 70; depression in, 204; developmental tasks in, 103–4, 111n11; emotional abuse in, 108; hostility in, 135–36; limit setting in, 105–6, 107, 108–10, 210; peer relations in, 67, 104, 107, 109, 110, 202; punishment in, 108, 110, 136; self-discipline in, 106–7, 108–10; sexuality in, 107; teasing in, 149. *See also* children

affectional current, 198

Africa, 44n6

aggression, 24n18; of animals, 39; definition of, 31, 43n1, 71n2; good, 30–31; in infants, 8–9; model of, 31;

as normal, 7; parenting and, 27–28; primary narcissism and, 48; trends of, 35–41, 115–16. *See also* anger; high-level hostile destructiveness; hostile aggression; hostile destructiveness; nondestructive aggression

aggression profile, 8; in adolescence, 29; conversion of, 29; experience in, 42; formation of, 9–10, 28–29; parents' role in, 9–10, 11–12, 42–43

aggressive behavior: categories of, 32–35; definition of, 31; disorders, 3

Ainsworth, Mary, 211n1

alcohol, 107

allowance, 110

ambivalence, 28, 121–22, 126, 190; defense mechanisms against, 125, 131–32; intensity of, 78–79; of parents, 189

anger, 19; being mean *vs.*, 115–18; bullying and, 140, 147–48; of children, 113–14, 123; towards children, 85–86, 87, 208, 209;

communication and, 147; definition of, 36; from emotional pain, 116; explanation of, 123; with limit setting, 85–86, 87; of parents, 85–86, 87, 208, 209
animals, 39, 44n6
annoyance, 116
anticipation, 66
anxiety, 205; counseling for, 206; of infants, 203–4; separation, 16–17, 94, 194; stranger, 15–17, 191–92, 193–94
apology, 140, 208–9
arguing, 127–28
assertiveness, 31, 38; ambivalence for, 79; bullying and, 149; fostering, 119
attachment: affectional current and, 198; to father, 10; history of, 211n1; imprinting for, 190–91; of infants, 16; to mother, 10; with parents, 10, 11–12; trauma and, 10–11
Attachment Theory, 211n1
authoritarianism, 47, 48, 53–54, 72n14
authority figures, 14
autonomy: in adolescence, 109; compliance and, 77, 110n1; from emotional pain, 42; of infants, 48–49, 195–96; interference with, 128–29; limit setting and, 181, 182–83, 184; nondestructive aggression from, 38–39; obedience and, 47–48; of toddlers, 48–49, 68–69, 91, 124

baby-proofing, 92
Baum, L. Frank, 71n2
Beebe, Beatrice, 11, 193
Bible, 52–53
birthing, 44n9
biting, 130
blame, 133
Bohleber, Werner, 47–48, 53, 55, 62–63, 71n4
books, 92

Bowlby, John, 211n1
brain. *See* cognitive functions
Brazelton, B., 11
Brenner, Ira, 11
Brisch, Karl-Heinz, 93
bullies, 143, 145–46, 155–56
bullying: in adolescence, 148, 156–57; by age, 153–58; anger and, 140, 147–48; assertiveness and, 149; blame for, 138; causes of, 143, 146; consequences of, 1–2, 138, 143, 148, 157; cyberbullying, 138, 158; definition of, 139, 140; with elementary school-age children, 155–56; from emotional pain, 15, 146; families and, 157; gender and, 156–57; hate and, 140; hitting back with, 152, 153, 154–55; from hostile destructiveness, 2, 8, 12, 14, 140, 148; from insufficient compliance, 57; with Internet, 1; interventions with, 152, 153–56, 157, 158–59; parents and, 152, 153–57, 158–59; as process, 139–40; research on, 150–51; sexting as, 158–59; solutions to, 151–53, 154, 155; suicide from, 148; from taunting, 143; from teasing, 143, 145; in toddlers, 153–54; victims of, 139, 143, 148–50, 151, 156–58

car, use of, 110
caregivers. *See* parents
caricaturing, 19, 134
causality, 66
children: 1 to 6 year-old, 9; 2 to 5 year-old, 93–98; 2 to 6 year-old, 66–67, 115; 2 to 8 year-old, 69; 3 to 6 year-old, 67; 4 to 8 year-old, 69–70; 5 to 8 year-old, 98–102; 6 to 12 year-old, 67; 8 to 14 year-old, 70, 102–3, 118; 12 to 15 year-old, 103–8; 14 to 19 year-old, 70; 15 to 18 year-old, 109;

adaptive functions of, 65, 76, 204; ambivalence of, 28, 78–79, 121–22, 125, 126, 131–32, 189–90; anger of, 113–14, 123; anger towards, 85–86, 87, 208, 209; apology to, 140, 208–20; cognitive functions of, 65, 66–67; communication with, 136–37, 146–47, 176–77, 184; coping by, 30–31, 60, 114, 122, 207–8; counseling for, 186–87, 205–7; demands on, 79–80; disposition of, 80, 81–82, 135–36, 140–50, 156–57, 172; emotional engagement with, 58–59; empathy of, 137, 139–40; expectations of, 62–63; frustration of, 77, 100, 124–25; guilt of, 121, 129, 199–200; harshness of, 54; high-energy, 111n5; in Holocaust, 11; hyperactivity in, 111n5; manipulation by, 178; medication for, 111n5; of Nazis, 143–44; optimizing relationship with, 189–90, 202–3; power for, 60–61 71n6; reactivity of, 118; reconciliation with, 208–9; rights of, 207; self-reflection for, 147; shame of, 143–44, 207–8; special needs, 73n21; as "spoiled brats," 60, 72n17, 182; will of, 51. *See also* adolescence; elementary school-age children; infants; peer relations; preschool age children; toddlers; *specific subjects*
"The children of the perpetrators–the after-effects of National Socialism on the following generations" (Bohleber), 71n4
chimpanzees, 44n6
chores, 64, 102, 107
classical conditioning, 66, 73n19
Clementi, Tyler, 138, 148, 158
coercion, 66
cognitive functions, 65; in adolescence, 105, 148, 158, 210; for compliance, 66–67; development of, 9; hate in, 21

colic, 179–81
Columbine High School, 1, 57, 138, 148, 157
comforting: after limit setting, 86, 87, 91, 125, 126, 132, 177–78; after rage reactions, 183–84; after temper tantrums, 177–78; for infants, 180–81, 194; internalization of, 181; from parents, 86, 87, 91, 125, 132, 177–78, 180–81; with separation anxiety, 194; with stranger response, 193–94
communication: in adolescence, 136–37, 146–47; anger and, 147; with infants, 28–29, 146–47, 182; with parents, 136–37, 146–47, 176–77, 184
Communism, 52, 54
compliance: in 2 to 8 year-olds, 69; in 4 to 8 year-olds, 69–70; in 8 to 14 year-olds, 70, 102–3, 118; in 14 to 19 year-olds, 70; in adolescence, 70; autonomy and, 77, 110n1; cognitive functions for, 66–67; definition of, 46; in education, 70, 99, 101–2; effect of, 47; of elementary school-age children, 100; excessive vs. insufficient, 54–61; with expectations, 65–70, 101; fears around, 110n1; of infants, 66, 68; insufficient, 55–57, 59–61, 110n1; limit setting for, 75–76, 77; obedience vs., 43, 45–46, 51; purpose of, 49–50; rationale for, 77, 78; resistance to, 77–78, 81–82, 83; of toddlers, 68–69, 92; ways to obtain, 75–77
compromise, 111n4
conscience: families and, 67; harsh, 121–22; revisions in, 104
control, 39
Cooney, Elizabeth, 105
coping, 30–31, 60, 114, 122, 207–8

counseling, 186, 187, 205–7. *See also*
therapist
curfew, 64
cursing, 127
cyberbullying, 138, 158
Cyrulnik, Boris, 160n16

Davis, Stan, 152, 153, 154, 155
day-care, 58
declarative memory, 72n18
defense mechanisms, 19, 51; against
ambivalence, 125, 131–32; as coping
strategy, 30–31; of infants, 134;
inhibitions from, 132–33; power
and, 60–61; purpose of, 50. *See also*
*specific defense mechanisms*
deliquency/crime, 8, 15
denial, 19, 134
depreciation, 19, 134
depression: in adolescence, 204;
counseling for, 206–7; of infants,
187n1, 203–4; of mother, 164;
recognizing, 204–5
disappointment, 60
disapproval, 120
discipline: definition of, 75; necessity
of, 80. *See also* self-discipline
displacement, 19, 50, 51, 133–34, 144,
146
distraction, 182
drugs, 107
dyslexia, 101

East Germany, 72n14
education: compliance in, 70, 99,
101–2; fundamentalist, 52; grades,
64–65, 106; hate in, 21; insufficient
compliance in, 56–57, 61; for
parenting, 7, 22n3, 186; parents
and, 99; for socialization, 21
Egeland, Byron, 11
ego psychology, 211n1
Electra complex, 198–201, 212n9

elementary school-age children: 5 to 8
year-old, 98–102; 8 to 12 year-old,
102–3, 118; bullying with, 155–56;
compliance of, 100; frustration in,
100; limit setting, 100, 102; peer
relations for, 201–2; punishment
for, 100–101, 102; self-discipline
in, 118; time outs for, 101. *See also*
children
emotional abuse, 13; in adolescence,
108; consequences of, 97;
narcissistic injury from, 14, 97; of
preschool age children, 97–98
emotional pain: anger from, 116;
autonomy from, 42; awareness of,
114; from biologic make-up, 41;
bullying from, 15, 146; cause of, 37;
duration of, 135; enjoyment causing,
117; hostile destructiveness from,
13–14, 41, 51, 115–17, 145, 170;
intensity of, 37–38, 42, 116, 159n1;
from limit setting, 123–24; from
parents, 20, 49, 77; repair of, 79,
119; self-generated, 15; tolerable,
137–38, 151
emotions: duration of, 126; expression
of, 90, 119–22, 125, 126–27, 128,
150. *See also specific emotions*
empathic relatedness, 159n5
empathy, 137, 139–40, 160n9; of
therapist, 159n5; with time outs, 147
Erikson, Erik, 66, 95, 103
ethnocentrism, malignant, 143
expectations, 69; of children, 62–63;
comparison of, 67; compliance
with, 65–70, 101; compromise with,
111n4; desirable, 64; for infants,
68; internalization of, 85–87, 95;
obligatory, 63–64, 94; special
needs and, 73n21; for toddlers, 68;
understanding, 98–99; wished-for,
64–65
explicit memory, 72n18

fairness, 67
families: bullying and, 157; conscience
    and, 67; distancing from, 109;
    membership in, 18; peer relations
    and, 136; siblings, 94–95, 100, 144,
    197; single-parent, 62, 200; stability
    from, 16. See also specific family
    members
father: attachment to, 10; as
    authoritarians, 47, 53–54; emotional
    engagement of, 59; limit setting by,
    97; love of, 23n9; teasing by, 138
fetus, 73n19
Fonagy, Peter, 160n9
food, withholding of, 103
Freud, Sigmund, 23n9
frustration, 77; in elementary school-
    age children, 100; by mother, 124; of
    parents, 179–80; of toddlers, 124–25

gender: bullying and, 156–57;
    determination of, 104
genocide, 143
The German mother and her first child,
    71n4
Germany, 55, 71n4, 71n7, 72n14. See
    also Nazis
golden rule, 210
Goodall, Jane, 44n6
"good mother," 86, 87
grades, 64–65, 106
grandparents, 180, 192, 193–94
gratification, delaying, 181
grounding, 88, 110
guilt, 121, 129; about sexuality, 199–200

Handling Children's Aggression
    Constructively: Toward Taming
    Human Destructiveness (Parens), 2
Haneke, Michael, 53
hate, 19, 36; bullying and, 140; in
    cognitive functions, 21; definition
    of, 37; in education, 21; expression

of, 120–21, 122, 127, 128; love and,
    126, 128; reaction to, 120–21, 122,
    128–29; self-, 194; undoing of, 117
HD. See hostile destructiveness
Herschkowitz, Norbert, 66, 73
high-level hostile destructiveness
    (HLHD), 161, 170, 171; discharge
    of, 173, 175. See also rage reactions;
    temper tantrums
History of Genocide, 52
hitting: by age, 117–18; bullying and,
    152, 153, 154–55; by infants, 114–
    15, 117; limit setting with, 129–31;
    morality of, 117–18; of mother, 129,
    130, 131; prevention of, 118–19;
    punishment for, 129, 130; self-
    discipline about, 118
HLHD. See high-level hostile
    destructiveness
Holocaust, 11, 143–44
homework, 99, 102, 213n13
hostile aggression, 12; causes of,
    40–41, 115; definition of, 13, 24n18,
    35–36; hostile destructiveness and,
    38, 41, 116–17; nondestructive
    aggression and, 42; pleasure-related
    destructiveness, 33–35, 38; purpose
    of, 36–37, 115; in toddlers, 34. See
    also hostile destructiveness
hostile destructiveness (HD), 71n6;
    accumulation of, 114; bullying from,
    2, 8, 12, 14, 140, 148; constructive
    expression of, 118; definition of,
    24n18; discharge of, 14, 118, 145,
    146, 170; from emotional pain,
    13–14, 41, 51, 115–17, 145, 170;
    hostile aggression and, 38, 41, 116–
    17; malignant prejudice from, 21;
    results of, 8, 12; teasing from, 140;
    of toddlers, 165
hostility, 19, 36; in adolescence,
    135–36; blaming, 133; bullying
    from, 140; causes of, 119; coping

with, 114, 122; direction of, 130–31; discharge of, 119–20, 122, 127–28, 135, 136; displacement of, 133–34, 144; as episodic, 140; of infants, 197; from internalization, 87; of parents, 77–78, 176–77; reduction of, 117; verbalization of, 136
hygiene, 107
hyperactivity, 111n5

identification, 17–18
identification with aggressor, 50, 51
imitation, 17–18
implicit memory, 65–66, 72n18
imprinting, 190–91
impulsivity, 159n3
infantile sexuality, 197–201
infants: aggression in, 8–9; anxiety of, 203–4; attachment of, 16; autonomy of, 48–49, 195–96; biologic make-up of, 41; birthing of, 44n9; coercion of, 66; with colic, 179–81; comforting for, 180–81, 194; communication with, 28–29, 146–47, 182; compliance of, 66, 68; defense mechanisms of, 134; demands of, 81; depression of, 187n1, 203–4; expectations for, 68; feeding, 179–80, 181–82; hitting by, 114–15, 117; hostility of, 197; identification of, 17–18; limit setting for, 80–81, 90–91; memory of, 65–66; prenatal development of, 23n7, 73n19; punishment of, 90–91; rage in, 32; rage reaction in, 179–81, 182, 186; self-experience of, 194–95; separation anxiety of, 16–17, 94, 194; separation-individuation theory of, 160n8, 194–97; smiling, 16; stranger anxiety of, 15–17, 191–92, 193–94; trauma for, 202–3; trust for, 66. See also attachment; children
inhibitions, 132–33

initiative, 95
insults, 147
internalization: of comforting, 181; of expectations, 85–87, 95; hostility from, 87; for preschool age children, 95; of rage, 50, 132
Internet, 1
intolerance, 8
irritability, 116, 162
irritability, of the protoplasm, 37

Jared Benjamin High, 138
Jensen, Frances, 105, 210
judgment, 51, 52

Kagan, Jerome, 66, 73
Kestenberg, Judy, 11
Kiernan, Ben, 52
"Killer apes on American Airlines or how religion was the main hijacker on September 11" (Thompson), 44n6
kindling, 173, 187n6
Koehler, Lotte, 47–48, 55, 71n4
Krystal, Henry, 23n9

learning dysfunction, 101
libido, 198
limit setting, 28–29; in adolescence, 105–6, 107, 108–10, 210; by age, 68–70; anger with, 85–86, 87; autonomy and, 181, 182–83, 184; changes in, 84–85; comforting after, 86, 87, 91, 125, 126, 132, 177–78; for compliance, 75–76, 77; consistent, 78; constructive, 79–80; definition of, 76–77; for elementary school-age children, 100, 102; emotional pain from, 123–24; excessive, 92; explanation of, 83; by father, 97; with hitting, 129–31; for infants, 80–81, 90–91; insufficient, 92; model for, 83–85; by mother, 97; for preschool age

children, 93–94; principles of, 82–83; quality of, 78–79; rage reactions from, 169, 182–83; reactions to, 80, 81–82; resistance to, 77–78, 124–25; with taunting, 142–43, 145–46; with teasing, 142–43, 145–46; for toddlers, 91–93, 124–25, 141, 144, 182–83. *See also* punishment
Logan, Jessica, 138, 158
Lorenz, Konrad, 191
love: of father, 23n9; hate and, 126, 128; of mother, 23n9; self-, 194; "tough," 135–36

magical thinking, 133
Mahler, Margaret, 62, 160n8, 168, 194
manipulation, 178
mean, angry *vs.*, 115–18
media, electronic, 107
Medical College of Pennsylvania, research project, 6–7, 8, 22n3
medication, 111n5
memory: explicit, 72n18; implicit, 65–66, 72n18; of infants, 65–66; of trauma, 213n10; words for, 67
mental health professionals. *See* therapist
mentalization, 160n9
*la Milice*, 71n7
Molotov cocktails, 55, 63
morality, 67, 117–18
mother: attachment to, 10; depression of, 164; first-time, 179, 180; frustration by, 124; good, 86, 87; hitting of, 129, 130, 131; limit setting by, 97; love of, 23n9; self-care of, 23n7; separation from, 187n1; smiling by, 191; working, 57–59, 61. *See also* good mother

narcissism, 60; primary, 48
narcissistic injury, 50; from emotional abuse, 14, 97; rage reactions and, 181

Nazis, 47; children of, 143–44; non-German, 71n12; parenting under, 71n7; passive obedience under, 50, 54–55
Nixon, Charisse, 152, 153, 154, 155
non-affective destructiveness, 33; definition of, 12, 39; purpose of, 40, 115
nondestructive aggression, 32–33; from autonomy, 38–39; definition of, 12; hostile aggression and, 42; primary narcissism in, 48; purpose of, 42, 115
normal symbiotic phase, 195
Nuremberg Laws, 71n12

obedience: autonomy and, 47–48; compliance *vs.*, 43, 45–46, 51; definition of, 46; effect of, 47; in history, 52–53; origins of, 51–52; passive, 50, 52, 54. *See also* passive obedience
obligation, 63
*OED. See Oxford English Dictionary*
Oedipus complex, 198–201
Ornstein, Anna, 23n9
*Oxford English Dictionary (OED)*, 46, 138–39

packs, 50
pain. *See* emotional pain
pain, physical, 13, 159n1, 169
panic attacks, 206
Parens, H., 2, 7
Parens, Rachel, 212n9
parenting: aggression and, 27–28; education for, 7, 22n3, 186; empathic relatedness in, 159n5; in Germany, 55, 71n4, 71n7, 72n14; growth-promoting, 43n2, 61, 211; harshness in, 47, 53–54, 172; strategies for, 30
*Parenting for Emotional Growth* (Parens), 76

parents: aggression profile role of, 9–10, 11–12, 42–43; ambivalence of, 189; anger of, 85–86, 87, 208, 209; apology of, 140, 208–9; attachment with, 10, 11–12; of bullies, 155–56; bullying and, 152, 153–57, 158–59; comforting from, 86, 87, 91, 125, 132, 177–78, 180–81; communication with, 136–37, 146–47, 176–77, 184; criticism by, 207, 209; education and, 99; embarrassment of, 125, 126; emotional investment of, 10, 58–59; emotional pain from, 20, 49, 77; emotional unavailability, 209–10; encouragement by, 99–100; frustration of, 179–80; hostility of, 77–78, 176–77; peer relation interventions by, 147–48; power over, 60–61; rage reactions and, 170, 171–72, 183–84; relationship with, 42, 189–90, 202–3; ridicule by, 156; self-trust of, 207; in sense of self, 195; separation from, 176–77; support for, 186; teasing assessment by, 149; temper tantrums and, 162–63, 170–72, 174, 175–78; threats by, 174; trauma from, 10–11, 20, 184–85; trust in, 51, 66. *See also* compliance; expectations; father; limit setting; mother; obedience; punishment

passive obedience, 50; in Communism, 52, 54; rationalization of, 52

passivity, 52

peer relations, 201–2; in adolescence, 67, 104, 107, 109, 110; families and, 136; parent interventions with, 147–48; pressure in, 67, 107, 110; with siblings, 94–95, 144, 197

personality, formation of, 9

physical abuse, 13; authoritarianism and, 53–54; consequences of, 97;

extent of, 96–97; punishment as, 89, 96

Piaget, Jean, 16

Pinheiro, Paulo S., 96

playing, 67

pleading, 83–84

pleasure-related destructiveness, 33–35, 38, 141

post-traumatic stress disorder, 207

power, 60–61 71n6

prejudice, 15; benign, 18–19; definition of, 24n21; malignant, 19, 20–21, 134–35, 140, 143

pre-rage state, 174

preschool, 58

preschool age children: emotional abuse of, 97–98; internalization for, 95; limit setting for, 93–94; punishment for, 95–96; self-discipline in, 115. *See also* children

pre-tantrum state, 174

prey aggression, 39

primary narcissism, 48

primary relationships, 201

Prince, Phoebe, 138

privacy, 109

privilege, withdrawal of, 88, 101, 103, 108, 110

problem solving, 133

procedural memory. *See* implicit memory

projection, 19, 133, 146

*Psychiatric News*, 150–51

psychic pain. *See* emotional pain

punishment: in adolescence, 108, 110, 136; age-appropriate, 88–90; amount of, 88, 95–96; definition of, 76; for elementary school-age children, 100–101, 102; for hitting, 129, 130; of infants, 90–91; inflicting pain, 88, 89; physical, 108, 136; as physical abuse, 89, 96; for preschool age children, 95–96; principles of,

87–89; reduction of, 79; spanking, 83, 89, 96; threat of, 52, 65; time out as, 93; of toddlers, 93; warning of, 84; withdrawing privilege, 88, 108, 110, 136

racism, 140, 143
rage, 36; definition of, 37, 117; in infants, 32; internalization of, 50, 132; from narcissistic injury, 50; taunting and, 141; teasing and, 141
rage reactions: abandonment during, 182; age with, 167; category 1, 169, 172, 179–81; category 2, 169, 175, 181–84; category 3, 169–70, 175, 184–87; causes of, 169; from colic, 179–81; comforting after, 183–84; consequences of, 171; counseling for, 186; damage-repair of, 166; disorganization in, 175; distraction from, 182; from events, 169–70; in infants, 179–81, 182, 186; kindling, 173; from limit setting, 169, 182–83; narcissistic injury and, 181; parents and, 170, 171–72, 183–84; from physical pain, 169; pre-rage state, 174; prevention of, 166, 174; structure of, 166, *167*; temper tantrums and, 161–66; trauma and, 163–66, 169–70, 171, 172, 184–86; trust and, 184–85. *See also* temper tantrums
rationalization, 19, 52, 134
reactivity, 118, 159n3, 162
reading, 92
reality-distorting defenses, 19, 51
rebellion, 8, 110
recidivism, 185
reductionism, 19, 134
relationships, 201–2. *See also* peer relations
resilience, 11, 137, 160n16
retribution, 34

revenge, 24n18; of toddlers, 34, 38, 142, 144–45; from trauma, 20
Rostock, youth of, 55, 63, 72n14

Sacco, F., 138, 139, 143
sadism, 117, 145
scolding, 85, 86, 87
secondary relationships, 201
*The Secret in their Eyes*, 187n3
seizure disorders, 187n6
self, sense of, 48, 49, 110n1; age with, 167–68; as bad, 120, 121–22, 123; parents in, 195; primitive, 194; temper tantrums and, 167–68
self-care, 23n7, 107
self-discipline, 75, 94; in adolescence, 106–7, 108–10; in elementary school-age children, 118; about hitting, 118; in preschool age children, 115
self-esteem, 99
self-hate, 194
self-identity, 103, 136
self-image, 87
self-love, 194
self-reflection, 147
self-righteousness, 52
self-trust, 207
self-value, 23n9, 48
separation anxiety, 16–17, 94, 194
separation-individuation, 160n8, 194–97
sexting, 158–59
sexual drive, 198
sexuality: in adolescence, 107; emergence of, 197–201; guilt about, 199–200
shame, 110, 143–44, 207–8
shaming, 110
sharing, 65
siblings, 94–95, 100, 144, 197
Sifford, Daryl, 213n11
smiling, 16, 191
socialization, 21
social smiling response, 191

spanking, 89, 93, 96
special needs, 73n21
Spitz, Rene, 16, 168, 187n1, 190–91
Spock, Ben, 92
Sroufe, Alan, 11
stranger anxiety, 15–17, 191–92, 193–94
stranger response, 191, 193–94
stubbornness, 110n1
sublimation, 104, 200
suicide, 148
swear words, 127

Target, Mary, 160n9
taunting, 137; bullying from, 143;
    definition of, 139, 140; limit setting
    with, 142–43, 145–46; rage and,
    141; of toddlers, 34–35, 153; victims
    of, 150, 153
teasing, 38; in adolescence, 149;
    bullying from, 143, 145; definition
    of, 138, 140; by father, 138; from
    hostile destructiveness, 140; limit
    setting with, 142–43, 145–46;
    parental assessment of, 149; as
    playfulness, 137, 148–49; rage and,
    141; victim of, 148–49, 153
teenager. See adolescence
temper tantrums, 124–26;
    abandonment during, 175–76;
    age with, 167–68; comforting
    after, 177–78; consequences of,
    171, 175; damage-repair of, 166;
    disorganization in, 175, 176;
    kindling, 173; parents and, 162–63,
    170–72, 174, 175–78; pre-tantrum
    state, 174; prevention of, 174–75;
    rage reactions and, 161–66; sense of
    self and, 167–68; structure of, 166,
    167, 173–74, 175, 177
texting, 158
therapist, 102, 205–6; empathy of,
    159n5; transference with, 203
Thompson, J.A., 44n6

threats, 84, 174
time outs, 88; age-appropriate, 93; for
    elementary school-age children, 101;
    empathy with, 147; for parents, 208
toddlers: autonomy of, 48–49, 68–69,
    91, 124; bullying in, 153–54;
    compliance of, 68–69, 92; denial
    by, 134; displacement by, 133–34,
    144; expectations for, 68; frustration
    of, 124–25; hostile aggression in,
    34; hostile destructiveness of, 165;
    limit setting for, 91–93, 124–25, 141,
    144, 182–83; projection by, 134;
    punishment of, 93; rationalization
    by, 134; reading to, 92; revenge of,
    34, 38, 142, 144–45; separation-
    individuation theory of, 196–97;
    stranger response in, 192, 193–94;
    taunting of, 34–35, 153. See also
    children
toilet training, 53, 94
tough love, 135–36
transference, 203
trauma: age at, 185; attachment and,
    10–11; cause of, 187n7; counseling
    for, 207; factors in, 20; for infants,
    202–3; memory of, 213n10; from
    parents, 10–11, 20, 184–85; rage
    reactions and, 163–66, 169–70, 171,
    172, 184–86; repair of, 186–87, 203,
    213n11; revenge from, 20
triadic relatedness, 197
trust: for infants, 66; in parents, 51, 66;
    rage reactions and, 184–85; self-, 207
Twemlow, S. W., 138, 139, 143

United Nation Children's Fund
    (UNICEF), 96
unpleasure-related destructiveness, 32

video-camming, 158–59
vilification, 19, 134
vulnerability, 185

Walker-Hoover, Carl, 138
warning, 84
warrior cultures, 54
Werner, Emmy, 23n9
will, 51
Wisel, Hope, 138, 158

*The Wizard of Oz* (Baum), 71n2
women, rights of, 57–59, 61, 72n16.
    *See also* mother
Women's Liberation Movement, 57,
    72n16
words, 127

# ABOUT THE AUTHOR

**Henri Parens**, M.D., FACPsa., is professor of psychiatry at Thomas Jefferson University, and a training and supervising analyst (adult and child) at the Psychoanalytic Center of Philadelphia.

He is the author of over 220 scientific and lay publications and multimedia programs, including 18 books, 9 authored: *Dependence in Man* (1971), *The Development of Aggression in Early Childhood* (1979, Revised Edition 2008), *Aggression in Our Children: Coping with it Constructively* (1987), *Parenting for Emotional Growth: The Textbook* (1997), *Parenting for Emotional Growth: A Curriculum for Students in Grades K Thru 12* (1997), *Parenting for Emotional Growth: The Workshops Series* (1997), *Helping Children Cope with Trauma Workshops* (1997) and *Renewal of Life—Healing from the Holocaust* (2004), as well as 9 books coedited, 5 scientific films, one documentary entitled, *The Urgent Need for Parenting Education* and one television series for CBS: 39 one half-hour programs entitled, *Parenting: Love and Much More*.

The recipient of many honors and awards, his principal research and prevention efforts include the development of aggression in early childhood; the prevention of violence and malignant prejudice, and the prevention of experience-derived emotional disorders; as well as methods of education for parenting. Dr. Parens is a Holocaust survivor.

CPSIA information can be obtained at www.ICGtesting.com
Printed in the USA
BVOW070801131211

278229BV00002B/1/P